HOMELAND SECURITY AND SAFETY

WALKING THE GROUND

THE PIED PIPER OF HISTORY

A MEMOIR OF EDWIN COLE BEARSS

HOMELAND SECURITY AND SAFETY
ROBERT IRVING DESOURDIS - SERIES EDITOR –
DESOURDIS COLLABORATION, LLC, OLYMPIA, WASHINGTON, US

Walking the Ground: The Pied Piper of History. A Memoir of Edwin Cole Bearss
Edwin Cole Bearss and Robert Irving Desourdis
2020. ISBN: 978-1-53617-658-2 (Softcover)
2020. ISBN: 978-1-53617-659-9 (eBook)

Walking the Ground: Making American History. A Memoir of Edwin Cole Bearss
Edwin Cole Bearss and Robert Irving Desourdis
2020. ISBN: 978-1-53616-953-9 (Softcover)
2020. ISBN: 978-1-53616-954-6 (eBook)

Walking the Ground: From Big Sky to Semper Fi. A Memoir of Edwin Cole Bearss
Edwin Cole Bearss and Robert Irving Desourdis
2020. ISBN: 978-1-53616-935-5 (Softcover)
2020. ISBN: 978-1-53616-936-2 (eBook)

God Was Our Pilot: Surviving 33 Missions in the 8th Air Force. The Memoir of Bernard Thomas Nolan
Bernard Thomas Nolan and Robert Irving Desourdis
2020. ISBN: 978-1-53617-685-8 (Hardcover)
2020. ISBN: 978-1-53617-686-5 (eBook)

Human Collaboration in Homeland Security
Robert Irving Desourdis and Kuan Hengameh Collins (Editors)
2017. ISBN: 978-1-53611-935-0 (Hardcover)
2017. ISBN: 978-1-53611-956-5 (eBook)

HOMELAND SECURITY AND SAFETY

WALKING THE GROUND

THE PIED PIPER OF HISTORY

A MEMOIR OF EDWIN COLE BEARSS

EDWIN COLE BEARSS

EDITED BY
ROBERT IRVING DESOURDIS

Copyright © 2020 by Nova Science Publishers, Inc.

All rights reserved. No part of this book may be reproduced, stored in a retrieval system or transmitted in any form or by any means: electronic, electrostatic, magnetic, tape, mechanical photocopying, recording or otherwise without the written permission of the Publisher.

We have partnered with Copyright Clearance Center to make it easy for you to obtain permissions to reuse content from this publication. Simply navigate to this publication's page on Nova's website and locate the "Get Permission" button below the title description. This button is linked directly to the title's permission page on copyright.com. Alternatively, you can visit copyright.com and search by title, ISBN, or ISSN.

For further questions about using the service on copyright.com, please contact:
Copyright Clearance Center
Phone: +1-(978) 750-8400   Fax: +1-(978) 750-4470   E-mail: info@copyright.com.

NOTICE TO THE READER

The Publisher has taken reasonable care in the preparation of this book, but makes no expressed or implied warranty of any kind and assumes no responsibility for any errors or omissions. No liability is assumed for incidental or consequential damages in connection with or arising out of information contained in this book. The Publisher shall not be liable for any special, consequential, or exemplary damages resulting, in whole or in part, from the readers' use of, or reliance upon, this material. Any parts of this book based on government reports are so indicated and copyright is claimed for those parts to the extent applicable to compilations of such works.

Independent verification should be sought for any data, advice or recommendations contained in this book. In addition, no responsibility is assumed by the Publisher for any injury and/or damage to persons or property arising from any methods, products, instructions, ideas or otherwise contained in this publication.

This publication is designed to provide accurate and authoritative information with regard to the subject matter covered herein. It is sold with the clear understanding that the Publisher is not engaged in rendering legal or any other professional services. If legal or any other expert assistance is required, the services of a competent person should be sought. FROM A DECLARATION OF PARTICIPANTS JOINTLY ADOPTED BY A COMMITTEE OF THE AMERICAN BAR ASSOCIATION AND A COMMITTEE OF PUBLISHERS.

Additional color graphics may be available in the e-book version of this book.

Library of Congress Cataloging-in-Publication Data

Names: Bearss, Edwin C., author. | Desourdis, Robert Irving.
Title: Walking the ground / The Pied Piper of History. A Memoir of Edwin Cole Bearss.
Description: New York : Nova Science Publishers, [2019] | Series: Homeland
  security and safety | Includes bibliographical references and index. |
  Contents: [Vol. 1] From Big Sky to Semper Fi -- [vol. 2] Making
  American History |
Identifiers: LCCN 2019056805 (print) | LCCN 2019056806 (ebook) | ISBN
  9781536169355 (v.1 ; paperback) | ISBN 9781536169539 (v.2 ; paperback) | ISBN 9781536176582 (v.3 ; paperback)
  | ISBN 9781536169362 (v.1 adobe pdf) | ISBN 9781536169546 (v.2 adobe pdf) | ISBN 9781536176599 (v.3 adobe pdf)
Subjects: LCSH: Bearss, Edwin C. | World War, 1939-1945--Personal
  narratives, American. | United States. Marine Corps--Biography. |
  Historians--United States--Biography.
Classification: LCC E175.5.B39 A3 2019 (print) | LCC E175.5.B39 (ebook) |
  DDC 940.54/8173--dc23
LC record available at https://lccn.loc.gov/2019056805
LC ebook record available at https://lccn.loc.gov/2019056806

Published by Nova Science Publishers, Inc. † New York

To the American Wounded Warrior

Semper Fidelis
Never give up
and
To the Practical Historians of the National Park Service
Stay in the Field

CONTENTS

Foreword		ix
	Jerome A. Greene and Bill Vodra	
Preface		xxi
Editors' Note to the Readers		xxxv
Biographies		xxxvii
Acknowledgments		xlvii
Chapter 1	Becoming History's Pied Piper	1
Chapter 2	Grant's Vicksburg Campaign Tour	21
Chapter 3	Gettysburg: The Third Day Tour	57
Chapter 4	John Wilkes Booth Escape Tour	73
Chapter 5	Sioux Indian Wars Tour	91
Chapter 6	The Great War Tour	173
Chapter 7	The Bearss in History	241
Afterword		277
	Robert Irving Desourdis	

About the Editor	**279**
Index of Terms	**285**
Index of Names	**297**

FOREWORD

Jerome A. Greene

Edwin Cole Bearss has been a mainstay in my life for more than forty-five years. In July, 1973, when I entered the National Park Service (NPS) permanently as a research historian at the onset of the American Bicentennial program, I joined a coterie of seasoned professionals at the newly established Denver Service Center that included such luminaries as Merrill J. Mattes, Erwin N. Thompson, and the indefatigable Ed Bearss. He was already a legendary scholar of wide repute for his Civil War research and interpretive skills while serving at Vicksburg National Military Park in Mississippi and the then-Richmond, Virginia, regional office during the 1950s and 1960s. It was also the period of the newly legislated National Historic Preservation Act – a time often referenced today as the golden years of cultural resources protection in NPS.

At the time, our Denver team worked for then-Chief Historian Robert M. Utley, himself a widely respected scholar and administrator who remotely oversaw our office from Washington, DC. Ed himself remained duty stationed in Washington, having been posted there since the sixties, and although administratively part of our research component, he had chosen to remain in the East rather than move with his family to Denver. Ed shortly gained national prominence with his appearances in the award-winning Ken

Burns PBS series about the Civil War. I first met him when he arrived in Denver within weeks of my appointment to attend meetings concerning the nation's Bicentennial history program. I found him at once outgoing, genuine, humorous, and easy to know, and we struck up an immediate friendship, one that would prove professional, mutually enjoyable, and enduring through coming decades.

Edwin C. Bearss and Jerome A. Greene at the Frederic Remington Museum, Ogdensburg, New York, July, 2018.

Since those early days, I've come to know Ed extremely well and to regard him as a cherished friend and colleague. I learned of his Montana upbringing and of his parents' ranching endeavors, and of his courageous service with the U.S. Marines in the South Pacific during World War II. I also learned of his later college and graduate education, and of his subsequent work with the Office of the Chief of Military History – all of which preceded his illustrious public history career producing voluminous studies for the NPS and climaxing with his tenure between 1981 and 1995 as the agency's longest serving chief historian.

Several times through the years, Ed and I have co-led tours to Indian wars sites in Wyoming, Montana, South Dakota, Colorado, and Canada. I've always been enthralled with his ability to communicate – both intellectually and – truly as well– vocally. Further, I've learned that whatever military conflict Ed interprets to his "Bearss Brigade" groupies, he always shows the utmost respect and compassion for all perspectives and players, be they Confederate or Union – or even Lakota warriors. He doesn't choose sides and he remains steadfastly objective and without favoritism in his presentations – the hallmark of the truly professional historian. Ed Bearss's stance while recounting either a battle action, momentous historical decision, or a player particular to his lecture – with eyes closed as he virtually evokes people and events long gone – , can be mesmerizing to see and to hear. His razor wit, moreover, often accompanies these orations.

Ed has been an inspiration to me in many ways, including my own take on history craftsmanship. Some historians go for broad conceptual viewpoints, while often muddying or ignoring details; others focus too much on trivia at the expense of solid thinking. Ed Bearss, fortunately, eschews such restrictive precepts to present full accountings of the people and events in history. He is a humanistic and master storyteller, and he fills his writings and lectures with requisite color, balance, clarity, and objectivity, as well as with grace and good humor. Mirroring Ed Bearss's inimitable methodology, I've attempted to so craft my own work, too. For Ed and me, because of its value in eliciting vital emotion and attention – so conducive to imparting overall meaning and comprehension among readers and listeners – properly used detail is welcome, even mandatory. It makes history all the more interesting and relevant.

Ed and I have taken jaunts together over the past dozen or so years. We've logged thousands of miles visiting battle and fort sites on the prairies and plains of Sioux War country in the Dakotas, Montana, Wyoming, and Nebraska, as well as places in New Mexico, Colorado, Oklahoma, Texas, and Utah. On these road trips, I always do the driving while we discuss the rogues and events of history, people we've known and places we've been, as well as sites we hope yet to visit. In a radical departure in 2018, we went east to upstate New York, visiting the grave of Capt. Myles Keogh (killed with Custer at the Little Bighorn), Secretary of State Seward's mansion in Auburn, Women's Rights National Historical Site in Seneca Falls, Fort

Ontario in Oswego, the War of 1812 village of Sackett's Harbor, the Frederic Remington Museum in Ogdensburg (where the staff graciously welcomed Ed), and the nearby Thousand Islands region of the St. Lawrence River.

As a long-abiding friend, how would I assess Ed Bearss? One of General George Crook's subalterns affirmatively described his chief as being "as plain as an old stick." That, to me, is also essentially Ed, in that it reflects at once the intrinsic beauty of this inordinately complex yet humble and resolute man. He is a special person, really a national treasure and as honest and forthcoming as the day is long – perhaps, indeed, his greatest attribute.

Ed possesses an unflagging spirit and a phenomenal pinpoint memory that never falters. He is unpretentiously loquacious, yet ever modest, affable, full of irony, and is an astonishing fount of knowledge, as those who know him can attest. The bottom line here is that I've been blessed to have this wonderful man's existence intersect with my own. It is altogether fitting that Ed Bearss's thoughts and memories can now be shared through the vision of editor Robert Desourdis. So please read and cherish this window into a remarkable American life, for to know Ed Bearss is to know the very best of men.

Jerome A. Greene, February 2020

Bill Vodra

In September 1987, the Smithsonian offered a pair of day trips to study the battles of Second Manassas and Antietam. Having recently read *Landscape Turned Red*, I signed up for both. The first trip departed at 8:00 am on a Saturday morning. Almost immediately, a voice came over the bus PA system. The guide summarized the course of the Civil War from April 1861 through June 1862. He then detailed the reorganization of both Union and Confederate armies that summer, providing thumbnail sketches of the officers of the Confederate Army of Northern Virginia and the Union Army of Virginia, starting with Lee and Pope, but continuing through Corps and

Divisions, and even to Brigades. By the time the bus stopped at Thoroughfare Gap, our guide had explained the strategies and troop movements leading to the clash in August. As we exited the bus, I asked the monitor what book the guide was using. "He doesn't use notes," came the reply. We systematically maneuvered following Stonewall Jackson's route to Manassas, visited Brawner's Farm, walked the assault of the Union on the unfinished railroad cut, and hiked along Chinn Ridge to understand Longstreet's attack that turned the battle. Having a guide proved a remarkably valuable experience.

Ed Bearss with Dru and Bill Vodra at Champion Hill, Mississippi, May 3, 2019.

On the way back to DC, our guide walked through the bus, answering questions and correcting any misunderstandings. Over the PA system, he addressed two questions of general interest: Why did Lincoln pick Pope to command the Army of Virginia? Why did the cavalry forces of the Union and Confederacy reverse their fortunes over the course of the war? Command of armies throughout history is based on seniority of officers, the guide explained. He then proceeded to list the 10 top generals in the Union Army, in order of seniority as of June 1862, with their combat records at that point. "Who would you have picked?" he asked, without giving his answer. (Pope was the obvious choice, however!) Our guide then launched into a discussion of each of the 10 or 12 factors that would determine cavalry effectiveness in mid-19th century, ranging from horse flesh, fodder, and shoes, to saddles and arms, to training and experience of riders, and finally to officers, tactics, and strategic uses of cavalry. Having established why each factor was important, he compared how Confederates and Federals evolved through the war. It became clear that the Confederates were unable to maintain high quality they had in 1861, while the Union consistently improved. All of this, without notes!

At the end of the trip, I concluded that the fellow guiding us had spent way too much of his life concentrating on one battle. Next week's trip to Antietam would not – could not – be as informative. I was wrong. For I had just encountered Edwin Cole Bearss. Over the next 30+ years, I would travel with and learn from him.

Fortunately, I live in the Washington, DC, area. Working with the Smithsonian, Ed led over 40 different tours to battlefields in the Eastern Theater of the Civil War, and to another dozen battlefields of the Revolutionary War from Monmouth, New Jersey, to Yorktown, Virginia, and the War of 1812 around the Chesapeake Bay. These tours were extremely popular even before Ken Burns made Ed a national celebrity in 1990.

The frequent travelers on these tours soon became friends. We shared a love of history, a desire to walk the ground where important things happened, and an unabashed willingness to be Ed's groupies! Somewhere along the way, we adopted a title, "The Bearss Brigade." Ball caps and T-shirts pronounced our loyalty. The Bearss Brigade is unique: it has no formal membership, no officers, no meetings, no newsletter, no organization whatsoever. It is bound together solely by admiration for Ed. On a trip in the mid-1990s, Ed mentioned that it was his birthday, so we treated him to a dessert. That started a tradition. Each year, we honor Ed with a birthday dinner and a fund-raising for a battlefield preservation cause selected by Ed. People come from around the country and send contributions if they cannot attend. Since 1997, the Bearss Brigade has raised at least $150,000, and perhaps more than $200,000, in Ed's honor. How does a group with no organization do this? Thankfully, Wendy Swanson is a leader.

Ed also led multi-day tours for the Smithsonian, for various Civil War roundtables, and for professional tour companies. He teaches, entertains, and encourages people to want to learn more. He welcomes questions and treats every inquiry with dignity. As on that first trip to Manassas, most of the questions are serious and sincere. Occasionally, however, a newcomer will try to "stump the expert." When asked the name of the Confederate General whose son was a U.S. Army general in WW2 and where did the son die, Ed proceeded to give biographical sketches of CSA Lt. Gen. Simon Bolivar Buckner and his son, Lt. Gen. S. B. Buckner Jr., who was killed in the battle of Okinawa in 1945, 80 years after the Civil War. At no time did Ed act as though the question was a trick; instead, he thought the fellow was genuinely curious. Another time, after explaining that the name of the Settlement of Ninety Six, in South Carolina (site of several important battles in the Revolutionary War) referred to the mileage to the nearest Cherokee village, he was asked, "How far were the Indians from here?" He patiently replied, "A little over 95 miles."

Ed also acknowledges the limits to his information, rather than faking it. Asked the origin of the name "Manassas" on that first trip, Ed said he did not know but would look it up for the questioner. Another time he told a heart-warming story how CSA [Confederate States of America] Major Gen. Stephen Ramseur's wife passed through the lines to be with her dying husband after the battle of Cedar Creek. A recent book about this battle said that Mrs. Ramseur had given birth to a child only days before in South Carolina, that Ramseur was informed of the birth on the morning of the battle, and that he had died only one day after he was wounded. It seemed impossible that his wife could have gotten word of his wounding, left a newborn infant, and traveled to Virginia in 24 hours. I showed Ed the book – in private, to minimize my own potential embarrassment at believing the author and doubting Ed. He looked at it and said, "I'll have to verify and change my narrative."

Since 1989, my wife and I have followed Ed down the Mississippi from Island No. 10 through Vicksburg to Fort Jackson; through historic sites in Ohio, Florida and Texas; onto battlefields of the wars of Little Turtle and Tecumseh, Black Hawk, the Seminoles, the Lakota, and the Nez Perce; and over the Height of Land with Benedict Arnold to Quebec and back to Lake Champlain and West Point. When Ed began giving tours overseas, we sailed with him to Guadalcanal and up the Slot to Guam, and explored Malta, Sicily and the World War II battlefields in southern Italy. I conservatively estimate that I have spent over a year of my life on some bus, someplace, with Ed Bearss. It has been a wonderful ride!

Ed has displayed some fascinating but often overlooked talents on these trips. At Mill Springs, Kentucky, on a damp Memorial Day in 1990, Ed gave us an exciting and detailed interpretation of the battle, showing where the Confederates marched up the road, where the Union artillery was, where the Union cavalry charged, and finally where Confederate General Zollicoffer died. After taking questions, he quietly said, "This is very pretty; I've never been here before." In Saltville, Virginia, we dismounted and hiked up a steep hill to the vantage point Ed wanted. My wife and I were the first ones to reach the top after Ed, who turned to look at his group, straggling upward from the bus. "It's a damn shame people cannot keep up with a 75-year-old man," Ed muttered. I asked, "Who is 75 on this bus?" Ed responded, "I am!" (Anyone who has ever heard Ed speak can imagine exactly the sound of his voice at this point!) And on a tour to the Second Day at Gettysburg, Ed addressed our group standing on the rocks in front of Little Round Top. Ed's booming voice carries, and his vivid descriptions grab attention. Soon, other tourists stopped, and the crowd grew large. Ed was enjoying the chance to educate anyone who cared to stop. At the end, one participant commented, "The Sermon on the Mount must have been like this."

Ed taught important lessons for touring battlefields:

1. Use a guide, at least for your first visit. A good guide makes the land come alive and orients you to the events. In many American battlefield parks, the visitor's centers and signage are very helpful, but not a complete substitute. Elsewhere – especially on battlefields outside the US – there are often no monuments, kiosks, or signs to tell the stories. You will get 100 times more understanding of any battlefield with a guide.

2. Read something about the battle before touring the field. There are usually dozens of excellent books on any major fight, offering short, broad overviews or in-depth discussions of individual units or parts of the field. New books appear regularly and recent scholarship often offers important reinterpretations of a battle that was believed to be well-understood. If you don't have time to devour several hundred pages of a book, however, at least go on line and find an article that summarizes the events. Wikipedia is a readily accessible source, if not always fully reliable. Other excellent sources are the American Battlefield Trust (www.battlefields.org), the American Battle Monuments Commission (www.abmc.gov), and the United States Army Center for Military History (www.history.army.mil).
3. Take maps. One simply cannot understand a battle without maps showing the location of woods, open fields, roads, bridges, and buildings at the time, and the movements of the soldiers during the fight.
4. Get out of your vehicle and walk the land, even going off the main trails now and then. You will find that the terrain contains surprises not readily visible from a seat on a bus or from a high viewpoint. For instance, walking the route of Pickett's Charge at Gettysburg, you will experience undulating folds in the ground that are invisible from the roads. Moreover, the pace of walking permits one to appreciate what soldiers say and did.
5. Wear hiking boots. Sandals, sneakers, and leather shoes are fine for fair weather walks on maintained trails. But a surprise rain or snow, or an excursion off the trail into woods or wetlands, can ruin that footwear. And you never know when you might want to plunge into a forest to see something!
6. Read more about the battle when you finish your tour. Once you have seen the terrain, the literature will make more sense.
7. Be cautious about criticizing the commanders or soldiers, particularly about the mistakes that seem obvious in hindsight. Armies learn to fight the enemy and adapt as tactics and weapons change. This evolution is not obvious when you focus on individual

battles. [See Ed's masterpiece, The Vicksburg Campaign (three volumes published 1985-86), to learn how Grant tried a variety of strategies, tactics, technologies, and resources, to take the key to the Mississippi.] Ed also emphasizes that neither side in any war has a monopoly on ingenuity or stupidity. Victory often belongs to the side that makes fewer mistakes, and success is frequently a close-run thing.

Ed sticks to the historical record. When asked (as he often is), "What if they had done such-and-such," he answers, "As FDR used to say, that is an 'iffy' question." He will then lay out what the soldiers knew at the time, what options they realistically had (given the challenges of communications and transportation, for instance), and what they later said about why they made the choices they did – while noting that memoirs rarely admit mistakes and usually omit embarrassing failures.

Over the battlefields on which Americans fought and died, Ed has led tens of thousands, possibly hundreds of thousands of people, over 64 years. Whether students at Vicksburg or staff rides for the Army and Marines, Ed has promoted both history and preservation. He helps groups like the American Battlefield Trust; state, regional and local preservation groups; Civil War Round Tables; Congressional committees; Smithsonian; and tour companies such as Pete Brown's HistoryAmerica Tours. He also lectures around the country. Retirement is not an option for him. Simply stated, *Ed is the greatest public historian of his generation.* To honor him, the American Battlefield Trust erected a monument in his honor on the Champion Hill Battlefield, unveiled in May 2019. I was privileged to give a few remarks, reminding Ed that we stood together at this crossroads exactly 30 years earlier, on a multi-day tour of the Vicksburg campaign. In 1989, none of that pivotal battlefield was preserved. Now over 1100 acres are protected, and the site is joining the Vicksburg National Military Park. Ed has "championed" Champion Hill as one of the most important – and underappreciated – battles of the entire Civil War. The monument to Ed could not be put in a better place.

Foreword

Battlefield touring is more than an academic study to Ed. He is a wounded combat veteran and understands what it is like to be at the sharp end of the spear. Like so many Americans today, I never served in the military. Ed has made me appreciate the motivation of men to enlist, and then to kill and risk being killed. He describes how, despite training and orders, when men go into combat, they adjust their kit to meet realistic needs and abilities – and discard the accoutrements that serve little function in the field, no matter how essential they might have seemed to somebody behind a desk thousands of miles away. Like most soldiers, Ed knows that both sides in opposing armies contain men with courage, generally backed by a home front willing to sacrifice to support their troops. They also contain those ill-equipped mentally or emotionally for combat, some who have been pushed to the limits of human endurance, and even some cowards, while dissent at home can sap morale.

Ed pays careful honor to those who died young, fighting for their comrades and on orders of their government. In addition to American National Cemeteries in the US and overseas, I have walked with Ed through German, Italian, Japanese, British, Canadian, Australian, Polish, and French cemeteries of World War II, stood by the graves of leaders of Indian tribes who opposed Custer, and visited numerous Confederate cemeteries. He practices respect for any soldier who paid the ultimate price. In my own travels, I always set aside significant time to visit military cemeteries, to wander among the graves, to recall that each marker represents not only a man, but parents, siblings, wives or sweethearts, and perhaps children who also suffered from the death of that soldier.

Ed Bearss, thank you for sharing a lifetime of learning and caring about America.

Bill Vodra, July 2019

PREFACE

THE PIED PIPER OF HISTORY

Why "Pied Piper"?

The credit for seeing Edwin Cole Bearss as the "Pied Piper of History" belongs to John Waugh and those who assembled the Ed Bearss's 2003 biography, which included in its title, "History's Pied Piper."[1] His first memoir book, *Walking the Ground: From Big Sky to Semper Fi*, shows he was out in front, scouting for his squad, platoon, company and regiment, when he was hit four times by Japanese bullets at Suicide Creek.[2] From the second memoir book, *Walking the Ground: Making American History,* we know Ed Bearss believes "you must be out in front" of your tour group, and leading their emotions in his stories to bring the past alive for them. With a string of people behind him, because historically he is faster than most and

---

[1] Waugh, John. Edwin C. Bearss: History's Pied Piper: A Biography by John C. Waugh, A Concise Illustrated Biography of the Life and Times of America's Impresario of Public History. Washington, DC: Edwin C. Bearss Tribute Fund, Inc. and Dallas, Texas: HistoryAmerica Tours, 2003.

[2] See Chapter 2 of the first Ed Bearss memoir book, *Walking the Ground: From Big Sky to Semper Fi.*

knows better where to stand the ground on a battlefield for interpretation, the "Pied Piper" moniker fits well.

We have appropriately drawn on that title in this third memoir book, which includes summaries of a few characteristic Ed Bearss's history tours,

Ed Bearss as *History's Pied Piper*, leading a tour at Antietam. Courtesy of Mary Gane of South Mountain Expeditions.

though representing only a small fraction of his repertoire. In this way, we hope to give the reader a sense of being on one of his tours as well as hope to inspire them to visit the hallowed ground around the world. To do so, we have included Ed Bearss's spoken interpretation of key historic places and events in Chapters 2 through 5. We chose these specific tours both because they offer truly excellent examples of his style as well as the memoir theme of "walking the ground."

OUR PURPOSE

Reading the description of Ed Bearss tours in this third book far from experiencing the places and events on tour. Nevertheless, these tour experiences are presented to give the reader a sense of being on his tours.

The other hope in presenting them is to encourage more people to experience America and its history, as well as its history in Europe, Asia and the Pacific, for themselves. You have to read the history, have to walk the ground, see the buildings and roads, and if very lucky, meet those who were there or whose relatives (2nd hand) can relate the human experience.

Hearing about what men and women did in the terrain you stand on or in the building you stand in, like the spots where Lincoln and then Booth were killed; on Last Stand Hill with Custer, his brother and friends, and the Indians who's families he'd just attacked; standing in an Easy Company[3] foxhole in the woods above the town of Foy outside Bastogne; in the quiet atrium of a University of Munich main building (the Scholl siblings)[4] and Dachau;[5] the Montfaucon American Monument,[6] and perhaps most of all, in the many cemeteries[7] around the world, such as the Meuse Argonne,[8] gives you a sense of why Ed Bearss and practical historians love their work. You can't just read about it; you have to be there to *feel* it.

On Tour

In what follows, we present abridged tour experiences from the perspective of a member of the history-touring group. Photographs pulled from video taken during these tours is used to illustrate Ed Bearss's descriptions as we walked (and drove) the ground. The lead-in and explanatory text surrounded Ed Bearss's words on the tours presented have been edited by Ed Bearss.

---

[3] Online: http://www.easy506th.org/ or
   https://en.wikipedia.org/wiki/E_Company,_506th_Infantry_Regiment_(United_States).
[4] Online: https://en.wikipedia.org/wiki/White_Rose.
[5] Online: https://en.wikipedia.org/wiki/Dachau_concentration_camp.
[6] Online: https://www.abmc.gov/cemeteries-memorials/europe/montfaucon-american-monument.
[7] Online: https://www.abmc.gov/.
[8] Online: https://www.abmc.gov/cemeteries-memorials/europe/meuse-argonne-american-cemetery.

Creating an Ed Bearss Tour in Narrative

The images in this book are pulled for the most part from video clips on tour, not carefully staged and professionally captured images in the proper lighting. Sometimes you can't get your fellow tour goers to conveniently move to the side for you, but doing so disturbs their tour experience. Also, sometimes audio is lost due to other people talking, vehicles passing by, wind across the microphone, and other causes. In such cases, mostly in the Vicksburg tour quotes of Ed's words and his talk at Belleau Wood in the World War I tour, you will see the ellipsis ("…") when this happens.

We also used the ellipsis when we abridged his talks to focus primarily on events and not the myriad of fascinating cause-and-effect relationships or personal details of historic figures he knows so well. These details bring these people to life for the tour goer, and this is Ed Bearss intent – as with his fallen comrades at Suicide Creek (see the first memoir book, *Walking the Ground: From Big Sky to Semper Fi*) – to keep their memory alive.[9] Sometimes, his spoken words are edited for ease of reading the narrative, but we have tried to demonstrate in book form as much of Ed Bearss's wit, colorful expressions, unique mannerisms, and, of course, knowledge of the past as possible in this third memoir book. We are trying to some extent to describe the Ed Bearss experience in words and photos, any imperfections in a real-life tour then become a part of the third book of the Ed Bearss memoir.

Constant Reference to Maps

Maps are critical to understanding the flow and timing of historical action, and this is Ed's forte from his childhood, covered in the NOVA Publisher's Ed Bearss memoir book, *Walking the Ground: From Big Sky to Semper Fi*. Ed Bearss is always getting tour goers to hold their maps in the orientation of the ground they stand on, so they can know where they are relative to the action happening in his interpretation. You'll experience this map reference in these chapters as on an actual tour. In this book's tour chapters, we have tried to include enough map detail so the reader can

---

[9] We have complete manuscripts of the Vicksburg tour we hope to publish in future.

understand where the events occur. We have also used annotated satellite images in the editor's Chapter 6 WWI tour addendum to provide actual tour locations when tracking down where York's Medal-of-Honor fight occurred. You will also see Ed Bearss's occasional reference to the "Gane Atlas," which is a tour publication of images, narrative and maps that Ed Bearss and Marty Gane provide, but Marty assembles and prints for her private tour groups.

Live Ed

Voice

Ed has a distinctive commanding voice that carries well, wherever he is and whenever he belches it out, drawing immediate attention as he begins, often drowning out other sounds, and other people talking, wherever he is walking, standing or sitting. He is unmistakable with it, perhaps from the Ken Burns series, and people still recognize him from that voice in faraway places. Of course, the voice will not come through these written words, but there are many YouTube (and other) videos of him on line where you can experience it and I may create movies in future from the hundreds of hours I have captured.

Eyes Closed

Ed Bearss has heard the complaint that he closes his eyes during an interpretative talk. Well, he is also complemented by those who say they know he is envisioning the person, place or event he is describing, and he is envisioning his subject while minimizing the distraction of the surroundings and people nearby. He says he does some of his best interpretations with his eyes shut. He has said that he's living the story he's telling vicariously, trying to imagine being there. He is helping himself into the past to bring his story to life. It is nothing to complain about, it is to be valued.

Talking Over Others

He has also been told that he talks over people, well, he says he didn't hear they were talking (they should have been listening to him). Also, he is trying to stay in his interpretation and follow his storyline, not hearing any interruptions until he asks if there are "any questions." Tour goers have paid to hear him, not themselves, and this should be remembered in the coaches, on the walks, and in the stands (selected places to stop to see and hear the story)

Animated

Ed will use his pointer or walking stick to point at key features of the terrain. The photos try to show it when it happens, and then show the target of his pointing in the same or adjacent photograph. He will sometimes punch or gesture with his right arm to add emphasis (see his book Dedication), or "punch up," a key action or event. Many times, he will draw a map in loose dirt on the ground. All of these mannerisms are a fundamental part of an Ed Bearss tour.

Teasing

As you see from historian Harry Butowksy's reminiscences from working many years with Ed (see the second Ed Bearss memoir book, *Walking the Ground: Making American History*, Ed is a great teaser. Ed displays this interaction with selected people in his tour groups, certainly the ladies, but everyone in general. He generally aligns them with one or more people or units from their State, and tells them how excited they are to see people from their state in action in Civil war battles. Sometimes he'll give one or more of them the persona of a personality from history throughout the tour, referring to them as "General this" or "Private that."

Repetition

If you are on tour and stay with the history interpreter, and have a large group (say, 25 tour goers), people will be "all over the place." Also, they will seem to ask a question that was answered 30 seconds ago, but before they were present or started to actually listen to the speaker. They will not stay in a tight and well-disciplined group. Ed Bearss tries to capture these outliers through repetition, which you will detect in the tour chapters of the book. This repetition is more prevalent when the tour involves longer trail walks and people are spread out, such as in Chapter 5 "Sioux Indian Wars" on the Rosebud Battlefield, which Ed Bearss says, "… is the most pristine battlefield in the United States."

Like It Is

Ed will use his sense of humor and infrequent, but effective, uncensored language. We have only "lightly" abridged the chapters with Ed's quotes, so Ed's words are as much as possible what he actually said. We have allowed most of what he said, particularly when he was quoting some historical figure like George S. Patton. Perhaps one of the most relevant and interesting expressions comes from another Ed Bearss characteristic, his expressive t-shirts he wears on tours (when the weather allows). Although there are many, one of the most relevant sayings is "I'd rather be historically accurate, than politically correct."

THE CHAPTERS IN THE PIED PIPER OF HISTORY

Having this background, the *Walking the Ground: Pied Piper of History* chapters describe his tour experiences, often in the words of those planning and managing a tour as well as those who have experienced his tours (read Bill Vodra's Foreword). The most amazing thing is that his talks are not scripted, he has no notes – just maps – and all the facts and details are burned in, almost infused in, Ed Bearss. He is clearly the "Google" of American history, certainly Civil War history, and much more. So, as you read Chapters 2 through 5, remember his quoted words (captured in video taken on tour), as he spoke them are from his memory only. It is at the heart of the amazing oratory skill that Ed Bearss possesses that makes him truly unique.

Chapter 1: Becoming History's Pied Piper

Chapter 1 presents the overall practice of being a tour historian, where how all the facets of his personality and experience come together to do his favorite vocation and pastime rolled into one. We describe the attributes of a good tour, those considerations of the tour planners that make the experience of the tour goer the best it can be. This chapter describes the typical activities of Ed Bearss's third career, following his WWII years in the Marines and hospitals (1942-1946), colleges and first jobs (1946-1955), then 40 years in the NPS (1955-1995), culminating in the title NPS Chief Historian, Emeritus. These earlier periods in his life are covered in the first two NOVA Science Publishers of Ed Bearss memoir books.

Chapter 2: Grant's Vicksburg Campaign Tour

The first tour experience we present comes from Marty Gane's South Mountain Expeditions[10] *Vicksburg – A Sesquicentennial Commemoration: February 25/27-March 4, 2013*. Having lived in Vicksburg for a decade, this tour arguably best represents Ed Bearss's extensive knowledge and experience for a critical Civil War campaign that had a major impact on the outcome of the war. We provide Ed Bearss's words at key locations and points in Grant's Campaign to invest the city and its control over a key bend in the Mississippi, blocking Union transit of what Lincoln called "the father of waters."[11]

Chapter 3: Gettysburg: The Third Day Tour

Chapter 3 provides a brief summary description of an Ed Bearss "Third Day at Gettysburg" tour. This tour summary is brief and hits the major

---

[10] Online: http://www.smountainexpeditions.com/.
[11] Online: https://www.nps.gov/gett/index.htm.

places we visited, but many sites are not described and the reader should visit the park. Most importantly, we capture highlights (but not all) of Ed Bearss's oratory as we cross the "Pickett's Charge" field to the famous Stone Wall at the Angle.

Chapter 4: John Wilkes Booth Escape Tour

In this chapter, we present highlights of Ed Bearss's oratory along the route followed by John Wilkes Booth after assassinating President Abraham Lincoln. Again, we "walked the ground" where the chase for Lincoln's killer occurred, from inside Ford's Theater, to the back where Booth emerged from the theater after the act, through to where he was finally shot down.

Chapter 5: Sioux Indian Wars Tour

On another South Mountain tour, Ed Bearss leads us through the Fetterman Fight, the Battle of the Rosebud, and the Battle of the Little Big Horn. One of Ed's best friends and peers, Jerome A. Greene (also once an employee of the National Park Service), a well-known author of books on the American Indian's plight under the 18th century U.S. Government, shares the tour lead-historian workload with Ed Bearss.

Chapter 6: The Great War Tour

Chapter 6 provides a summary description of the Ed Bearss' World War I tour, where our experienced lead history guide was Mike Kelly takes us to Ypres, Verdun, Fleury and Douaumont, the Somme, and the Meuse Argonne, among others. Ed Bearss interpretation on the U.S. Marine fight at Belleau Wood is presented word for word. We also visit several major American WWI monuments and cemeteries. Chapter 6 also includes an

Addendum where the memoir editor was able to experience at least a small part of the discovery of history Ed Bearss has lived countless times. In this case, reliving discovery of what in all probability is the true site of Sergeant York's Medal of Honor action near Chatel-Cherery in France. Historian and tour guide Michael Kelly, author of *Hero on the Western Front: Discovering Alvin York's WWI Battlefield* led this subsequent tour as well. Though Ed was not present, I learned much from him that I applied during the experience and he reviewed and edited my account for inclusion in his memoir. Here, I best applied what I had learned from my several Ed Bearss's tours and "walking-the-ground" education to understand the action by living vicariously and "being there" at Chatel-Cherhery on October 8, 1918.

Chapter 7: The Bearss in History

This chapter documents most, but certainly not all, of Ed Bearss accomplishments in "making American history" (see his second memoir book). It also describes the history accomplishments of his late wife Margie Riddle Bearss and his late daughter Sara Bearss's with for the Library of Virginia. Clearly, Ed Bearss was not the only historian in his family. We also take you with Ed Bearss as he throws out the first pitch in Nationals Stadium, in Washington, DC.

IMAGES AND FOOTNOTES

There were occurrences of images containing maps or pictures, most of which we extracted from video taken during the tour. As such, the images are imperfect, and it is sometimes difficult to clearly distinguish details on them from a photograph extracted in this way, in varying light, angles, and video focus. Similarly, the audio is sometimes lost from wind noise, particularly on the Great Plains, other people talking, and other causes – the tour is not a soundstage and in general you cannot stop the tour and inconvenience other tour goers by constantly creating quality photographs or asking Ed Bearss to repeat himself. One does not want Ed Bearss to do as he says in Chapter 5, "find out how a man throws a temper tantrum." Moreover, these tour chapters are intended to demonstrate the tour experience as best as one can in an illustrated narrative. In this regard, being on tour is also an imperfect experience, and you miss sights, miss interpretations, only see maps in shade and sunlight or while bouncing a bit on busses. You will have this static experience – with some aids to make maps and sights more evident – in what follows.

As in the tours themselves, you have to include enough detail and unique emotive stories to provide at least a passing interest for the well-read tour goer. However, there are also people on the tour with no background in the subject at all, and the tour was their way of getting exposure to the subject. The reader of these Ed Bearss sample tours will span this range of people as well. Ed Bearss's interpretations presented in the sample tour descriptions require significant historical background knowledge to fully appreciate. To this end, we have tried to provide online sources for any place, person or thing with which the reader may not be familiar. We provide URLs so the reader can do a "deep dive" on any person, place, or thing.

Our selection of online sources followed, perhaps imperfectly, the following priority:

1. Non-commercial Worldwide Web URLs, though there had to be exceptions when no other reference could be found. So, the first priority was to use links to the actual place we visited if one existed, particularly, we tried to use National Park Service URLs if they (i) could be found, and (ii) were not dead links, which we found (Harry Butowsky points out dead National Park Service URL links in the Ed Bearss memoir book 2, *Walking the Ground: Making American History*).
2. Wikipedia references provided most of the URLs we used. Arguably, these references are not "academically pure" references by experts in the field, so we checked for articles with extensive supporting references. We also realized that Wikipedia references are viewed worldwide and can be improved over time as new

information becomes available. No printed work has this real-time advantage, though these books are generally the source of references for many Wikipedia articles. Moreover, many readers cannot locate printed books we reference as well, particularly if not available from online sellers, but they can easily access Wikipedia and other online sources. These references provide quick access to further details on the times, people and places Ed identifies online, without having to track down a hard copy.
3. Any URL that provided additional information or sources on the person, place or thing referenced in the text.

Finally, we are trying to replicate the Ed Bearss's tour experience, not teach history, and we hope the many footnotes for online sources and the bibliography at the end of each chapter can provide what you need for a deep dive into the far-more-extensive academic history than provided in the tour descriptions. This deep dive would be best done just before going on an Ed Bearss interpretive tour, or other highly rated, history tour, or before visiting one of our National Battlefield Parks to "walk the ground" You can be sure Ed Bearss was there before you.

DEDICATION

The full-on Ed Bearss's tour experience can only be hinted in print, but you must have the real experience to appreciate all he knows and has experienced himself. He shares this full Ed Bearss in every tour, book or article he has written, his 140 National Park Service reports,[12] with the Americans (and others) he has served throughout his life, even as a wounded Marine. Ed Bearss's wounding at Cape Gloucester did not "disable" him, it actually "enabled" him to be far more successful in life, as he has said, then if he'd not been hit four times by Japanese bullets that day in January 1944. Ed's life should be an inspiration to any wounded warrior of what's possible

---

[12] Ninety of the 140 are described and a URL provided for download in the second memoir book.

in America. It is for this reason we dedicated the book to these men and women as well as the practical historians of the National Park Service.

Robert Irving Desourdis
Fairfax, Virginia, August 2019,
and Olympia, Washington, February 2020

Editors' Note to the Readers

Ed Bearss Memoir Books

The third book in the Ed Bearss *Walking the Ground* memoir:

The Pied Piper of History – Ed's third career as a lead tour historian is described in this book in the words of those who know his lessons taught from hundreds of hours walking history's hallowed ground. Of course, the American Civil War is the landscape of his most-walked ground, but he has also lead tours spanning the breadth of American sacrifice in WWI and WWII in Europe and WWII in Pacific. This book summarizes a few of these tours and provides a foretaste of potential future books detailing these Ed Bearss tours.

This second book of Ed Bearss "Walking the Ground" memoir is entitled:

Making American History – Ed's National Park Service career from the Park Historian at the Vicksburg National Military Park to the Chief Historian, investigating and documenting historic sites/events and developing what Americans will be told happened at these sites.

The first book in the Ed Bearss "Walking the Ground" memoir includes:

From Big Sky to Semper Fi – Ed's early history in Montana (and elsewhere), the United States Marines, his wounding and recovery, college, and the road to his National Park Service career.

IMPROVEMENTS

This book is derived from many sources and integrated into the Ed Bearss memoir book series. Although Ed's memory is truly extraordinary, it has fringes of recollection where certain specifics could be supplemented. As a reader, and natural critic, please send any errata, clarifications, or recommendations that "may" affect future editions to: Email: edbearssmemoirs@gmail.com.

We may not check these emails for some time or respond to them, but we will reference them for any future editions.

In this regard, we also ask that you provide feedback on the form and format of the word-for-word narrative and illustrations in Ed Bearss talk at Belleau Wood in Chapter 7. We have several major WWII tours completed in this format and seek your feedback to improve them, including the D-Day tour and the Italian Campaign, from Sicily to Rome – we will acknowledge valued recommendations in the proposed books.

Thank you.

BIOGRAPHIES

Jerome A. Greene

Contribution: The first Foreword in the book, and tour co-historian with Ed Bearss for Chapter 5 "Sioux Indian Wars Tour" with bibliography. Jerry Greene's Foreword also appears in the second Ed Bearss memoir book, *Walking the Ground: Making American History*.

Bio: Jerome A. Greene is a retired research historian, curator, and manager with the National Park Service, and the author of 23 books. A native of northern New York State, he is a U.S. Army veteran and a graduate of Black Hills State University and the University of South Dakota. Greene's interest in Native Americans was promoted during his early youth growing up in the Algonkian and Iroquois country, where he often searched for artifacts along the shores of Lake Ontario. As a Boy Scout and a member of the YMCA, he participated in classes devoted to Indian dancing and crafts and learned the lore of various tribes, hobbies that soon fostered an allure with the history of the conflicts between the U.S. Army and the Indian peoples of the Great Plains.

Following military service, Greene attended college in South Dakota and Oklahoma, settings steeped in Indian wars history. He drew encouragement for his interests from noted undergraduate and graduate professors Lura G. Camery, Donald J. Berthrong, Arrell M. Gibson, and Savoie Lottinville. While in graduate school, he served summers as a ranger-historian at Montana's Custer Battlefield National Monument (present Little Bighorn Battlefield National Monument), a position that further fixed his penchant for research and writing. Greene later taught American Indian history at Haskell Indian Nations University, served on the council of the Western History Association, as well as on editorial boards of the Western Historical Quarterly, South Dakota History, and Montana The Magazine of Western History. During his National Park Service career, 1973-2007, he worked with, and garnered inspiration from, Historians Edwin C. Bearss, Robert M. Utley, Don Rickey, Erwin N. Thompson, and Merrill J. Mattes. His own tours at Little Bighorn, wherein Greene often accompanied Bearss, were largely grounded in the field study and file research he had completed as a ranger there.

Among Greene's books is *American Carnage: Wounded Knee, 1890*, published by the University of Oklahoma Press, and which won the Spur Award for Best Western Historical Nonfiction from the Western Writers of America in 2015. His latest volume is January Moon: *The Northern Cheyenne Breakout from Fort Robinson, 1878-1879*, forthcoming from the University of Oklahoma Press in 2020. Greene resides in Colorado.

William Vodra

Contribution: The second Foreword in this third Ed Bearss memoir book, written as long-time Ed Bearss tour-goer. Bill also provided an excellent review of material in all three Ed Bearss memoir books.

Bio: Bill Vodra, JD, retired from the active practice of law at Arnold & Porter, LLP, in 2010 after more than 30 years with the firm, specializing in crisis management and regulatory issues involving medical products. Before joining Arnold & Porter, he served in the Food and Drug Administration and the Drug Enforcement Administration. Mr. Vodra has authored or coauthored more than 35 published papers and book chapters on legal and regulatory matters. He received his JD from Columbia University and a BA in economics from the College of Wooster. He and his wife have identified 21 direct and collateral ancestors who served in the Civil War (all wearing blue uniforms), as well as others who served our nation in wars from the Revolution through Korea. They have been in the Bearss Brigade since the late 1980s.

Marty Gane

Marty Gane with Ed Bearss.

Contribution: Contributed Ed Bearss meeting and business start history, Chapter 1 "History's Pied Piper," provided tour "read-ahead" lists for several chapter bibliographies and several important Ed Bearss tour stories and photographs.

Bio: Marty Gane has over 35 years of experience designing, operating, and escorting study tours for numerous clients including the Smithsonian Travel Program, World Wildlife Fund and National Geographic Expeditions. Since 1979, she has led educational groups to many corners of the world: from the Himalayas to the Great Barrier Reef; and from the archaeological wonders of Greece and Egypt to the Anazasi ruins of the American Southwest. She designed two unique itineraries for the Smithsonian: an Atlantic crossing aboard the four-masted tall ship *Sea Cloud* in commemoration of the 500th anniversary of Columbus' 1492 voyage; and a seven-day "University at Sea" cruising the Aegean Islands in partnership with Oxford University.

In 2006, at the urging of Ed Bearss, Marty established her own company, South Mountain Expeditions. South Mountain operates 4-5 history tours each year in the U.S. and overseas. Popular tours have included "Attack on

Pearl Harbor," "Normandy to the Rhine River," "Sherman's March Through Georgia," "The Battle of Little Bighorn," and "Greece, featuring the WWII Battle of Crete." More information about her tour plans and results can be found at: http://www.smountainexpeditions.com/ and Tel: (301) 988-1852, email: tours@smountainexpeditions.com.

In 2014, Marty acquired Civil War Tours, a company that has offered in-depth tours of our nation's most significant Civil War Battlefields since 1999. See: www.civilwartours.org.

A native Washingtonian, Marty received a degree in Greek Classics at the University of Virginia. A civil war buff, Marty resides in the shadow of South Mountain just down the road from the Antietam Battlefield.

Pete Brown

Pete Brown and wife Julia.

Contribution: Approval for use of the John C. Waugh biography of Ed Bearss,[13] narrative and photos of Ed on a HistoryAmerica Tour to the South Pacific, including vignettes of some of his photographed moments.

---

[13] Waugh, John C. *Edwin C. Bearss: History's Pied Piper: A Biography by John C. Waugh, A Concise Illustrated Biography of the Life and Times of America's Impresario of Public History*, Edwin C. Bearss Tribute Fund, Inc., Washington, DC, and HistoryAmerica Tours, Dallas, Texas, 2003.

Bio: Pete Brown and his wife Julia founded HistoryAmerica Tours in 1990. In the process, they soon met Ed Bearss. Using small ships, riverboats, vans, and busses, HistoryAmerica Tours offered 80 tours with Ed at the helm from Guadalcanal to the Rhine. This does not include numerous scouting trips. Military history was the principle subject offered under Bearss' tutelage, but he had the ability to lead tours featuring a multitude of themes and did so. The business was sold in early 2007. Pete and Julia reside in suburban Dallas. Prior to 1990, they were in the construction business. Pete Brown majored in history at the University of New Mexico in Albuquerque where he graduated in 1963.

Michael Kelly

Contribution: Mike provided an excellent leadership of the South Mountain Expeditions World War I tour in 2017. In 2018, Mike did another WWI tour, and this time brought the tour group (with Robert Desourdis) to the York fight site behind the village of Chatel-Chéhéry in France, then showed all the site locations where artifacts were recovered. While doing so, he took us through the actions that happened there on October 8, 2018, described in the addendum — which he reviewed and improved — as an Addendum to Chapter 6.

Bio: He was educated at the University of Hull, obtaining a degree in history. Michael had joined the Royal Navy at the age of 15. Upon leaving, he joined the British Police and became a police detective; working on serious crime and homicide for 25 years. Upon his retirement, he started guiding on the Great War Battlefields. He worked with the Elderhostel Group for five years, guiding on the American sectors.

He is also an accomplished guide on the D-Day Landings. Together with his good friend Dr. Nolan, a retired MTSU Professor; Michael assisted in the formation of the Sergeant York Project. (Now known as the "Nolan Group.") This initiative was an attempt to locate the scene where Alvin C. York fought in 1918. Between 2004 and 2009, research and field visits by professional historians, geographers and archaeologists, resulted in the discovery of incontrovertible evidence as to the whereabouts of the fight site.

Unit artefacts were located and the records of the U.S. Grave Registration Service, which gave coordinates of the temporary burial locations of the six Americans killed in the fight, enabled the Group to trace further artefacts. This, the true site is 800 meters from the present York Memorial. His book *Hero on The Western Front: Discovering Alvin York's WWI Battlefield*, describes this work and settles the true York-site search. His next book, *Behind Enemy Lines with the SOE*, will be published in 2020.

Michael is available for guiding and he can be contacted at: apollobattlefieldguide@gmail.com.

His book, *Hero on The Western Front* is available at: www.battlehistorianguy.com.

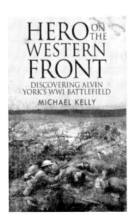

Rebecca Blackwell Drake

Contribution: Documentation about Margie Riddle Bearss and her history accomplishments, including narrative and photographs.

Bio: Rebecca Blackwell Drake of Raymond, Mississippi, is the author of ten Civil War books:

- *The Battle of Raymond and Other Collected Stories*
- *In Their Own Words, Soldiers Tell the Story of the Battle of Raymond*
- *A Soldier's Story of the Siege of Vicksburg: From the Diary of Osborn H. Oldroyd*
- *Lone Star General, Hiram B. Granbury* (co-authored with Thomas Holder)

- *My Dear Wife: Letters to Matilda: The Civil War Letters of Sid and Matilda Champion* (co-authored with Margie Bearss)
- *Darwina's Diary: A View of Champion Hill in 1865,* (co-authored with Margie Bearss)
- *Collected Stories of the Vicksburg Campaign* (co-authored with Margie Bearss)
- *Leaves: The Diary of Elizabeth Meade Ingraham, Rebel Sister of General George Meade* (co-authored with Sue Burns Moore)
- *Lift High the Cross: The History of St. Alban's Episcopal Church* (co-authored with Kenon Ruska)
- *Owl Roost Plantation: The Civil War Letters of Samuel and Caroline Townsend of Bovina.*

She is the recipient of numerous awards including the *William D. McCain Publication Award* (2002) presented by the Mississippi Division of Sons of Confederate Veterans and a Resolution of Commendation (2003) presented by the Mississippi Department of Archives and History for her contributions to historic preservation. Along with her husband, James L. Drake, they format and edit the Champion Hill website: www.battleofchampionhill.org.

Profits from the sale of her books are donated primarily to the preservation of Sid Champion's portion of the Champion Hill Battlefield and to St. Alban's Church, Bovina, which was used as a hospital after the Battles of Champion Hill and the Big Black River.

David R. Smith

Contribution: Reviewed and commented on all chapters, and Implemented Ed Bearss' edits and "scribblings" as well as provided editorial recommendations. David introduced the Editor Desourdis to South Mountain Expedition tours and Ed Bearss in 2011, which has culminated in the Ed Bearss memoir books.

Bio: Dr. Smith received a BS in Physics from Randolph-Macon College in 1967, an M.S.E.E. from Georgia Tech in 1970, and a PhD in Electrical Engineering and Computer Science from The George Washington University in 1977. He has worked as an electrical engineer and manager within the Department of Defense, and held adjunct, visiting, research, and regular faculty positions at Georgia Tech, George Washington University and George Mason University. Dr. Smith also consulted for several companies, has written technical books and technical articles, and has lectured worldwide, in the areas of digital and wireless communications. Now mostly retired, his current interests include traveling and spending time with his ten grandchildren.

ACKNOWLEDGMENTS

This third book in the Ed Bearss memoir includes inputs from many people with whom he has engaged over decades as a lead tour historian. They have made important contributions we were not able to reach in the time we had available, but in the hope of future editions, we could include relevant submissions at that time (see the Editor's Note).

We thank Ed's close friend and peer, Jerome A. Greene, for providing the first Foreword and editing Chapter 5, "Sioux Indian Wars Tour," supporting the Little Big Horn portion of our experience. His expertise on this battlefield, which he helped preserve and interpret as a National Park Service employee, was invaluable to us on the tour.

We thank Bill Vodra for his excellent second Foreword, covering his experience on over 95 tours with Ed Bearss. His words provide not only due praise for Ed Bearss's in-depth knowledge of American and World history, but also his emotive speech and detailed stories of the historic figures that once walked our toured ground.

We thank Martha Gane, a close friend of Ed Bearss and owner/operator of South Mountain Expeditions, Ed's preferred tour company for Marty's expertise as a detail-oriented tour director/manager. First, we thank her for providing Ed with the best possible business foundation for tour customer satisfaction, ensuring that each of her customers detailed needs are addressed so they can focus on the history being revealed. Marty also provided an excellent narrative on how she and Ed met and describing Ed's promotion of her starting her company. She also provided tour "read-ahead" bibliographies and several important photographs of Ed, including those with her late best dog friend, Jack.

We thank Michael Kelly of the UK for his excellent WWI South Mountain Expeditions history tour in France and Belgium in 2017. He also reviewed and greatly improved Chapter 6 "The Great War Tour," in which the tour description is provided, including review of the Sergeant York battle site Addendum.

We thank Pete Brown, the founder of HistoryAmerica Tours in 1990. Pete has led extensive history tours with Ed, including to the Pacific islands, and contributed entertaining vignettes found in Chapter 2.

Ed and I thank historian and history preservationist Rebecca Blackwell Drake for material about Ed's late wife Margie, which pays proper tribute to Margie's work as a historian in her own right. Rebecca had also read a letter during our Vicksburg tour (Chapter 7) that Matilda Champion wrote to her husband during the Civil War. Her recitation is in the word-for-word tour description, unfortunately cut from the published summary description, but possibly included in a future NOVA publication.

We also thank Pete Brown for permission to draw from the John C. Waugh book *Edwin Cole Bearss: History's Pied Piper: A Concise Illustrated Biography of the Life and Times of America's Impresario of Public History*, the Edwin C. Bearss Tribute Fund, Inc., Washington, D.C., and HistoryAmerica Tours, Dallas, Texas.

Ed and I thank his daughter Ginny for making several important editorial (and censorial) comments about the text and helped us portray the lives of her mother and sister in the right context. We also thank her for providing great photos of the latest two generations of the Bearss family descendants of Ed and Margie.

We thank Ann E. Henderson, Mari Julienne, and John Deal of the Library of Virginia for providing permission to publish their memoriam notifications about the passing of Sara Bearss and her significant contribution to Virginia history in Chapter 7 "The Bearss in History."

Acknowledgments

We thank Wendy Swanson for planning and operating the annual Ed Bearss Birthday Bash events, describing her history with Ed Bearss in the "Bearss Brigade," and providing photographs of Ed seeing his installed monument at Champion Hill in Chapter 7.

We thank Ed's friends, such as Earl and Sharon Clough for taking Ed to the All-Star game festivities and other events, helping him practice his "first pitch" for the game, inviting him into their home on various special occasions, and writing this story for Ed's memoir in Chapter 7 "The Bearss in History."

We acknowledge the help of Jennifer Romanoski, Museum Educator, and staff at the Johnson County Jim Gatchell Memorial Museum for their providing photographs (with permission) of the Metzger bugle and plaque on display in their museum used in Chapter 5 "Sioux Indian Wars Tour."

Of course, we thank the many people who have played key roles in Ed's life, many mentioned in this book, who we were not able to contact for their contribution. If anyone would like to add to a possible future edition or just for Ed's reading, the Editor's Note gives an email address for submissions: Email: EdBearssMemoirs@gmail.com.

Bob Desourdis thanks his wife Betty for her patience, as well as reviewing and editing the final prefaces, and daughters Danielle, Nicole and Amanda for having an absentee father and grandfather during the two years it has taken to create the Ed Bearss memoir books.

Finally, we thank Nova staff and of course, Nadya Columbus, the NOVA President, whose foresight is bringing you this impressive Ed Bearss memoir.

Chapter 1

BECOMING HISTORY'S PIED PIPER[14]

HISTORY TOUR GUIDE

Serving as a lead tour historian requires a verified logistics plan of the vignettes we will visit, which is tightly integrated with the tour-manager's plan beforehand. Given the many places we intend to visit within the time available, travel times and the physical needs of a diverse group of tour goers, we cannot afford any major uncertainties. All hotel stays from airport to airport, hotel and restaurant schedules, rest stops on highways and roadways, refueling stops, and all other visits along the tour route are scheduled oftentimes months in advance.

Tour goers receive materials and recommended bibliographies of books to read or videos to watch well ahead of the tour, so those on the tour have the necessary historic background to best appreciate the events we will be recounting and the people you'll be meeting (virtually). Ed Bearss usually does background lectures on the coach before arrival, timed to account for

---

[14] A reference to the 2003 book Edwin Cole Bearss: *History's Pied Piper, A Biography by John C. Waugh. A Concise Illustrated Biography of the Life and Times of America's Impresario of Public History*. Edwin C. Bearss Tribute Fund, Inc., Washington, DC, and HistoryAmerica Tours, Dallas, Texas. 2003

the key information needed to know why, as well as where, the action we are surveying happened when and where it did.

The Tour Manager makes all arrangements well beforehand so the tour groups can focus on "walking the ground" and hearing my interpretations, not wondering where their luggage is, where they'll eat next and where they'll find a pitstop. Of course, these details as well the sites we'll visit are worked our months earlier between the Tour Director and Ed Bearss, as lead tour historian. Of course, options and "free time" are worked in, but all other arrangements, mostly to the minute, must be worked out in advance.

Of course, the buses or other transportation we get is very important. The large tour buses are great for good straight roads with no tight turns, but then there are places in some parks in the U.S. and American battlefields in Europe that become inaccessible, so often smaller buses scheduled for certain locations are better. Of course, you also have to have good drivers that are capable of getting us where we want to go, and sometimes they have to know that bus well to negotiate the turns and hills we encounter. There is always some risk-taking at low speed in these tight places with the bus. Of course, the buses must have a microphone so Ed Bearss can give his interpretation as a set up for each stand, that is, place we will stop, walk and "stand" for a few minutes, before we get there.

HISTORY TOUR DIRECTORS

Pete Brown and Marty Gane were largely, though not exclusively, responsible for Ed Bearss's third career as a history tour leader, easing the end of his NPS career and continuing to make it possible for him to "walk the ground" for the last few decades. Here, we have included their words describing their experiences with Ed Bearss.

Pete Brown's "Things You Might Not Know about Ed Bearss"

Pete Brown provided the following memories for Ed Bearss's memoir in April 2019.

Ed Bearss the Showman

Not everyone knows that in another world Ed would have loved to be on stage. On a cruise or a tour, he would do whatever it took to have tour members rolling in the aisles. For example, nobody on the *Delta Queen*[15] riverboat believed Ed had it in him to dance with the ladies in an on-board talent show, but there he is going at full blast. Check the picture.

On the *Delta Queen*. Provided with permission by Pete Brown.

Given a chance to be King Neptune[16] with a shipload of uninitiated "pollywogs" in 2005, Ed jumped at it. The ship crossed the equator heading north from the Solomon Islands to Guam. Ed threw away the carefully prepared script and came out of the event as star of the show, transforming all the passengers into "shellbacks" by making them kiss a dead fish and other indignities. Of course, Ed first crossed the equator on a troop ship in 1942 heading from San Diego to Samoa and knew the ropes. It was a lot more fun to be King Neptune. Again, check the picture.

---

[15] Online: https://deltaqueen.com/ and https://en.wikipedia.org/wiki/Delta_Queen.
[16] Online: https://en.wikipedia.org/wiki/Neptune_(mythology).

People have little clue that Ed has a fine sense of rhythm when the situation calls for it. While leading the "Deluge in the Delta," tour dealing with the great Mississippi flood of 1927,[17] Ed took his group to the Great Hinds Street Missionary Baptist Church[18] in Greenville, Mississippi, by pre-arrangement on a Sunday morning. Ed the Showman emerged when the time came for gospel music. He could not hold still and shouted out every word, much to the delight of all in attendance. Sadly, we don't have a picture, but Ed was written up in the *Delta Democrat Times*[19] the next morning. His right arm was still sore by using it to keep time. The locals, of course, loved him.

Ed Bearss as King Neptune. Provided with permission by Pete Brown.

Ed and the Rubber Boat Incident

Here's an Ed WW2 story you may not know. On September 20, 1942, he volunteered to serve in the Third Raider Battalion and was eventually sent to Espirito Santo in the archipelago of the New Hebrides for amphibious combat training.20 Serving with this unit considerably upped his chance of seeing combat. Assigned to carry the Browning Automatic Rifle (BAR) for his squad, they all became very proficient in handling such a boat. Marines in rubber boats lightheartedly dubbed themselves the "Condom Navy" but knew how critical this training could be for upcoming combat. Ed was not

---

[17] Online: https://en.wikipedia.org/wiki/Great_Mississippi_Flood_of_1927.
[18] Online: https://www.greaterhindsmbc.org/our-history#!.
[19] Online: https://www.ddtonline.com/.
[20] See the Ed Bearss first memoir book, *From Big Sky to Semper Fi*, also by NOVA Science.

about to go all the way from Montana to the South Pacific in order to miss out on being in the action.

A BAR man in the bow of the rubber landing craft provides covering fire as the 10-man boat crew reaches the undefended beach of Pavuvu in the Russell Islands. Department of Defense Photo (USMC) 54765.

The enclosed picture does not show Ed's particular squad, but gives an idea of what the rubber boats looked like. The BAR man sits at the bow of the boat, his weapon poised for action. One day, being towed back to port by a much larger and more powerful Higgins boat, they hit a wave head on and their rubber boat flipped completely over, dumping the whole squad in the ocean. Ed was especially weighed down with BAR ammo belts and in no time found himself sinking quite rapidly. Somehow, he stayed calm, dumped the ammo belts and finally headed up instead of down. He was mighty happy to finally break the surface, gulp some air and get fished out by the Higgins boat swabbies. Other than getting shot about four months later, this was his closest call as a WW2 Marine.

Ed at Suicide Creek

To know Ed is to know he ran into a Japanese machine gun on January 2, 1944, on the west end of the island of New Britain. It took him 26 months to recover from his many wounds in three different U.S. Naval Hospitals, all in California. The question here, how many of you know the location of New Britain? And furthermore, do any of you know the actual location of Suicide Creek? The banks of the creek mark where he and a large number of fellow

Marines were killed or wounded that fateful day. Ed's squad was point for several hundred Marines on patrol.

Ed sat down with me several years ago and using Google Earth we came up with a set of coordinates which are very close to where all the action took place. The coordinates are 5° 29' 27.21" S, 148° 24' 57.26" E. Of the eleven men in Ed's 7th Marine Regiment squad that day, five were killed and three were badly wounded. The disaster led to the battalion commander being relieved before sundown. New Britain, by the way, remains part of Papua New Guinea to this day. See if you can find it, and if not, the map drawn by Kieran McAuliffe, should help you understand the important geography of the most pivotal event in Ed's young life.

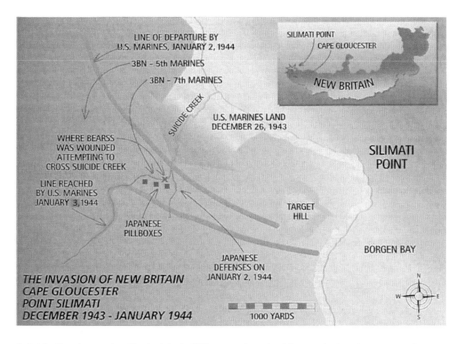

Suicide Creek map by Kevin McAuliffe reproduced with permission from John C. Waugh's Edwin Cole Bearss: History's Pied Piper: A Concise Illustrated Biography of the Life and Times of America's Impresario of Public History Public History. Provided by Pete Brown.

Sports Fan and Athlete

Ed does not talk about this a whole lot, but sports played a big role in his life, especially as a young man. On July 6, 1933, Ed went with his father to the first-ever Major League Baseball (MLB) All Star game. They sat in the right field bleachers at Comiskey Park, Chicago, and watched Babe Ruth hit a home run. Ed can name every athlete imaginable in at least three sports: football, baseball and boxing, all his favorites. He played varsity football at Hardin High School, Montana, as a pulling guard and remembers virtually every play. He boxed while in the Marine Corps and was quite good, especially when he employed the rope-a-dope. Ask about any championship fight in the 1930s and he'll tell you in detail how it unfolded.

After the war, Ed managed a local softball team and on October 3, 1951, he danced on a bar in Washington, DC, when Bobby Thomson hit his famous homer to win the pennant for the New York Giants over the Brooklyn Dodgers. Ed had season tickets to the Washington Senators for a number of years and was a big fan. Just last year Ed was a guest of honor at the MLB All Star game[21] in Washington, DC, home of the Washington Nationals the year before they won the World Series. Sports continue to be a big factor in Ed's life.

---

[21] Online: https://www.mlb.com/all-star.

Public Speaker

Ed has given thousands of talks to groups large and small over the last 70 odd years. He's very good at it, but it didn't start out that way. This story came from his wife Margie and Ed has confirmed it. The first significant speech he ever gave took place during the time he was working at Vicksburg National Military Park (VNMP) in the late 1950s. The preparation got his full attention, to the point he wrote his talk out word for word. Given a mic attached to a long cord, Ed had only his one good hand to manage his notes and the mic. The speech simply had to go well, but it didn't come close. Standing still proved impossible, and he ended up hopelessly tangled in the cord with the notes scattered on the floor. The very next day Ed promised himself there would never be a repeat of that. In my 29 years of knowing him, I've never seen him use notes or a mic with a long cord. I doubt if you have either.

If Ed stands at a podium, he sometimes looks down while talking, but he's not reading anything. He feels very strongly that a speech, to be fully effective, must not be read from notes. His storied public speaking career offers proof of this point. No notes.

Marty Gane's "How I Met and Worked with Ed Bearss"

Martha "Marty" Gane provided her memories for Ed Bearss's memoir in August 2019.

Despite the fact that I grew up in Arlington and rooted for the "Generals" and the Blue & Grey at Washington-Lee High School, I didn't visit my first Civil War battlefield until I was in my 30's(?!). In fact, I distinctly remember my father and my husband (now x-husband) sitting around the kitchen table discussing the Civil War and my walking out of the room due to my lack of interest. My interest in the American Civil War was kindled years later when I watched Ken Burns' series on PBS. After watching that amazing program, I began researching my Great Grandfather, Frank Haskell. I made visits to the National Archives and learned that he had fought for both the 5th Maine and the 17th Maine; that he had fought in all the major battles of the Eastern Theater.

Ed Bearss and Marty Gane.

I was telling a friend of mine at work about some of my findings. She said that if I were interested in the Civil War, I should take the Smithsonian Resident Associates' day trips to a Civil War battlefield. She and father had taken several, and told me, "You get on a coach at the Castle at 8 in the morning and spend all day at a battlefield like Fredericksburg then return to the Smithsonian at 5:30-6 PM," and she said, "The best part was that the tours were led by Ed Bearss." I replied, "Who's Ed Bearss?" She laughed, chucked me on the shoulder, and said "Marty! Ed Bearss. He was in the Ken Burns series." I said, "You mean that strange old man?" And she said," Yes, but he's completely different on a battlefield; he's amazing."

I met Ed Bearss when I took my first Smithsonian day trip in the summer 1994 to Manassas. On the First Manassas tour, Ed showed me exactly where my great grandfather's unit (the 5th Maine) stood on Chinn Ridge to fire their one and only volley before they took off skedaddling. I was hooked. I took a few more tours as a paying participant and then volunteered to go on the trips as the Smithsonian tour assistant (so I could take the trips for free).

Over the next several years, I tour-managed nearly all of Ed's Smithsonian Civil War tours and often I would drive him home after the tours. Ed and I became good buddies. One day in 2000 he said, "Margie wants to meet you." I had only spoken to Margie two or three times on the phone and was delighted and honored to get the chance to meet Mrs. Bearss. Margie was in very poor health with congestive heart failure. She had basically been house bound in a wheelchair for several years before I met her.

"George Washington"
October 18-28, 2010

"The Chesapeake"
August 20-27, 2009

"Boston: An Early American Sampler"
September 21-27, 2009

"The Attack on Pearl Harbor"
December 4-11, 2008

"Joshua Chamberlain & The 20th Maine"
May 2007

"Benedict Arnold: Path from Patriot to Traitor"
August 2007

Ed's tours for me [Martha Gane] August 2007 to October 2010. Provided with permission by Marty Gane.

We three went out to dinner. I spent the evening grilling Margie about Ed, where and how they met and Ed courting her. She told me about the time Ed came calling when he brought her three books and a Hotchkiss shell. "Most other women get roses. I got a cannon ball." Margie told me about their marriage in 1958 and the "honeymoon from hell," a month-long, 10,000-mile road trip where they started at 5:30 am each morning and reach a motel by night fall. They visited historic sites all over the western states except four.

Ed's tours for me [Martha Gane] August 2010 to April 2013. Provided with permission by Marty Gane.

More dinners followed. Then one day I got the "OK" from Ed to drive Margie to Gettysburg to meet a young ranger who had a copy of Margie's book *Sheridan's Meridian Expedition: The Forgotten Campaign*. She met the ranger and autographed her book, then I took her on an abbreviated tour of the battlefield. We had a ball!

I got to take Margie to see the *Hunley*. Due to my tour schedule, the only time I had available was in the middle of the week, but the *Hunley* facility was only open on weekends. Ed made some phone calls and they opened up the museum just for Margie and me. They had two security guards, an excellent tour guide, and two women in the gift shop. We spent an hour and half in there. Margie was ecstatic! When we told Ed about our trip he remarked, "I only get to spend 30 mins. when I bring a group!"

Ed's tours for me [Martha Gane] 2013-2018. Provided with permission by Marty Gane.

Ed and Margie Bearss became dear, dear friends; family really. I lost my mom to cancer when I was 19 and my dad died of cancer 10 years later. Ed has been more than a mentor and friend; Ed's been like a father to me.

When I met Ed in 1994, I was working for a tour operator named Academic Travel Abroad (ATA) located in Washington DC. They organize educational tours for non-profit organizations such as the Smithsonian, *National Geographic*, the World Wildlife Fund and Harvard Alum.

I worked for ATA from 1987 to 2001. Initially I was hired as the "Southeast Asia & Pacific Program Designer." In 1989, I added the Caribbean to my bailiwick when I organized several programs on the four-masted tall ship *Sea Cloud* for the Smithsonian. After I met Ed Bearss, Ed and I designed and led several Civil War itineraries for the National Trust for Historic Preservation and *National Geographic*. By that time, the marketing department was referring to me as "ROW," the "Rest of the World," because I had a basket of about 18 different countries where as other program designers typically handled tours to just one country: Russia, China, England, France, or Italy etc.

All along, I was asking to design tours to Greece, since I had a degree in Greek Classics. In 1996, ATA created a new position for me: Africa and the Middle East. And so, it was on September 11, 2001, I had a group flying home from Turkey which was diverted to Halifax, another group trying to fly to Turkey that afternoon, and a group stranded in Greece for 4 extra days. By September 12th, all of my tours for the balance of 2001-2002 were canceled as no one desired to tour Egypt, Jordan, Syria, Morocco, or Turkey.

ATA had to let go nearly a quarter of their staff, but they offered me a full-time job of tour managing and so in 2002 I tour managed 16 tours all over the world, including countries like Iceland, Russia, France and Italy, and others that weren't "my" countries.

Ed had introduced me to Pete Brown, owner of HistoryAmerica Tours, back in 1999. Pete had hired me to manage a few of his tours, including a history of the State of Florida tour. Over 15 years, Ed had led scores of tours in the U.S. for Pete Brown, but nothing overseas. Apparently, Pete had been trying for some time to convince Ed to repeat a WWII tour that Ed had done in 1999, but Ed refused. He had had such a disastrous experience with the company who made the arrangements, that Ed had sworn he would never set foot in Europe again.

In 2002, unbeknownst to me, Ed put a bug in Pete's ear and said that he would agree to lead a WWII tour from Normandy to the Rhine River if, and only if, Pete hired me to design it and tour-manage it. That's how I was hired to design and lead tours for HistoryAmerica from 2003-2006, including "The Great Battlefields of Europe: From Normandy to the Rhine River" led by Ed; "The Battle of Britain" led by Vice Air Marshal Ron Dick; and "The Anazasi of the American South West" led by Scott Thybony.

When Pete Brown decided to sell HistoryAmerica Tours, Ed gave me a call and asked if I would "do four tours for me next year." His call came in April, just as I was about to set off to manage four tours, nearly back-to-back, for ATA. My first reaction was one of doubt; lots of doubts. I remember thinking…what me? Me start a company? By myself? Are you kidding? I couldn't do that even if I had the time. I worried about the risk and the responsibility and, after all, Ed was 83 years old!

But it was such a great opportunity, I had to say, "yes," even if it ended up being only for a year or two. So, I said I would do two tours in 2007 for him; we decided on "Joshua Chamberlain and the 20th Maine" and "Benedict Arnold: Path from Patriot to Traitor." In between tour managing assignments, I found a name (South Mountain Expeditions, basically because I didn't have time to do a name search and I knew the odds were that no one else was using that name); a logo (beautifully designed by my college roommate, Marty Ferraro); I developed a website from software I bought at Costco; formed an LLC; bought liability insurance; designed a brochure; and I was off!

Cowboy Ed at Buffalo Bill's museum in Golden Colorado. Provided with permission by Marty Gane.

I can now say whole-heartedly that it was the best decision of my life. I honestly don't know where I'd be today if Ed hadn't encouraged me to start my own company. I presented Ed with an antique compass at the farewell dinner of South Mountain's inaugural tour, telling him that he had changed the course of my life and I would be forever grateful.

South Mountain Expeditions is a small travel company that offers four to five history tours a year in the US and Abroad. We have operated tours focusing on the American Revolution, the Civil War, WWII, WWI and, a two-week history tour of Greece, where Ed led the four-day portion on the WWII Battle of Crete. Our popular "State" series began in 2008 where we spend 10-days visiting historic and cultural sites and national parks in a state. To date we've explored the states of Montana, Wyoming, Colorado, New Mexico/Arizona, Missouri, Kentucky, Maine, Texas, the Chesapeake region, New Hampshire and Vermont, New York and Michigan. It's a fantastic way to see the country. I always mention at the welcome dinner that Ed is the only person on the planet that could lead a tour of historic sites in a state. If he had to cancel due to broken ankle, I would most likely have to hire five to seven people to take his place.

"Classical Greece"
May 18-June 1, 2010

"Great Battlefields of Western Europe From Normandy to the Rhine River"
September 2011

"WWII Invasion of Italy"
Sept 30-October 12, 2014

"Bonnie Scotland"
May 2015

"Third Reich Germany"
September 2018

"WWII England"
September 6/7-16 2016

"World War I, The Great War"
October 2017

"Normandy"
October 2018

Ed's South Mountain Expeditions international tours Ed Bearss did for me [Martha Gane]. Provided with permission by Marty Gane.

Marty Gane: When I realized that my two best buddies were going to turn 91 years old in 2014, I knew I wanted to capture a photo of this momentous event. Ed turned 91 in June and when my dear sweet Jack turned 13 in December (13 x 7 dog years = 91), I took this snapshot of the two Nonagenarians. Provided with permission by Marty Gane.

EXPERIENCING AN ED BEARSS TOUR

The Pied Piper of History

Ed Bearss has been giving tours since his first days at Vicksburg, and these had been done under the auspices of the National Park Service[22] as one of its employees. Later, his expertise advanced, he came to be doing "staff rides" for both NPS and military officers at major battlefield parks, like Gettysburg and Antietam. Inevitably, people – including the Smithsonian Institution and private companies – would use him be the history lead doing tours for them, and in the latter case, he could be paid outside the Government. Of course, there were several stipulations that came with this permission. That meant he was not allowed to use any materials produced by the National Park Service and, of course, he could not do them when he was paid by the Government. So, nights, holidays, vacations and weekends offered the only times for such outside work.

Well before his last days at the Park Service, he was in high demand to do private tours, particularly after the Ken Burns Series[23] aired. He would go on to lead tours for HistoryAmerica Tours, the Smithsonian Institution[24] and eventually South Mountain Expeditions[25] (among others). As his expertise at multiple parks grew, and national interest in the Civil War, he became a highly desirable tour historian. Few knew more about the people, plans, events and consequences at a specific battlefield park as Ed Bearss, and absolutely no one knew as much about as many battlefields and other sites as he did. So, when his last day at the Park Service was set, and he took the Government's "buy out" opportunity to leave after 40 years at age 75, he was ready for a third era of his work, as a lead tour historian.

---

[22] Online: https://en.wikipedia.org/wiki/National_Park_Service.
[23] Online: http://www.pbs.org/kenburns/civil-war/.
[24] Online: https://www.smithsonianjourneys.org/.
[25] Online: http://www.smountainexpeditions.com/.

Experience, Not Theory

From firsthand experience, there is no better way to appreciate history than on an Ed Bearss tour. Few tour historians can claim in their experience to have the following advantages:

- Lifelong love of history, starting as a young boy from a ranch in Montana by mapping the progress of Italian and Ethiopian armies on his parent's living-room ranch wall in 1935
- Trained soldier, a U.S. Marine willing to kill or be killed taking his objective, and recovering for 27 months in hospitals from New Guinea to Australia to California
- A sense of humor, being able to take on the *Mummy* persona under Nurse Molly Padlow's kidding care,[26] and would use this humor on his tours
- A recognized master historian who remade and interpreted the basic history of many of our Nation's Parks.

The Heart

If you read Ed Bearss's response to the Pete Shed Shiloh tour in Chapter 4 of the first Ed Bearss memoir book, *Walking the Ground: From Big Sky to Semper Fi*; and read Mr. Bearss's words about public speaking, that is, you must "be emotive, don't read from notes, speak from the heart," you understand the Ed Bearss draw. This draw is all part of Ed Bearss's learned behavior to compel his listeners. You can't really know history unless you can put yourself "in the shoes" of the human beings that lived the experience, to "feel," even if just a little bit, what it must have been like. This point is tied to what Pete Shed told Ed Bearss about the difference between an academic historian and a practical historian, which motivated Ed Bearss to join the National Park Service to the benefit of all Americans.

---

[26] From Chapter 3, *Walking the Ground: From Big Sky to Semper Fi*.

Asked why he was so driven to give these people a voice, many under stone markers in cemeteries from the Pacific and across countless American graves in cemeteries in Western Europe and Italy, Ed Bearss said he would speak for those who now cannot. Those like his comrades at Suicide Creek, with whom he'd lived, laughed and shared the "Band-of-Brothers"[27] trust and togetherness in combat, who were in a moment shot down, stilled, and made silent forever. As he said, they were never able to speak again to their families, never able to write their memoirs (as he has done). So, he was driven to tell their stories.

The Means

The background he provides on the way to a tour site, helps you go back in time. His chosen words – often in the present tense - speak simply to his audience. No arrogance, just facts, but facts emotively conveyed. You can easily read history in a book, but you can't *feel* it unless you stand where the history was made, whether on a ridge, in a coulee, on ridge line, in an old theater, and most movingly, in a cemetery. A practical historian, Ed Bearss's passion made possible by his profession, putting you in their shoes, to best understand the people and their times. The effect of doing so is to appreciate history through an emotive experience, and the emotions stirred seem to burn experiences into the mind.

In parallel with what Lincoln[28] said in his Gettysburg Address,[29] people will not remember the facts and dates Ed Bearss and other historians say on the tour, but they will remember how they felt. They will hopefully have some respect and appreciation for what the men and woman experienced and survived, or didn't survive, what they sacrificed and what was gained and lost. So, the history-tour guide must evoke an emotional experience in their audience, from hearing about the people that lived, died or thrived for a time, to feeling with and, hopefully, *for* them.

---

[27] Online: https://en.wikipedia.org/wiki/Band_of_Brothers_(miniseries).
[28] Online: https://en.wikipedia.org/wiki/Abraham_Lincoln.
[29] Online: https://en.wikipedia.org/wiki/Gettysburg_Address.

Chapter 2

GRANT'S VICKSBURG CAMPAIGN TOUR[30]

This chapter presents brief vignettes of Ed Bearss as he led the South Mountain Expeditions tour of General Ulysses S. Grant's Civil War campaign to capture the City of Vicksburg, Mississippi. Vicksburg at the time sat to the east of a big bend in the Mississippi River. Her cannon could rake anything moving on the river, but bluffs along the Yazoo River north of the city were also defended. Grant needed to get around them on the high ground north and east of the city.

BATTLE OF MEMPHIS[31]

Our tour starts in Memphis, Tennessee, where Ed Bearss explained where we are in the war's timeline and gets us into the actions at Memphis between the Union and Confederate Navies here on the Mississippi.[32] Ed picks up the action beginning with the Battle of Memphis from the Memphis

---

[30] This chapter is an abridged version of a much longer manuscript giving the word-for-word Ed Bearss tour of the campaign. We have extracted notable quotes during his ten-day tour for this chapter.
[31] Online: https://en.wikipedia.org/wiki/First_Battle_of_Memphis.
[32] Online: https://www.nps.gov/abpp/battles/tn004.htm and
https://en.wikipedia.org/wiki/First_Battle_of_Memphis.

shore overlooking the Mississippi across from Mud Island[33] about where the Battle of Memphis occurred.

Ed Bearss by footbridge to Mud Island, Memphis, Tennessee, on February 26, 2013, describing the Battle of Memphis.

The Union wanted to split the Confederacy down the Mississippi river and clear the river for their own commerce. To do so, Memphis and Vicksburg had to be in Union hands. On the night of June 5th, the Union Brown-water Navy[34] is two miles upstream from Memphis. They include the *Cairo*[35] and four of her sister ships, the City Series ironclads,[36] the flagship *Benton*, and they have two new vessels [*Queen of the West*[37] and *Monarch*[38]]. Now, everybody in Memphis, which has a population of about 20,000, know they're going to have a big naval battle here the next day.

Capt. [James E.] Montgomery has eight Confederate rams, which mount usually one or two guns, besides using the reinforced bows, which did well

---

[33] Online: https://en.wikipedia.org/wiki/Mud_Island,_Memphis.
[34] Online: https://en.wikipedia.org/wiki/Brown-water_navy.
[35] Online: https://en.wikipedia.org/wiki/USS_Cairo.
[36] Online: https://en.wikipedia.org/wiki/City-class_ironclad.
[37] Online: https://en.wikipedia.org/wiki/USS_Queen_of_the_West_(1854).
[38] Online: https://en.wikipedia.org/wiki/USS_Monarch_(1862).

against the ironclads at Plum Point Bend[39] on the 10th day of May. That was the only time the Confederates ever won a fleet engagement. So, since Marty Gane[40] lives here [representing Marty as a typical Memphis belle], she will dress in her best clothes and is down here with everybody else. A bigger crowd than came out to watch First Manassas,[41] cause they're sure they're going to win.

Unfortunately for them, coming downstream with the force of the current are the two Eads[42] rams,[43] *Queen of the West* out in front trailed by *Monarch*. And just as they're cheering here, the *Queen of the West* rams into the *Lovell*[44] as she starts to turn, drives her bow deep into the *Lovell's* vitals. The crowd moans and groans, as the *Lovell* disappears beneath the swirling brown waters of the river [group chuckles]. Next to come in successively, the *General Price*[45] comes in and tries to ram *Queen of the West*, she turns her bow and sheers off one of *Price's* sidewheels, and [then] the *Price* limps over to the Arkansas shore. The crowd is undoubtedly beginning to moan even more so. Now comes *Monarch*.

So, *General Price* is out, but she's ashore, *Lovell* is sunk, and the next thing *Monarch* crashes into the *General Bragg*[46] and seriously damages her and she pulls over to the shore. We now have one Confederate ram sunk with heavy casualties, two of them have gone aground, and the *Little Rebel*[47] finds herself isolated, because now the ironclads have turned around. They're coming downstream with the current and the *Little Rebel* surrenders as does the *General Sumter*.[48] So, now the Confederate fleet is down to two vessels, and they'll proceed downriver and we'll hear about them later.

---

[39] Online: https://en.wikipedia.org/wiki/Fort_Pillow_naval_battle.
[40] Our tour manager and owner of South Mountain Expeditions who planned our tour with Ed Bearss.
[41] Online: https://en.wikipedia.org/wiki/First_Battle_of_Bull_Run.
[42] Online: https://en.wikipedia.org/wiki/James_Buchanan_Eads.
[43] Online: https://en.wikipedia.org/wiki/United_States_Ram_Fleet.
[44] Online: https://en.wikipedia.org/wiki/CSS_Colonel_Lovell.
[45] Online: https://en.wikipedia.org/wiki/Laurent_Millaudon_(1856).
[46] Online: https://en.wikipedia.org/wiki/USS_General_Bragg_(1851).
[47] Online: https://en.wikipedia.org/wiki/USS_Little_Rebel_(1859).
[48] Online: https://en.wikipedia.org/wiki/USS_Sumter_(1863).

The Total Annihilation of the Rebel Fleet by the Federal Fleet under Commodore Davis. On the Morning of June 6th 1862, off Memphis, Tennessee." Lithograph by Middleton, Strobridge & Co. In the foreground, the print depicts the Confederate ships (from left to right): *General M. Jeff Thompson* (shown sinking); *Little Rebel* (shown burning); *General Sterling Price*; *General Beauregard* (shown being rammed by the Ellet Ram *Monarch*); *General Bragg* (shown aground) and *Colonel Lovell* (shown sinking). In the background are the Federal warships (from left to right): *Queen of the West*; *Cairo*; *Carondelet*; *Louisville*; *Saint Louis*; a tug; and *Benton*. The City of Memphis is in the right distance, with a wharf boat by the shore. Courtesy of the Naval Historical Foundation. Public domain. Retrieved from https://upload.wikimedia.org/wikipedia/commons/a/a4/Memphis_h42367.jpg.

So, by this time the crowd has dissipated, just like a basketball team or your football team getting crushed, and the Confederates are getting out of Memphis as fast as they can. Late in the day, they have a race to see who can get into Memphis first, the Indiana soldiers, but the one-upmanship by Charles Rivers Ellet,[49] the son of the builder of the vessels, he races in, goes up to the Custom House and pulls down the Confederate flag and runs up the United States flag, and the flag will be flying over here the rest of the war. So, the Battle of Memphis is over. It's now a Union base.

It will become a city of sin, because all Union troops passing south of here will stop, and I hate to say it, "Boys will be boys." This and Nashville

---

[49] Online: https://en.wikipedia.org/wiki/Charles_R._Ellet.

will be the two biggest cities of sin in this part of the South. What Washington, DC, is in the North and Richmond in the South.

Eventually, Grant moves south and decides to get above the City of Vicksburg on the same side of the Mississippi River. He will make several attempts using the rivers and bayous of the complicated terrain above the city. Map 1 shows each of the four initial attempts. They are numbered in the order of their start dates, not their ending dates. Note that three of the four attempts overlapped in time as Grant probed where he hoped to find the best approach to Vicksburg east of the Mississippi. Our tour visited the locations where each attempt came to its end, never achieving the intended objective of getting to the same side of the Mississippi as Vicksburg.

1. BATTLE OF CHICKASAW BAYOU[50] (DECEMBER 26–29, 1862)

General William Tecumseh Sherman[51] wants to get north of Vicksburg on the same side of the Mississippi. As he sees the river is rising, he is forced to make a frontal assault with his men in a column marching along an east-west causeway that wasn't yet under the waters of the Chickasaw Bayou. They would have to march toward the Confederate defense lines which were laid along a north-south road and railroad line athwart a causeway, the only line of Union advance. Ed Bearss describes the tactical situation.

Sherman now prepares to attack on the morning of the 29th [of December] … He's going to attack along the causeway … [which] isn't any wider than this road, which means the Confederates can converge their fire on you from all these different directions, and it's not going to be a happy time.

---

[50] Online: https://en.wikipedia.org/wiki/Battle_of_Chickasaw_Bayou.
[51] Online: https://en.wikipedia.org/wiki/William_Tecumseh_Sherman.

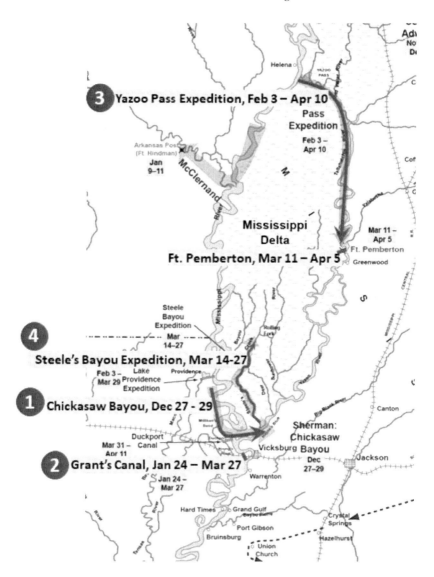

Map 1. Map of the Vicksburg Campaign December 62 - March 63 of the American Civil War. (1) Sherman's Chickasaw Bayou attempt. (2) Grant's Canal attempt. (3) Yazoo Pass attempt, stopped at Ft. Pemberton. (5) Porter's Steele's Bayou attempt. Drawn in Adobe Illustrator CS5 by Hal Jespersen from a public domain resource of the U.S. Government. Source: Map by Hal Jespersen, www.posix.com/CW. License: https://creativecommons.org/licenses/by/3.0/deed.en and transformative fair use of owned image. Retrieved and used with label additions from https://upload.wikimedia.org/wikipedia/commons/3/3e/VicksburgCampaignDecember62March63.png.

The Attack Goes In

We drove to the causeway on which the Union attacked, [John F.] DeCourcy's and [Francis P.] Blair's[52] brigades attacked, and debussed beyond Chickasaw Bayou right in front of what was the Confederate lines, infantry and cannon lines, now a residential area. Ed Bearss explained the tactical situation here as we walked back towards the direction from which DeCourcy's men approached the Confederate lines and then reversed direction and walked back following the path they took on January 29, 1863, toward the rebel guns.

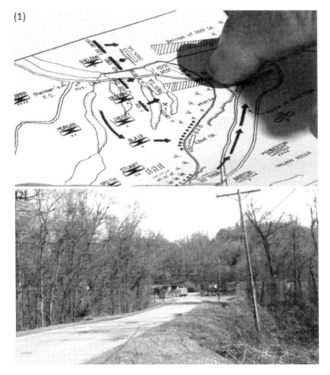

We are here on the map crossing the bayou and the Confederate line with artillery is up just pass the bus, and none of us [as Union troops] will get that far. (1) Looking back down the causeway, the Confederate picket line is at the rail line in front of the bus; (2) Our location on the battle map. Transformative fair use of owned image.

---

[52] Online: https://en.wikipedia.org/wiki/Francis_Preston_Blair_Jr.

From here, the Confederate main line of resistance is [pointing] along this road. Now we're going up to the causeway. Now, we're going to be on the causeway in a minute. The causeway's going to extend to a position where we saw those houses on stilts. That means if we go off to the left or right, we're into a bog. ... We're gonna see water up here on both sides of the road. Chickasaw Bayou coming up to our left and to our right.

So, his attack is going to be a two-pronged attack. Two brigades, that is, out of his 32,000 men, that's about 3,000 men. In the Brigades commanded by Frank Blair, and the Brigade commanded by DeCourcy.

So, that means that then on the sides of the slopes behind it [the Yazoo City Road embankment], is the Confederate artillery. It's the Confederate dream to get Sherman into position where he's going to order an attack in this situation. That means that DeCourcy's and Blair's chances are slim and none, and few if any of them are going to get halfway to where our bus is [on the Confederate line] before their attack is going to break up.

Here we go across the causeway [DeCourcy's attack], the Confederate skirmishers falling back, and we're never going to reach the Yazoo City Road [beyond the bus]. That's the Confederate earthworks. They're [the Confederates] right beyond the railroad. None of them [the Federals] are gonna reach that. That means we're soon gonna be skedaddling out as they [the Confederates] counterattack. It is not going to be a good day for the Federals, either here or down at the Indian Mound [where Blair attacked, further south]. The Indian Mound being downstream about ¾ of a mile, down in that direction [pointing to the right of the causeway facing the Confederate line] where we're standing.

Assaulted and Failed

So, none of the Union troops are going to be breaking the line and they're going to be repulsed. By noon, it's all over, and Sherman has lost 1776 men, the Confederates, 208. Sherman then will describe what happened this day. Now, an interesting thing, they did not teach military history at West Point at that time. They did not teach a "Great Captains" course. That means that Sherman checked out books. Now, if you read military history, for the 1840's the library records are extant. They show that Sherman checked out a lot of military history. Grant checked out romance novels. [Big group laughs.] So, what you read is a little different than you would expect.

Thus, General Sherman cannot take the Walnut Hills bluffs overlooking the Bayou above Vicksburg. Sherman knows Caesar well. What does he say when he crosses the Etowah, he crosses the "Rubicon," getting that right out of Caesar? Caesar's most famous words are, "I came, I saw, I conquered." So, Sherman will paraphrase it, [writing] "I landed at Vicksburg at the time appointed, assaulted and failed."

2. Grant's Canal[53]

The Union attempts to build a canal across the sharp turn in the Mississippi to get south of the Vicksburg river batteries – Ed Bearss speaks at the short remaining section of the canal.

Arriving here is our hero, U. S. Grant on the 30th of January with orders that he's to reorganize the Army. Sherman's orders as he camps in this area here and in high waters, this area will flood, even today, then much more. And Sherman is told to go to work and make happen what [Brig. Gen. Thomas] Williams[54] had [earlier] tried to do. Williams, from hell, where he's helping stoke the Devil's workshop, is probably saying, "Those sons-of-bitches will probably fail just the same as I did." So, again, they begin working on the canal. And, on March 30th, and they're going to start using floating dredges, four in all, and a lot more manpower, and they go to work on the canal.

---

[53] Online: https://www.nps.gov/vick/learn/historyculture/grants-canal.htm.
[54] Online: https://en.wikipedia.org/wiki/Thomas_Williams_(Union_general).

(1) The Confederate artillery was there; (2) Confederate earthworks where the road sits parallel to the rail line; (3) Confederate skirmishers falling back through here; (4-5) Walking back along the causeway up which the Union columns came; (6-7) Chickasaw Bayou on either side of causeway (8) Indian Mound that way.

Remains of Grant's Canal, a big operation.

[Walking to other plaques] So, let's move down here. This is a big operation. Grant, when he writes his memoirs, he probably becomes even smarter. Since Lincoln is dead, he captured Vicksburg, been President of the United States, and has become a great hero. I don't think he's as smart about it as he has you believe in his memoirs. In his memoirs, he takes the position that an idle man is an unhappy man, something that even lieutenants believe in the Army, and the Navy, and the Marine Corps, that an idle man is an unhappy man. So, let's have work for them. This time it's a big operation. They have dipping dredges. The canal is to be 60 feet wide, just as wide as this scar we can see in the open fields [here]. It's to be eight feet deep, and it is to run one and one-half miles. They're doing pretty well by the 7th day of March. The Confederates, however, have nullified it. They're positioning batteries south of Vicksburg, at Grand Gulf … to have a backup position if this canal should succeed.

Ed Bearss describes the two efforts to build a canal across the De Soto Peninsula to create a channel for Union river traffic to bypass Vicksburg's guns.

But the river is rising fast, and it's going to crest, and Sherman's men are going to flee for any high ground around here. Otherwise, all the area is under water. At the same time, the Yazoo Pass Expedition and the Steele's Bayou Expedition are beginning to run into serious trouble. By the 22nd, they're back to work on the canal, but by the 27th, Yazoo Pass has become a disaster, Steele's Bayou a disaster, the canal a failure, they're up by Lake Providence, a roundabout and a disaster is in the making, and Grant will make that decision on a reconnaissance up the Yazoo River with Porter on the 27th of March. An examination of the Confederate defenses at Drumgold-Snyder's and Hayne's Bluffs, and that's when he says, "It ain't gonna work." And then we're back where we picked everybody up 48 hours ago when Grant makes his decision, "I'm going to move down the west bank of the river." The canal is a failure.

Now, all that remains of the canal is these 300 yards. When I first came here, it had a few more remains here, because there was no highway Interstate 20. So, the canal extended at that time to old Highway 80, but on the other side of old Highway 80, it had all but disappeared into farmland. Time goes fast, about 20 years ago, the local landowner, wrote to the Conservation Fund, donates this land here, and the Park Service has been able to preserve the only surviving vestige of the Williams-Grant Canal. And, about ten years ago, they opened up this little parking spot here, and you can see [on the plaque] it becomes as big business as you can have and as high-tech as you could have at that time from a pick-and-shovel project that Williams sought to undertake.

Sherman and [Gen. James Birdseye] McPherson,[55] cautious West Pointers,[56] will urge Grant, "Take your army back to Memphis, Tennessee, and resume the overland advance. So, that's one of Grant's options, backed and supported by his two favorite corps commanders. The next option is to launch an amphibious attack on Vicksburg across the river from the Louisiana shore. This would be a "Fredericksburg,"[57] or worse, and Grant would be out of a job, and [Maj.Gen. John Alexander] McClernand[58] would be leading the Army. His third alternative, the one opposed vigorously by Sherman and McPherson, since Sherman is more vocal, he'll be taking the lead, is to move his army south through the parishes of Louisiana, cross the river by Madison and Tensas parish ferries.

---

[55] Online: https://en.wikipedia.org/wiki/James_B._McPherson.
[56] Online: https://www.westpoint.edu/.
[57] Online: https://www.nps.gov/frsp/index.htm and
    https://en.wikipedia.org/wiki/Battle_of_Fredericksburg.
[58] Online: https://en.wikipedia.org/wiki/John_Alexander_McClernand.

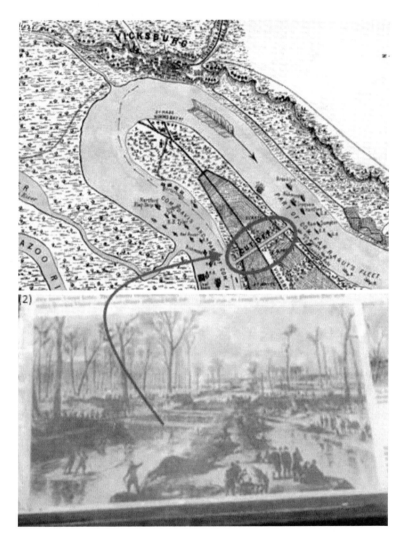

(1) Detail from View of Vicksburg and plan of the canal, fortifications & vicinity surveyed by Lieut. L. A. Wrotnowski (note that North is to the left). Public domain. Retrieved from https://upload.wikimedia.org/wikipedia/commons/3/35/Grants_Canal_detail.jpg. (2) Plaque picture showing large-scale canal work at the remaining canal scar and marker site.

3. YAZOO PASS EXPEDITION[59]
(FEBRUARY 3 – APRIL 12, 1863)

Sherman has to get on the same side of the Mississippi and its connecting waterways, the rivers and bayous, another way to flank [Confederate Lt. Gen. John Clifford] Pemberton's[60] Vicksburg defenses on the bluffs at Chickasaw Bayou. Sherman's next attempt is to outflank the Chickasaw Bayou defenders by crossing the Yazoo above the well-defended bluffs. We go to the place where the Yazoo Bypass comes out of Moon Lake, the beginnings of the Yazoo Pass Expedition. There is much timber and vegetation to be cleared to get these tall-masted ironclads down these narrow bayous and rivers.

We drive to the location of Fort Pemberton,[61] which was hurriedly built along with river blockades along the Tallahatchie River to stop the Union fleet from passing this point headed south. Ed Bearss describes the action here, which consists only of a marker, and stand where Battery No. 8 of the fort was positioned.

So, in the afternoon of the 11th [of March], the two ironclads, *Chillicothe*[62] and [*Baron*] *DeKalb*,[63] start downriver. As they round that bend, they're about 700 yards from our position as Battery No. 8, and we're going to open fire on them. We're going to bounce some shells off *Chillicothe*, and she doesn't take battery fire very well. So, after about an hour's duel, the two gunboats, the ironclads, withdraw around that bend and head upriver. Now remember, in addition, you've got two barriers here. You have the *Star of the West*[64] scuttled athwart [i.e., sunk across] the river here, and downstream a little bit from us, we have a raft.

---

[59] Online: https://en.wikipedia.org/wiki/Yazoo_Pass_Expedition.
[60] Online: https://en.wikipedia.org/wiki/John_C._Pemberton.
[61] Online: https://www.battlefields.org/visit/heritage-sites/fort-pemberton., not to be confused with the "Fort Pemberton" in South Carolina.
[62] Online: https://en.wikipedia.org/wiki/USS_Chillicothe_(1862).
[63] Online: https://en.wikipedia.org/wiki/USS_Baron_DeKalb.
[64] Online: https://en.wikipedia.org/wiki/Star_of_the_West.

(1) Yazoo Pass is coming out of Moon Lake; (2) Levee two miles across Moon Lake; (3) Where Yazoo Pass debauches from Moon Lake; (4) Yazoo Pass is beginning to choke up; (5) Levee breached and big clods of earth are washed downstream; (6) Clearing timber. Transformative fair use of owned images.

The Union have not done any good on the 11th, so they draw off to think about it. They decide, [since] the area is inundated, we have 4,000 men, there's no place to put them ashore. There's no place we can get by them unless we blast the Confederate fort into smithereens. Late on the 11th, *Chillicothe* comes down alone, takes some more hits, and heads [back] upstream.

On the 13th, [Lt. Cdr.] Watson Smith is beside himself. This cowardly bunch of Navy people will not close with the enemy. So, this time they decide to come down the river with *Chillicothe* leading and *DeKalb* trailing, and down they came. Almost immediately, we [the Confederates] get a lucky hit. Just as they're loading one of the 11-inch bow guns on *Chillicothe*, it causes an explosion of the projectile they're loading and a number of Union sailors are killed or wounded. We back off again. They're going to try one more time on the 16th. They're going to land two 30-pounder Parrotts[65] and set them up in that field where you can see they set up two guns, land men and attack Ft. Pemberton, the battery.

(1) USS *Chillicothe* (1862). Public domain. Author: Troy McClure. Retrieved from https://upload.wikimedia.org/wikipedia/commons/c/c8/USSChillicothe.jpg. (2) USS *Baron DeKalb*, an Eads class ironclad. Public domain. Retrieved from https://upload.wikimedia.org/wikipedia/commons/f/f8/USS_Baron_DeKalb.jpg.

---

[65] Online: https://en.wikipedia.org/wiki/Parrott_rifle.

[Maj. Gen. William Wing] Loring,[66] the commander at Ft. Pemberton, is having a field day, as he strolls along the top of the parapet shouting, "Give them blizzards, give them blizzards, men!" On the 16th, [Brig. Gen. Leonard Fulton] Ross,[67] Wilson and Smith meet, and they decide, "We can't cut the mustard." The Confederates are here, … this thing that Wilson had bet his career on, as well as Grant, and we leave here, and we start upstream.

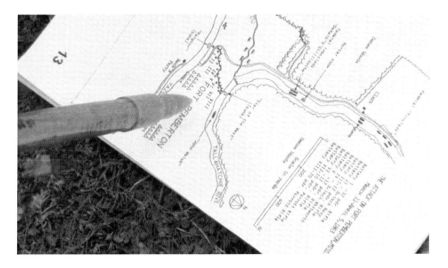

Map showing our "Stand" at Battery No. 8 in the hastily built Fort Pemberton. The location of the sunken Star of the West blocking the Tallahatchie across from the cannon is also shown. I am pointing at it with Ed's classic .50-caliber bullet-tipped pointer. Transformative fair use of owned image.

When they're upriver, halfway between Ft. Pemberton and Yazoo Pass, they run into reinforcements coming down. These are coming the same way that we followed, under General [Isaac Ferdinand] Quinby,[68] and they will be back at Ft. Pemberton between the 18th and 21st / 22nd day of March when they learn from General Grant, he's scrubbing the Yazoo Pass route. It's a place of no return and possibly the loss of two divisions of troops. … So, on the 22nd, the message has come all the way from Vicksburg by boat [no radio, no cellular, no Internet], up thorough Elk, Arkansas, all the way down this

---

[66] Online: https://en.wikipedia.org/wiki/William_Wing_Loring.
[67] Online: https://en.wikipedia.org/wiki/Leonard_Fulton_Ross.
[68] Online: https://en.wikipedia.org/wiki/Isaac_Ferdinand_Quinby.

long chain of rivers, and the decision that Grant has made, is gonna take four days in getting here. So, Quinby says, "Boys, we're going back." Grant has cut bait. So, we go back on the rivers, and they're going to be damn glad, when the leave Yazoo Pass, on the 5th day of April, and this has not been a pleasant move for the Federals.

Meanwhile, they have heard by the grapevine in reading the Vicksburg papers that pass through their lines that the Confederates are savoring the situation up at Ft. Pemberton, and the Confederates are beginning to think maybe we can knock of those two divisions, McPherson's and Ross's Divisions, and if it's reinforced by Quinby's Division, knock it off, and we can ruin General Grant's reputation.

4. STEELE'S BAYOU EXPEDITION[69] (MARCH 14–27, 1863)

Next, we have Adm. David D. Porter's[70] attempt to get to the Yazoo River above Vicksburg by traversing the linking waterways to get to the Yazoo, and we go to key points along that third failed attempt to get above the city on the same side of the river. As we drive north above the Yazoo River, Ed Bearss explains the intent of the Steele's Bayou Expedition. It will be another attempt to get above the Walnut Hills and Synder's Bluff where they were stopped at Chickasaw Bayou and get on the same side of the Mississippi as Vicksburg. This time, it begins as a Navy plan.

Porter and the Idea

… David Dixon Porter I believe probably has the greatest ego of a service of men with great egos of any in their time and continued to our time. The Navy is now in charge of the inland Navy. That has been a bureaucratic decision made and it's implemented in the mid-October, 1862. The Navy gets their independence. In the Navy earlier, they were under administrative control of the Army. So, it's important that the Naval Officer in charge, and

---

[69] Online: https://en.wikipedia.org/wiki/Steele%27s_Bayou_expedition.
[70] Online: https://en.wikipedia.org/wiki/David_Dixon_Porter.

Grant and Sherman get along well with Porter. He's no longer bound by taking orders when he is under administrative control of the Army. He's an independent man with a great deal of ability and tremendous ego. So, he has been supporting the naval operations of the Army in the Vicksburg area ever since early December 1862. He had not been on the site, but he'd been administratively responsible when they lost the *Cairo* on the 12th day of December.

He will be with Sherman when we're talking about the Battle of Chickasaw Bayou that will take place between the 26th day of December and the 1st day of the new year [1863] in which he tries to be helpful, but the Army isn't doing well. He [Porter] will be much less impressed with McClernand.

Porter will have a decent working relationship with Grant and Sherman, but he does not get along with political generals, whether it is General John A. McClernand or General Nathaniel Prentice Banks[71] or [General] Benjamin Franklin Butler.[72] He'll be very demeaning to them and will be very uncooperative, but he does work with McClernand along with Sherman when they go up to Arkansas Post on the 4th day of January and the capture of Arkansas Post on the 11th day of January in which they knock off a Confederate garrison of about 4500 men and capture a fort that guards the approaches to Little Rock [Arkansas]. So, he's back operating on the Mississippi and he decides maybe I can star you. The Army is not doing well. The canal across the DeSoto Peninsula[73] [Grant's Canal] is a bust. The Army is in serious trouble up at Yazoo Pass, and McPherson is doing no better at Lake Providence.[74]

He looks at his maps, he talks to blacks, talks to the people of the area, and he thinks, "I know how we can bail those Army fellows out up at Ft. Pemberton and reach the Yazoo River upstream from Vicksburg and be heroes of the occasion.

---

[71] Online: https://en.wikipedia.org/wiki/Nathaniel_P._Banks.
[72] Online: https://en.wikipedia.org/wiki/Benjamin_Butler.
[73] Online: https://www.nps.gov/vick/learn/nature/rivers.htm.
[74] Online: https://www.nps.gov/vick/learn/historyculture/lake-providence-canal-february-march-1863.htm.

Now if you look at your map, probably Map 15 [in the Gane Atlas], it is probably the best, you get more detail, Map 11, inset D, if you're not interested in detail. Now, Steele's Bayou flows into the Yazoo River about 12 miles above where the Yazoo River joins the Mississippi. It is a fairly large bayou, much better than Yazoo Pass, and he thinks about it so much that on the 11th of March he takes a tug, goes up the Yazoo River, turns into Steele's Bayou, goes northward upstream on Steele's Bayou 30 miles, where he finds a connecting bayou. It shows up best on map 15. It's known as Black Bayou. It's only four miles in length, but they're going to find out it's a "can of worms" when you try to get vessels through it.

In fact, it's worse than Yazoo Pass, but they don't know it. Then it goes into a stream that's heavily used by small steamboats on Deer Creek. Deer Creek, we saw it yesterday, over there at Leland. It begins about 20 miles east of the Mississippi River and parallels it, and he knows, he finds out, "Yes, they've had steamboats up there, commercial steamboats up Deer Creek, and then he finds out there's Rolling Fork. Rolling Fork is a small connecting bayou that if it's practical, you can get from Rolling Fork over to the Big Sunflower River, which is used heavily by commercial steamboats before the war. Down the Big Sunflower River and you're in the Yazoo River halfway between Vicksburg and Yazoo City, and you're heroes. You not only have saved Grant's bacon up there at Yazoo Pass, but you've placed your fleet above Vicksburg and Grant can get on the bluffs and win it all.

So, Porter will go up, take the *Carondelet*,[75] which will be his flag boat during the operation, the most famous of the Eads City series ironclads, and he runs it up Steele's Bayou to the mouth of Black Bayou. He likes it even better, but he still hasn't tried to take a boat through Black Bayou. So, on the 15th he goes and tells U. S. Grant, "I think I have a winner," but I'm going to need some help of the Army.

He and Grant get aboard the *General Price*. This vessel has been in the Confederate River Defense Fleet,[76] badly damaged at Memphis, then repaired and incorporated in the Union Navy. Porter and Grant again go up Steele's Bayou only as far as the mouth of Deer Creek. Grant finds the

---

[75] Online: https://en.wikipedia.org/wiki/USS_Carondelet_(1861).
[76] Online: https://en.wikipedia.org/wiki/River_Defense_Fleet.

navigation on Steele's Bayou goes well, but neither he nor Porter have yet investigated seriously the possibility of taking the gunboats through Black Bayou into Deer Creek.

The Expedition Begins

Grant says, "Good," and on the 15th Grant issues orders to General Sherman, "You will cooperate with Admiral Porter and support him at least with one of your three divisions of troops." Sherman says, "Yes sir," and his men are going to begin… [wind noise].

Now, there was this big bend in the river, it's now Eagle Lake, and the Union troops will be shuttled up river from Young's Point, go ashore at Eagle Bend, march across on a road that goes along Muddy Bayou, and they have it relatively easy getting to Steele's Bayou a short distance before they have to leave Steele's Bayou and cross *en mass* to the Black Bayou, so off goes Sherman.

The Union does well. They take five City-series gunboats, *Pittsburg*,[77] *Louisville*,[78] *Cincinnati*,[79] *Mound City*[80] and *Carondelet*, and they have four mortars[81] mounted on scows,[82] and two work boats, and they start up Steele's Bayou. They have no trouble in reaching where Steele's Bayou flows into Black Bayou on the 17th. Everything is going good. I can see Porter patting himself on the back. I'm going to one-upmanship the Army. They're going to owe me a lot of Brownie points.[83] They may appreciate me more than my foster brother. He's very jealous of his foster brother, that would be David Glasgow Farragut.[84] He complains about Farragut being an old man and he [Porter] is young and vigorous and I would be a very good replacement. Now, Farragut is a physical culture man. Until his 64th birthday, he's able to

---

[77] Online: https://en.wikipedia.org/wiki/USS_Pittsburgh_(1861).
[78] Online: https://en.wikipedia.org/wiki/USS_Louisville_(1861).
[79] Online: https://en.wikipedia.org/wiki/USS_Cincinnati_%281861%29.
[80] Online: https://en.wikipedia.org/wiki/USS_Mound_City_(1861).
[81] Online: https://civilwarwiki.net/wiki/Civil_War_Era_Mortars.
[82] Online: https://en.wikipedia.org/wiki/Scow.
[83] Online: https://en.wikipedia.org/wiki/Brownie_points.
[84] Online: https://en.wikipedia.org/wiki/David_Farragut.

stand on the deck of a ship, jump up, do a double somersault, and land on his feet. [Group says, "Baloney."] But Farragut is a deep-water man [ocean], and Porter is now the brown-water man [silt-carrying rivers].

Now, they're going to run into lots of trouble when they try to take these ironclads – if you've seen *Cairo*, you know how big these boats are – getting five of them through Black Bayou, which would make Yazoo Pass look like a major waterway. It may be only four miles long, but it beats up the ironclads, particularly the wooden decking, the deck housing, and the chimneys take a beating.

They have another problem because the area's flooded and you run into large trees, and you may have a big -- and they become bigger when you have soldiers and sailors telling – [or] several large water moccasins[85] being knocked out of the trees, down on your decks. It is going to take them until the 17th to get through Black Bayou and to Hill's Planation. That will be our last stop on the Steele's Bayou Expedition, and that's where the fleet will be on the 17th, Sherman has detailed 100 pioneers to Porter to help cut a channel through the waterway.

Now the Confederates have only a small force in the Delta, commanded by a South Carolinian, a graduate of 1859 of West Point, Col. Samuel Wragg Ferguson.[86] He has a couple of companies of cavalry, he has six guns, and some infantry, and he's up here at Leland Plantation. Leland Plantation would be up there where we made our last stop yesterday. If you're a Confederate, he's a good guy, because he doesn't wait for orders. He realizes this could be a severe threat, and on the 17th he takes his cavalry and sends them southward and tells them to start impressing blacks and putting blacks to work chopping trees down, create obstructions, in Deer Creek to give the Union something to worry about. It's going to be late on the night of the 17th to the early hours of the 18th before Gen. Pemberton, who's heduqartered in Jackson, receives an encoded message from his commander in Vicksburg that the Yankees are about to give us some real trouble. They have reached

---

[85] Online: https://en.wikipedia.org/wiki/Agkistrodon_piscivorus.
[86] Online: https://en.wikipedia.org/wiki/Samuel_W._Ferguson.

Hill's Plantation. They've reached Deer Creek, which will be an easier waterway to master, we'd better do something about it.

Pemberton will send a message back to [Maj. Gen. Carter Littlepage] Stevenson[87] [commanding Vicksburg] to send troops and get your steamboats. I want you to send troops up the Big Sunflower River. It's no challenge at all, you go up the Big Sunflower River, you reach Rolling Fork, and you will support Colonel Ferguson. Ferguson is already at work using his men, he's rounded up blacks, and they're chopping trees and doing everything they can do to hinder the Union gunboats as they go up Deer Creek.

If they [Union] run into trouble at Deer Creek, they'll have to back down becase they've no room in Deer Creek to turn their gunboats around. So, you've got these five monsters, each of them 175-feet long and 50-and-1/2-foot wide at the widest point, creeping their way slowly up Deer Creek, and from the 18th on, having difficulty, as they're having to stop, put landing parties ashore, get out the hawsers, and tow and chop out the trees, and move them on.

Ed spoke at different points along the route of the failed Steele's Bayou Expedition, including (1-2) Black Bayou via Hill's Plantation, (3) Deer Creek and (4) Rolling Fork Bayou.

---

[87] Online: https://en.wikipedia.org/wiki/Carter_L._Stevenson.

Rolling Fork

By the 19th, they are going to be within Egremont Plantation and they think they have it made. They're only four miles short of Rolling Fork. This cross-stream that will allow them to move from Deer Creek across to the easily navibable waterway, the Big Sunflower River. But unfortunately by that time, Ferguson has brought his cannons up, no better than little popguns, but those big guns on the Union ironclads will be *no good at all* because they're below the level of the bank. They cannot elevate their guns enough to fire at the Confederate cannon, unless they put them on the Indian (burial) mounds [to provide height]. That means you're going to have to get poor old John McLeod Murphy,[88] skipper of *Carondelet*, to form a Naval landing force, they'll get out there "howitzer," for which they have to be the beast of burden pulling it, and they're going to take possession of an Indian mound they can see nearby and hopefully they can place their artillery there and be able to neutralize Ferguson's cannon.

Ed Bearss looking at an Indian Mound to provide some elevation in this flat Mississippi delta terrain where the *Carondelet* put ashore a Naval howitzer to disperse Ferguson's artillery. Deer Creek is behind him 50 years or so.

---

[88] Online: https://en.wikipedia.org/wiki/John_McLeod_Murphy.

We drive to Rolling Fork about halfway between Deer Creek and the Big Sunflower River, debus, and Ed Bearss describes how close Porter got to this spot.

Alright, this is Rolling Fork. To the west of us is Deer Creek going north and south. ... We are right there, here's Deer Creek and there is Rolling Fork, and if you come up Deer Creek, Rolling Fork will take you though to the Big Sunflower River. The Big Sunflower River, which is navigable, to good size steamboats and you're halfway between Vicksburg and Yazoo City. Ft. Pemberton is about 70 miles up the Yazoo from the Big Sunflower River. So, if you reach this point, and take your gunboats through, you have bailed out Yazoo Pass and you have the key to reaching the bluffs that are to the east of the Yazoo River. So, if the Confederates can stop them here, Porter is in a bad way. He's never going to get here. He's going to be stopped a mile south of here. So, we'll never know if he could have taken his five gunboats, his four scows with mortars, and Sherman's Division of troops through here, we'll never know. He never gets this far. He's going to be stopped on Deer Creek.

Plaque at Rolling Fork where Ed Bearss described the Porter's decision to end the Steele's bayou attempt at getting behind the Confederate defenses on the Yazoo River bluffs above Vicksburg.

So, here of course is a descriptive panel. It's the first time I've ever stopped here because they put these signs up fairly recently. Now, here is the Confederate hero of it. This is Samual Wagg Ferguson. He is a West Pointer, graduated in '59. Featherston didn't have the gonads this man [Ferguson] had. If he did, Porter might have to [blow up his gunboats, because] he would ever surrender them, and [then] escaping overland.

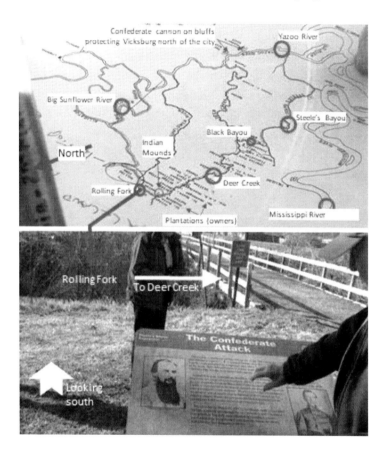

Ed Bearss explains the end of the Steele's Bayou Expedition. Transformative fair use of an owned image.

Now the confluence of Deer Creek and Rolling Fork is very close to here. [Pointing] it's that way from us, there's the Sharkey County Courthouse behind us, which wasn't there at the time. As it says here Ferguson arrives here on his own initiative on the morning of the 18th, and on the 20th, this will be when [Brig. Gen. Winfield Scott] Featherston[89] arrives. He comes by boat, coming up the Big Sunflower River, and lands his brigade of troops, and reinforces him [Ferguson]. On the 21st, we're going to be talking about the Confederates, who are going to drive the Yankees from the Indian mound, south of us here, and Porter, finally, on the 21st or 22nd, he says, "This ain't gonna work."

Now, his problem is he's going to have to have to back up all the route that he's come. He cannot turn his vessels around. The Confederates, as we're going to find out as we go down here to Deer Creek, are behind him. There even going to sink a coal barge behind him, and the Confederates having their positions there and unless Sherman can arrive, he [Porter] is gone, and that's what we're going to be talking about.

The Union Backs Out

They're going to have an artillery dual and the Confederates are going to lose, but, the Union can't manuver until Sherman arrives, he [Porter] is going to be out of action. So, about 5 PM Featherston arrives and the threatened Porter decides on the night of the 21st, I'm aborting it. He's going to send a message by a black man. He's going to tell the man, "You get down to Deer Cree. Find General Sherman somewere and tell him, 'I need help, bad.'" Sherman will, at Hill's Plantation, which will be our last stop here, Sherman will give General Giles Smith[90] 800 men and tell him, "You move up." On the evening of the 22nd, just as Porter's [situation] seems the blackest, Smith arrives, and Featherston will lack the initiatvie to attack. But, as I say, the Union never gets here [Rolling Fork].

The water [in Rolling Fork] would be much higher. The water table is higher, and remember the Union have crevaced the levy up at Yazoo Pass, so the water is higher, but not high enough for the gunboats guns to be level with the ground. They don't have enough elevation to see Confederates over

---

[89] Online: https://en.wikipedia.org/wiki/Winfield_S._Featherston.
[90] Online: https://en.wikipedia.org/wiki/Giles_Alexander_Smith.

there [north] or over there [south]. You couldn't get a motor boat through here nowadays, it shows the difference in water table then and now.

(1) Ed Bearss points along Rolling Fork towards its confluence with Deer Creek, looking west. (2) Big Sunflower River gets to the Yazoo here. (3) Gunboat guns cannot shoot over bank. (4) Water level on Rolling Fork during the Vicksburg Campaign.

But, it's still going to take five more days backing the steamboats up before they get into the Yazoo River and get out of this horrible period that Porter has had with his gunboats in the bayous of Mississippi and they come out, and it's an important day, the 27th, because Grant/Porter has failed again. Four failures [the Canal, Chickasaw Bayou, Yazoo pass, and now Steele's Bayou]. So, Grant and Porter will then go on a reconnaissance up the Yazoo River and see if he can have any opportunity at all of reaching the Yazoo River north of Vicksburg, and he's going to find out, "No, I can't do it, I've got to come up with another plan, and I am now in the eyes of the Administration, have wasted two months."

GRAND GULF TO THE SIEGE OF VICKSBURG

These four failed efforts by Grant were to get his army on the same side of the Mississippi River as Vicksburg, flanking the Confederate defenses that thwarted Sherman at Chickasaw Bayou or the bluffs overlooking the

Yazoo River north of Vicksburg. Finally, after a losing naval battle with the Confederate defenses at Grand Gulf,[91] he crosses at Bruinsburg,[92] south of Vicksburg, and moves northeast to fight at Port Gibson, Raymond, and then Jackson. He then turns his army west for the battles at Champion Hill[93] and Big Black River Bridge,[94] before laying siege to Vicksburg, where there is no protection from the Mississippi River. Our tour goes to each of these sites before approaching Vicksburg from the east as did Grant's army. Ed Bearss speaks at length at each one, describing the people and the battles that occurred there as well as the reaction of the locals to the Confederate defeats.

(1-2) Battle of Grand Gulf: We're standing on the remains of the parapet [of Ft. Cobun]." (3-4) Battle of Port Gibson: "This would be grown up in wild cane." (5-6) Battle of Raymond: "Davis is braver than he is bright."

---

[91] Online: https://en.wikipedia.org/wiki/Battle_of_Grand_Gulf and https://www.battlefields.org/visit/heritage-sites/grand-gulf-military-monument-park.
[92] Online: https://www.nps.gov/vick/learn/historyculture/bruincross.htm and
[93] Online: https://www.nps.gov/vick/learn/historyculture/championhill.htm and https://en.wikipedia.org/wiki/Battle_of_Champion_Hill.
[94] Online: https://en.wikipedia.org/wiki/Bruinsburg,_Mississippi.

Closing the tour, Ed Bearss closes his interpretation at the cemetery and describes the impact of Vicksburg's surrender on July 4, 1863, Independence Day in the Union. Ed then explains the consequences of Vicksburg being surrendered by Pemberton on July 4th.

(7-8) Battle of Champion Hill: "We're on the crest of Champion Hill." (9-10) Battle of Big Black Bridge: If it was a yard higher, we wouldn't be standing here right now." (11-12) Siege of Vicksburg. "He has just received a fine box of Havanas from home, and he has a premonition that he may not survive the attack."

In fact, Vicksburg will not celebrate the 4th of July from 1877 until 1947, it is not a National holiday. You go to work, unless you work for the United States Government, on the 4th of July. General Eisenhower, who will visit here in 1947, and that will be the first time they celebrate the 4th of July in Vicksburg since 1877, the end of Reconstruction. Even after that, it's not a big holiday in Vicksburg.

Ed Bearss contributed greatly to the understanding of the fight at Champion Hill, particularly the action at the Crossroads behind the hill. He was honored in 2019 with a plaque at this critical site in the battle.

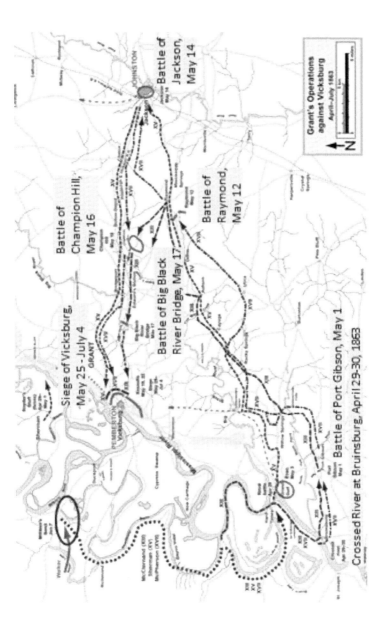

Grant's Operations against Vicksburg. Map of the Vicksburg Campaign of the American Civil War, drawn by Hal Jespersen. License: https://creativecommons.org/licenses/by/3.0/deed.en and transformative fair use. Retrieved from https://upload.wikimedia.org/wikipedia/commons/3/3c/VicksburgCampaignAprilJuly63.png. Cropping for size and larger labels overlaid for readability.

BIBLIOGRAPHY

The South Mountain Expeditions history tour highlighting Grant's Vicksburg Campaign, entitled "Vicksburg Tour – A Sesquicentennial Commemoration: February 25/27-March 4, 2013." Marty Gane provided her reading list compiled by Ed Bearss and herself as follows.

This short bibliography provides several recommended works on the Battle of Vicksburg.

Bearss, Edwin C. and Hills, J. Parker. *Receding Tide: Vicksburg and Gettysburg – The Campaigns That Changed the Civil War.* Sydney: Read How You Want, 2013.

Bearss, Edwin C. Hardluck Ironclad: The Sinking and Salvage of the Cairo, 2nd ed. LSU Press, 1980.

Bearss, Edwin C. Unvexed to the Sea: The Campaign for *Vicksburg.* Payson, Arizona: Morningside House, 1995.

Catton, Bruce. *Grant Moves South.* Edison, NJ: Castle Books, 2000.

Foote, Shelby. *The Civil War: A Narrative.* Vol. II. New York: Random House, 2005.

Loughborough, Mary Ann Webster. *My Cave Life in Vicksburg: with Letters of Trial and Travel.* Los Angeles: Hardpress Publishing, 2012.

Miles, Jim. *A River Unvexed: A History and Tour Guide to the Campaign for the Mississippi River.* Nashville, TN: Rutledge Hill Press, 1994.

Walker, Peter F. *Vicksburg: A People at War, 1860-1865.* Wilmington, NC: Broadfoot Pub. Co., 1987.

Winschel, Terrence J. *Triumph and Defeat.* El Dorado Hills, CA: Savas Beatie, 2015.

Winschel, Terrence J. *Vicksburg: Fall of the Confederate Gibraltar.*

Magazine

These back issues are available at www.bluegraymagazine.com or call 1 (800) 248-4592. Out of print copies might be available on eBay or elsewhere.

Bearss, Edwin C. and Terry Winschel. "The Vicksburg Campaign: Battles of Champion Hill and Big Black." *Blue and Gray Magazine*, Vol. 18, Issue #5, Columbus, OH: Blue and Gray Magazine, 2000.

Terry Winschel. "The Battle of Chickasaw Bayou." *Blue and Gray Magazine*, Vol. 26, Issue #3, Columbus, OH: Blue and Gray Magazine, 2009.

Bearss, Edwin C. and Terry Winschel. "The Vicksburg Campaign: Grant Moves Inland." *Blue and Gray Magazine*, Vol. 18, Issue #1. Columbus, OH: Blue and Gray Magazine, 2000.

Terry Winschel. "Grant's March Through Louisiana '63." *Blue and Gray Magazine*, Vol. 13, Issue #5. Columbus, OH: Blue and Gray Magazine, July 1996.

Terry Winschel. "The Siege of Vicksburg." *Blue and Gray Magazine*, Vol. 20, Issue #4, Columbus, OH: Blue and Gray Magazine, 2000.

Chapter 3

GETTYSBURG: THE THIRD DAY TOUR

Here is a short summary of an Ed Bearss tour that covers the main events on the third and last day of the Battle of Gettysburg, which occurred at the end of Grant's Campaign against Confederate Vicksburg, late June 1863. He does this tour as a single-day expedition, covering the third day at Gettysburg, July 3, 1863.

LEISTER HOUSE

We go to the "Widow" [Lydia Study] Leister[95] farm house, which was Gen. [George Gordon] Meade's[96] headquarters for the two days, July 2-3, 1863. Ed Bearss describes the Union response to the first two days and preparations for the third day.

Now this is where Meade establishes his headquarters on the morning of the second day of July. His headquarters will remain here until probably somewhere between 1:15 and 1:30 on July 3rd. Now General Meade, it's been a long day [the second day of the three-day Gettysburg battle] for both the leaders and the soldiers on the second day. It is the bloodiest day at

---

[95] Online: https://civilwarwiki.net/wiki/Leister_Farm_(Gettysburg) and
https://www.findagrave.com/memorial/14205480/lydia-leister.
[96] Online: https://en.wikipedia.org/wiki/George_Meade.

Gettysburg, and it could be argued if you could break out the Gettysburg losses on days one, two and three, it's quite possible, it's quite possibly bloodier than Antietam on the second day of July here. But you could never prove it, because you cannot breakout the losses for each of the three days at Gettysburg.

Meade will, at the end of the day, about 10 o'clock, will call a staff meeting. Before he has done this, he has sent a telegram to Washington telling them that there has been a terrible battle, particularly beginning about 4 PM on the second and continuing until well after dark. However, he thinks the general results favor the Union, and he's calling a meeting here.

Ed Bearss speaks at the "Widow" Leister house, damaged in the Confederate barrage, but restored.

Now if it was a meeting that would *not* be a Council of War,[97] there would be no problem with it. Now, a Council of War is when you call your leaders together and you set an agenda, you discuss it, and you vote on it. It's participatory democracy, and is *not* the way you run an army. Bonaparte

---

[97] Online: https://en.wikipedia.org/wiki/Council_of_war.

says, "Never hold one," the greatest soldier of the 19th Century, and [Confederate General Thomas J.] Jackson[98] will only hold one, and never again.

So, they're going to assemble here sometime after 10 PM. The improvements, the barns, the outbuildings, and the house are like they were at the time. So, they'll arrive here. All that's going to be in that room here, if you look in the window, the left window, all the furniture that's in the room is one table and one chair. Well, they come in and they're discussing the days actions. They've all lit up their cigars. You're probably glad they're lighting up the cigars because none of these guys have probably had a bath in one week and have been sweating a lot. There's going to be no organization [as] they talk about things, and then [Gen. Gouverneur Kemble] Warren,[99] in the far left-hand corner of the room as you look at it is going to be the smartest of them all. He's going to sit down in that corner and go to sleep, so he's not going to be a participant in the hearings, the discussions, and will sleep through it all.

Pickett's Charge

The bus takes the group to where the Pickett[100]-Pettigrew[101]-Trimble[102] charge[103] began across the open field and Ed Bearss addressed the group. He first described General Pickett and his wives to the group, adding some color to his story.

---

[98] Online: https://www.nps.gov/hafe/learn/historyculture/thomas-j-jackson.htm and https://en.wikipedia.org/wiki/Stonewall_Jackson.
[99] Online: https://en.wikipedia.org/wiki/Gouverneur_K._Warren.
[100] Online: https://en.wikipedia.org/wiki/George_Pickett
[101] Online: https://en.wikipedia.org/wiki/J._Johnston_Pettigrew.
[102] Online: https://en.wikipedia.org/wiki/Isaac_R._Trimble.
[103] Online: https://en.wikipedia.org/wiki/Pickett%27s_Charge.

Pickett

Now Pickett's Division, there's this aura about it. The line they used to have on the electric map was, "15 Virginia regiments, the flower of Lee's Army, pure unadulterated BS. I can name you a lot more troops from either Virginia, North Carolina, South Carolina, Mississippi, you can say that about, and you'd be more right than when you say it about Pickett's Division. Pickett's Division *is* 15 Virginia regiments, but they have fought as a unit very, very seldom. One brigade of them had been under Pickett at the Battle of Gaines' Mill[104] and Pickett had been wounded. Pickett does not return to duty until after June 27th until just before the Battle of Fredericksburg. His men see very little action at Fredericksburg and they see no action at all at [the Battle of] Chancellorsville. Where do they get this baloney, "the flower of Lee's Army?"

Now, Pickett himself, had graduated from West Point, in the Class of 1846, the bottom of the class, in which Gen. George B. McClellan[105] is No. 2. Thomas Johnathon Jackson is No. 17, and Pickett is No. 52. He'd been close to [Gen. James] Longstreet[106] since the Mexican War. Pickett will be assigned (now, if you're in the Mexican War,[107] if you want to be in a West Point class, you want to be in the Class of '46. It's the same thing as the Class of 1915, which is two years before we enter WWI,[108] and it's going to be the same thing. The stars are going to fall on it.

So, Pickett is assigned to the 8th infantry. Longstreet, … got out of West Point four years before George. Now, when he storms Chapultepec Castle,[109] on the 13th day of September, 1847, Longstreet is wounded, and he hands the colors of the 8th Infantry to George Pickett, and George Pickett plants the colors of the 8th infantry over Chapultepec Castle, and he becomes a protégé of Longstreet from that day.

---

[104] Online: https://www.nps.gov/rich/learn/historyculture/gainesmillbull.htm.
[105] Online: https://en.wikipedia.org/wiki/George_B._McClellan.
[106] Online: https://en.wikipedia.org/wiki/James_Longstreet.
[107] Online: https://en.wikipedia.org/wiki/Mexican%E2%80%93American_War.
[108] Online: https://en.wikipedia.org/wiki/World_War_I.
[109] Online: https://en.wikipedia.org/wiki/Chapultepec_Castle.

Now, Pickett, as he moves northward, he had married, and his wife No. 1 had died with a child who dies in childhood. He rose to a lieutenant, still in the 8th Infantry, and he's stationed out on Puget Sound. There, he falls for an Indian Maiden, and though there's no record of them ever being pronounced "man and wife" in the church, he said he married her by "jumping the broomstick,"[110] and by her he has a child.

Pickett will be at Ft. Monroe[111] when LaSalle Corbel[112] is five years old. Pickett is a bereaved widower at that time, and as LaSalle will write in the trivia and the trash she writes, a good romance novel for you ladies, and she saw Pickett there and decided she is going to marry him. He becomes her "soldier." In 1861, they begin seeing each other. Pickett's Indian Maiden, with whom he's jumped the broomstick, or united in matrimony by a priest, or a partisan chaplain, his second wife is deceased. So, they're going to exchange letters on the way up to Gettysburg.

Now, what she's going to do, LaSalle is going to write letters from George to herself, and she will reply, writing the letters to George by herself, so she writes both ways, and I've never seen such trivia. I don't want you ladies going to go buy her biography of Pickett. He is her "soldier," and she'll write this dribble. As he marches north to Gettysburg, "every tramp, tramp, tramp [steps forward] is thought, thought, thought, of you." I see [our tour manager] ready to swoon. She wished her husband, when he was courting her, had written such trivia as that. He'll [Picket] will reply, "She's the sweetest flower that he ever saw."

She is writing these letters and publishing after he's dead. He doesn't know he'd spoken this trivia, this crap. She's writing it and publishing it to show that he's a soldier. She also makes up the biggest baloney when Richmond falls. I'm just ... and then I'll get off this thing, my thing about it. When Richmond falls,[113] according to LaSalle, she has given birth to her first child by "her soldier" and who does she run into, on the 4th or the 5th of April, when Lincoln is up there she runs into Abraham Lincoln, and

---
[110] Online: https://en.wikipedia.org/wiki/Jumping_the_broom.
[111] Online: https://www.nps.gov/fomr/index.htm and https://en.wikipedia.org/wiki/Fort_Monroe.
[112] Online: https://en.wikipedia.org/wiki/LaSalle_Corbell_Pickett.
[113] Online: https://www.nps.gov/rich/index.htm.

[President] Abraham Lincoln[114] will take the child and kiss the child and say that he appointed Pickett to West Point. Pure unadulterated bullshit. What a vivid imagination she has.

Alright, so he has this division. He has three brigades. The brigade that is going to be deployed closest to the woods and the closest to this fence line, will be the five regiments commanded by Brig. Gen. [Richard Brooke] Garnett.[115] Now, Brig. Gen. Garnett is not an admirer of Thomas Jonathon Jackson. In fact, at the Battle of Kernstown,[116] on the 23rd day of March, 1862, he'd wisely ordered his command to retreat. Jackson brought charges against him, and he's relieved. So, he's going to request a court of inquiry. … Jackson is testifying. Garnett has a copy of the testimony, and every time Jackson opens his mouth, he writes, he doesn't have a good remembrance or is lying.

So, the news comes the Federals are advancing, the court martial is suspended, and never takes place. But Garnett has never recovered form this aspersion that Jackson had cast on him. So, he is very ill on this day, 102-degree temperature, but he's going into action, and will be one of the 23 Confederate officers that will ride a horse. He's not the only one, and he'll ride a horse forward at the head, and his men are deployed on the left.

On the right will be James [Lawson] Kemper,[117] a non-West Pointer, a lawyer, and a veteran of the Mexican War. He commands Longstreet's old Virginia Brigade. 1st Virginia,[118] 3rd Virginia,[119] 5th Virginia,[120] 11th Virginia,[121] 24th Virginia,[122] and he will be wounded very badly. Supporting him will be Gen. [Lewis Addison] Armistead,[123] Lo Armistead. Lo Armistead had been kicked out of West Point. Why is he kicked out of West Point? … for

---

[114] Online: https://en.wikipedia.org/wiki/Abraham_Lincoln.
[115] Online: https://en.wikipedia.org/wiki/Richard_B._Garnett.
[116] Online: https://www.nps.gov/cebe/learn/historyculture/first-battle-of-kernstown.htm and https://en.wikipedia.org/wiki/First_Battle_of_Kernstown.
[117] Online: https://en.wikipedia.org/wiki/James_L._Kemper.
[118] Online: https://en.wikipedia.org/wiki/1st_Virginia_Infantry.
[119] Online: https://en.wikipedia.org/wiki/3rd_Virginia_Cavalry.
[120] Online: https://en.wikipedia.org/wiki/5th_Virginia_Infantry.
[121] Online: https://en.wikipedia.org/wiki/11th_Virginia_Infantry.
[122] Online: https://en.wikipedia.org/wiki/24th_Virginia_Infantry.
[123] Online: https://en.wikipedia.org/wiki/Lewis_Armistead.

breaking a plate over Jubal Anderson Early's[124] head. He had then gone into the Army from civil life. He and [Union Gen. Winfield Scott] Hancock[125] are very close friends. When Armistead resigns from the Army, his last night on the west coast, will be in Hancock's headquarters, and Amoria Hancock will "tickle the ivories" as the soldiers will sing and weep with such tearjerkers as *The Morning and the Rest*. They'll say goodbye to each other and they're going to meet this day at Gettysburg.

[Looking at the map we're given,] you can see that Pickett does not go in a straight line. You can see this fence to our right. It's indicated on that map. This fence existed then and it exists now, and you're going to see that when the Confederates go up to that ridge there, Pickett's men are going to oblique, they're going to oblique 45 degrees, because they want to be touching Pettigrew's men when they cross the Emmitsburg Road. They want to have Pickett's leftmost men in the 8th Missouri[126] touching the rightmost men in the 53rd North Carolina when they reach the Emmitsburg Road. It's very important to understand that.

(1) Fence to our right then and now shows on our map. (2) we are marching to the copse of trees with left oblique" turn in direction. (3-4) Ed Bearss depicts the left oblique.

---

[124] Online: https://en.wikipedia.org/wiki/Jubal_Early.
[125] Online: https://en.wikipedia.org/wiki/Winfield_Scott_Hancock.
[126] Online: http://infantry8thmo.org/ and
    https://en.wikipedia.org/wiki/8th_Missouri_Volunteer_Infantry.

You're going to have these swales. At the time of the Civil War, there was no indirect firing. Whether it was artillery or rifles, small arms, you have to see the target if you're going to hit it. You do not have indirect fire. That means when you're in a swale you're as safe as in the arms of Jesus. When you're in the next swale, your as safe as in the arms of your mother. But when you come out of that swale, you're in hell.

The Charge Begins

We walk across the Pickett's charge field and get to the fence, about where the Confederates executed a left oblique. Ed Bearss describes the action.

All right, as you look at the map, you've got 36 Union guns (cannon) extending south from the Pennsylvania Monument. [Pointing] You can see that line of monuments there. Now they're able to fire on you. Up to we came to this point, [Maj. Freeman] McGilvery's[127] 36 cannon did not fire on us. Here we're going to do a left oblique. A left oblique is that your battle line, the most left man, when he gets there about 50 years in front of us, is going to no longer face this way [perpendicular to Union lines], he's going to face that way (45 degrees left to his left). That means the while line is going to change direction, because they want to reach that swale in front of us, because when they reach that swale, there no longer going to be subject to Freeman McGilvery's guns, or [Capt. Benjamin Franklin] Rittenhouse's[128] battery on Little Round Top.[129] Rittenhouse's guns are giving the Confederates hell now.

The Confederates extreme right will be Kemper, and he will go past the Klingle house,[130] barn and outbuildings. He'll be on that high ground and he's changing his direction too as you can see, because now, we're going to

---

[127] Online: https://en.wikipedia.org/wiki/Freeman_McGilvery.
[128] Online: https://en.wikipedia.org/wiki/Benjamin_F._Rittenhouse.
[129] Online: https://en.wikipedia.org/wiki/Little_Round_Top.
[130] Online: https://www.gettysburgdaily.com/gettysburgs-klingel-house-log-walls/.

be moving that way and we're going to be looking at that bus, because that's how we're going to reach the Emmitsburg Road.

Walking further, someone asked Ed Bearss, "Can the cannon fire over their own troops?" Ed Bearss responds, "*No*, their fuses are not very good. Because if you fire over your own troops, they'll halt in a defilade area and send a message back, "You sons of bitches, if you keep firing over our heads, we're going to fire on you. No, you don't have overhead fire at that time."

As Ed Bearss begins to cross the Pickett's Charge field, he remembers two men who made the charge with him years earlier.

Did anybody go back [from the charge]? They generally don't. Whenever they start looking at it [going back], I always tell about the two most exciting men that I ever walked this with. One is a Marine that lost both legs at the hip. His hands were reduced to two fingers on each hand, and he went across in a, ..., he had biceps on him like a weightlifter, and he went across this route that we're walking and he's up at the angle when the rest of us aren't halfway to the Emmitsburg Road.

The other one is a Vietnam veteran, has one leg off at the knee, and one leg off at the thigh. He had a plate in his skull, and he walked all the way. When we hit the angle, he fell. People extend their hands to help him up. He waves them to one side and gets up on his own. When you tell them about those two people, even the wimps, will generally decide maybe they had better walk too. If those two men with those terrible disabilities that these chaps have, well ... the person that has no legs at all, he of course, goes in a wheel chair. But his arms, his biceps, are like a weightlifter's, and he's at the angle when the rest of us aren't yet to the Emmitsburg Road.

After crossing the stone wall close to the famous "high water mark"[131] achieved by the Confederacy in the Civil War, Ed Bearss describes the final moments of the charge towards the Copse of Trees.

---

[131] Online: https://en.wikipedia.org/wiki/High-water_mark_of_the_Confederacy.

Canister Range

The guns firing cannister[132] at that short range will destroy Hodges Brigade, Hodges Regiment. The 14th Virginia will not get any closer to those cannon then that gentlemen in the yellow shirt over there when the regiment is destroyed. Now we're moving into the Col. Dennis O'Kane's[133] [Union] Regiment. He's an Irish bartender commanding an Irish regiment. He is familiar with Longfellow's poem, *Paul Revere*, in which he talks about Gen. Warren saying, "Don't fire until you see the whites of their eyes."

> Ed Bearss on cannon cannister fire.
>
> A standard cannister works on the same principle as your shotgun shell. The propellent charge throws it out. It has a very thin tin, where you have that cardboard thing at the end of your 12-gauge shotgun shell, and it's a black tin and the balls are in sawdust, so they come out. The balls can be generally a half inch in diameter, maybe as much as ¾ of an inch in diameter. If you get a bunch of cannister [and you fire it at] the men coming shoulder to shoulder, and you're about 50 yards off, you can hear the bones being crushed.

Now, the Confederates had been here, briefly, on the 2nd day of July. Here, he's [O'Kane] going to tell his men, "Gather up as many rifles as you can. Load them, and if you can, have four or five rifles," that's the real killers in the Irish Brigade, in the 69th… and when the 71st Pennsylvania[134] breaks, Col. O'Kane is killed, and his men, his right wing, fall back into the Copse of Trees. So, the Confederates have a breakthrough [over the wall].

---

[132] Online: https://en.wikipedia.org/wiki/Canister_shot.
[133] Online: https://www.findagrave.com/memorial/19069/dennis-o_kane and https://en.wikipedia.org/wiki/69th_Pennsylvania_Infantry_Regiment.
[134] Online: https://gettysburg.stonesentinels.com/union-monuments/pennsylvania/pennsylvania-infantry/71st-pennsylvania/ and http://www.pa-roots.com/pacw/infantry/71st/71storg.html.

Cushing's battery fires double cannister, and they'll never find Garnett's body.

Meanwhile, General Garnett, 102-degree temperature, his long frock coat,[135] riding a horse, he will be out in front of us about 50 yards, and [Lt. Alonzo] Cushing's[136] battery will open fire with double canister. The horse will come out of the grey smoke and they'll never find Garnett's body. His sword and watch will be hocked in Baltimore in the 1880's, so they know that some Yankee got them.

Breakthrough

The Confederates as a mob come over the wall here, they've got a breakthrough, and they're heading toward that monument where we can see the scroll. That's the monument put up to Armistead by the Union soldiers, because with Garnett killed, his horse badly wounded, Armistead is now leading men of [Brig. Gen. Brikett Davenport] Fry's[137] Tennessee Brigade, the two Alabama Regiments, and his Virginians. They're going to reach this point where we can see the scroll monument, and that is put here by the Union. That indicates where General Armistead will lay his hand on that gun five yards behind us, and he's shot down with a serious wound in the thigh.

---

[135] Online: https://en.wikipedia.org/wiki/Frock_coat.
[136] Online: https://www.nps.gov/gett/learn/historyculture/cushing-at-gettysburg.htm and https://en.wikipedia.org/wiki/Alonzo_Cushing.
[137] Online: https://en.wikipedia.org/wiki/Birkett_D._Fry.

The Union will now counter attack, coming in with the 19th Massachusetts,[138] 15th Massachusetts,[139] the 42nd New York,[140] and the 72nd Pennsylvania.[141] Only about a score of men of the 72nd Pennsylvania come forward.

The Confederates have a breakthrough.

If we stand here and look to your left, you're going to see a monument ... that's the high-water mark of the 26th North Carolina.[142] The Confederates have gone as far as they're going to go. General Hancock has been wounded, seriously, and he's heard reports that Longstreet is wounded and a prisoner. So, he'll send Capt. [Henry Harrison] Bingham,[143] a Mason,[144] down here to check and see if this is General Longstreet. He finds out it is General Armistead. Armistead and Bingham are Masons. Masons are not supposed to tell lies on other Masons. But what is going to happen, Armistead will ask, "How is General Hancock?" because Bingham is on his

---

[138] Online: https://archive.org/details/reminiscencesofn00adam/page/n8/mode/2up and
https://en.wikipedia.org/wiki/19th_Regiment_Massachusetts_Volunteer_Infantry.
[139] Online: https://www.nps.gov/anti/learn/historyculture/mnt-ma-15-inf.htm and
https://en.wikipedia.org/wiki/15th_Regiment_Massachusetts_Volunteer_Infantry.
[140] Online: https://dmna.ny.gov/historic/reghist/civil/infantry/42ndInf/42ndInfMain.htm and
https://en.wikipedia.org/wiki/42nd_New_York_Volunteer_Infantry_Regiment.
[141] Online: https://en.wikipedia.org/wiki/72nd_Pennsylvania_Infantry_Regiment.
[142] Online: http://26nc.org/History/history.html and
https://en.wikipedia.org/wiki/26th_North_Carolina_Infantry.
[143] Online: https://en.wikipedia.org/wiki/Henry_H._Bingham.
[144] Online: https://en.wikipedia.org/wiki/Freemasonry.

[Hancock's] staff. He [Bingham] said, "He's seriously wounded, but will live."

... that's the high-water mark of the 26th North Carolina.

Armistead said, "I'm glad to hear my old friend is going to live," and then he will say something that the Confederate's say a Mason would never say. Masons are not supposed to lie to other Masons. As Bingham remembers, Armistead will express regret at having taken up the old sword against the nation's flag. The Confederate's will say, "Baloney, he would have never said that." Masons will say, "Yes, he did say that," because one Mason would not tell a lie to another Mason. So, when they put a monument up in the expansion of the National cemetery, Mason's pledge over a million dollars to put up a monument interpreting the conversation between Capt. Bingham of Hancock's Staff and Armistead in which Armistead will express regret of having taken up the sword against the old flag. We won't know if he said it or not, because in 30 hours, Armistead[145] is dead.

---

[145] Online: https://www.findagrave.com/memorial/3493/Lewis-Addison-Armistead and https://gettysburg.stonesentinels.com/monuments-to-individuals/lewis-armistead/.

BIBLIOGRAPHY

A partial "Read Ahead" list for Gettysburg includes the following well-known references (there are many others):

Bearss, Edwin C. and Hills, J. Parker. *Receding Tide: Vicksburg and Gettysburg – The campaigns That Changed the Civil War*. Washington, DC: National Geographic, 2010.
Pfanz, Harry W. The Harry Pfanz Gettysburg Trilogy, Omnibus E-book: *Includes Gettysburg: The First Day; Gettysburg: The Second Day; and Gettysburg: Culp's Hill and Cemetery Hill, Civil War America series*. Chapel Hill, NC: UNC Press, 2011.
Pfanz, Harry W. *Gettysburg--The First Day, The Civil War America Series*. Chapel Hill, NC: UNC Press, 2010.
Pfanz, Harry W. *Gettysburg--The Second Day, The Civil War America Series*. Chapel Hill, NC: UNC Press, 1998.
Pfanz, Harry W. *Gettysburg--Culp's Hill and Cemetery Hill, The Civil War America Series*. Chapel Hill, NC: UNC Press, 2001.

ADDENDUM

Before we walked the ground of Pickett's Charge, a member of the group quoted a famous author on this moment, before the charge had happened.

I can't fill in what Ed did, but I want to leave you all with something else that happened after this was all over with. You're standing on ground that is, even if you're not a student of history, you've heard of Pickett's Charge. Yes, it should be Pickett's, Trimble's, Pettigrew's Charge, but everybody knows it as Pickett's Charge. This, in the 1870s and '80's, and as the veterans started to die out, this became a legendary piece of ground. If you went north, you went to Gettysburg, you had to go see where it was. It was such a big deal that probably Mississippi's most prominent novelist decided to put it into his *Intruder in the Dust*, William Faulkner. Permit me to read you a little bit about this, because it's *right* now.

> For every southern boy 14 years old, not once, but whenever he wants it, there is the instance when it's still not yet 2'o'clock on that July afternoon in 1863. The brigades are in position behind the rail fence, the guns are laid and ready in the woods, and the furled flags are already loosened to break out, and Pickett himself, with his long oiled ringlets in his hat in one hand probably and his sword in the other looking up the hill waiting for Longstreet to give the word, and it's all in the balance. It hasn't happened yet, hasn't even begun yet.
>
> It not only hasn't begun yet, but there is still time for it *not* to begin against that position and those circumstances which made more men than Garnett and Kemper and Armistead and Wilcox look grave. Yet, it's going to begin. Ya'll know that. We have come too far with too much at stake. That moment doesn't even need a 14-year-old boy to think, "This time, maybe this time, with all this much to lose and all this much to gain. Pennsylvania, Maryland, the world, the golden dome of Washington, itself de-crowned with desperate and unbelievable victory. The desperate gamble. The cast made two years ago.

This was part of the Lost Cause after the war, and even William Faulkner took it up, because this is the pinnacle that you were growing up with in the South. If you were a son of a veteran of the war who happened to be here at Gettysburg, it endures to this day in some parts of this country. It's part of the healing process that we go through. But when you go to Pickets Charge, like we're now about to step across, and you see that Copse of Trees over there, …, that's where the New America began.

Chapter 4

JOHN WILKES BOOTH ESCAPE TOUR

THE TOUR BEGINS

The John Wilkes Booth[146] Escape Route Tour is a day-long excursion that begins in Baptist Alley behind the Fords Theatre National Historic Site.[147] Ed Bearss first brings us to the back of the building in front of the exit door Booth exited after shooting President Abraham Lincoln.[148] We were awaiting our ticket time to here the NPS ranger describe the actual events that night as Booth's assassination plot unfolded. In what follows, we will present Ed Bearss's talks in the chronological order of history and not, out of tour necessity, in the order they were presented.

THE KIDNAP-TO-MURDER SPEECH

Ed Bearss provides extensive family background of the actor John Wilkes Booth, a vehement Confederate sympathizer, and at least in the

---

[146] Online: https://www.nps.gov/people/john-wilkes-booth.htm and https://en.wikipedia.org/wiki/John_Wilkes_Booth.
[147] Online: https://home.nps.gov/foth/learn/historyculture/index.htm.
[148] Online: https://en.wikipedia.org/wiki/Abraham_Lincoln.

south, known as "the handsomest man on stage." Ed then describes Booth's relationships with those who will become collaborators in his plans and escape long before the assassination as Booth plans to kidnap the President to force new prisoner exchanges. He then describes a watershed event in Booths change in plans from kidnapping Lincoln to murdering him.

> The Lincolns will get back in Washington [DC] on the 9th from City Point[149] to get the news that has come in that General [Robert E]. Lee[150] has surrendered at Appomattox Court House that day, that's how fast the Union had the telegraph functioning. So, on the 11th, there's going to be a big torchlight parade to celebrate the surrender of Bobby Lee and his army. The torchlight parade is going to end up in Lafayette Square[151] and in front of the north face of the White House.
>
> Lincoln is a glow and the audience is shouting, "Speech, speech, speech!" The bands are playing. They call for Lincoln to give a speech. Lincoln does not like to give off-the-cuff remarks, but he does. With Booth, [David] Herold[152] and [Lewis] Powell[153] in the audience, he makes a remark that with the war over, ... and Lincoln makes some remarks that I'm going to recommend to the Congress we give the vote to those blacks who served in the Union Army and to other well-disposed blacks. When he hears that, Booth turns to Powell and Herold, and say, "That's the last speech that son of a bitch will ever make." So, what had been a failed kidnap plot, is going to become a murder plot in a very short time span. That is the evening of the 11th. [154]

---

[149] Online: https://www.nps.gov/pete/learn/historyculture/city-point.htm and https://en.wikipedia.org/wiki/City_Point,_Virginia
[150] Online: https://www.nps.gov/arho/learn/historyculture/robert-lee.htm and https://en.wikipedia.org/wiki/Robert_E._Lee.
[151] Online: https://en.wikipedia.org/wiki/Lafayette_Square,_Washington,_D.C.
[152] Online: https://en.wikipedia.org/wiki/David_Herold.
[153] Online: https://en.wikipedia.org/wiki/Lewis_Powell_(conspirator).
[154] Online: https://www.nps.gov/parkhistory/online_books/hh/3b/hh3d.htm.

KILLING LINCOLN

Setting the Stage

(1) Inside Ford's Theater, operated by the NPS, showing (2) the Presidential Box seats and the stage below. (3-4) One of the interpretive signs near the entrance to the theater, with a depiction of Booth leaving the theater in Baptist Alley behind after exiting the theater back door and beginning his escape.

At the back of Ford's Theater building, where Ed Bearss describes Booth exiting the theater after shooting Lincoln and slashing Maj. [Henry Reed] Rathbone's[155] arm in Boxes 7 and 8, and then leaping to the stage – perhaps shouting the Virginia slogan "Sic Semper Tyrannis,"[156] ("Death to Tyrants") – yet not possibly breaking his leg there as is often stated. Ed Bearss describes our location and the infamous action here at a little after 10 PM, Good Friday, April 14, 1864.

We're at the back end of the Ford's Theater. The Ford's Theater ended at this standpipe. This is an addition as you face it to the right of the standpipe. There's lots of entrances here now because this building has been used for many things. The only entrance back here at that time was the door

---

[155] Online: https://en.wikipedia.org/wiki/Henry_Rathbone.
[156] Online: https://en.wikipedia.org/wiki/Sic_semper_tyrannis.

just behind me. This is the only entrance at the rear of the theater. If you go in that door, you've got a stairway going to the basement. Above the basement is the stage.

(1) An addition to the Ford's Theater at the time of the assassination. (2) Booth exited the door behind me. (3) Ed Bearss explains what's beyond the door in the theater. (4) Booth had trouble getting his right foot into the stirrup.

If you walk down that stairway, you're in the basement. You walk across the Ford's Theater to the south side of it where you have another ladder going up into the backstage with a door going outside. That's how Booth is going to access the theater.

Booth arrives at the theater about 8 AM. The Washington papers all say that [Gen. Ulysses S.] Grant[157] has just returned to Appomattox.[158] He arrived on the evening of the 13th. Now, if you think Lincoln's more popular than Grant at this moment, you'd better think another thought, because he's just accepted the surrender of Lee's Army, and of course, Lincoln is a politician.

---

[157] Online: https://www.nps.gov/ulsg/learn/historyculture/ulysses-s-grant.htm and https://en.wikipedia.org/wiki/Ulysses_S._Grant.
[158] Online: https://www.nps.gov/apco/learn/historyculture/the-surrender-meeting.htm.

Grant's first stop before he goes to the Willard's Hotel,[159] where his wife is staying, is of course at the White House. He goes in, and the President likes the theater, knows Grant is the most popular man in the United States. He says, "Of course, Mary [Todd Lincoln][160] and I are going to the theater tomorrow night on the 14th, on Good Friday,[161] they'll be a big crowd and you and your lady will come with me."

Good Friday

By that time, the paper had told that the Lincoln's guests that night at the theater are going to be the Grants. But Mrs. Grant and Mrs. Lincoln detest the very ground the other walks on. Grant may be Commander and Chief of the Union Army, but he's not the General and Chief in his household, particularly if Mary Lincoln is going to be a guest. The President knows they don't like each other. He's naïve.

Grant had probably thought to himself, "Shit, how do I get out of this." So, he goes home and goes to Julia [Boggs Grant][162] and says, "I've got news for you." We don't know his actual words, but he's a rather reticent fellow and he's going to tell her, "We're invited to the Ford's Theater tomorrow night and she says, "If anybody goes, you're going. I will not spend another night in the presence of that horrible woman." Now, they called each other, "woman." They have a violent dislike, and she's going to say, "We're going up and see our children up in Burlington, [New Jersey][163] tomorrow," and he'll say, "Yes ma'am, we are going." So, the next morning he has to go to the White House and tell the President that we're not going to the theater.

The President can't be that dense that he doesn't know that the two women detest each other. The papers don't say what theater he's going to. It

---

[159] Online: https://www.nps.gov/nr/travel/wash/dc36.htm.
[160] Online: https://en.wikipedia.org/wiki/Mary_Todd_Lincoln.
[161] Online: https://en.wikipedia.org/wiki/Good_Friday.
[162] Online: https://en.wikipedia.org/wiki/Julia_Grant.
[163] Online: http://www.tourburlington.org/SeeSites21-25.html.

can only be two. Either the Ford's Theater or the National Theater.[164] Booth, like all actors, picks up his mail at the theater. It arrives here. Except for the one-eyed horse that Powell will ride that night, Booth has sold all his livestock, and he's rented a horse at the Pumphrey Livery Stable[165] near the National Hotel near 8th and Pennsylvania, and he sees Henry Clay Ford[166] decorating Box 78. He asks, "What are you doing?" There was no Presidential Seal[167] at that time, and he's going to say, "Lincoln and the Grants are coming tonight." So, now Booth knows what theater they're going to.

He [Booth] is going to have a meeting later that morning in the Herndon House[168] with his close collaborators, he's going to outline a plan for that night. Tonight, Powell, you're going to come to the door of the theater with me and I'm going to assassinate the President and you're going to assassinate Gen. Grant. [George] Axerodt,[169] I've got you a room at the Kirkwood House[170] at 12th and Pennsylvania Avenue and it's right above where the Vice President has a room. The Vice President[171] didn't have a residence at that time, ... and he says that at about 10:00 or 10:30, you're going to knock at the door and when the Vice President answers the door, you're going to kill him. Harold, you'll be a general factotum helping us out.

Our American Cousin

In the afternoon, Booth rides up Pennsylvania Avenue.[172] As he's riding up Pennsylvania Avenue, who does he see coming out of the Willard's Hotel and getting in a hack? It's General Grant and his wife. Julia will remember

---

[164] Online: http://www.nationaltheatre.org/.
[165] Online: https://en.wikipedia.org/wiki/James_W._Pumphrey.
[166] Online: https://www.fords.org/lincolns-assassination/investigating-the-assassination/.
[167] Online: https://en.wikipedia.org/wiki/Seal_of_the_President_of_the_United_States.
[168] Online: https://www.gettysburgdaily.com/john-wilkes-booths-last-day-in-washington-5-with-gettysburg-lbg-mike-kanazawich/.
[169] Online: https://en.wikipedia.org/wiki/George_Atzerodt.
[170] Online: https://lincolnassassinationconspiracy.weebly.com/andrewjohnson.html.
[171] Online: https://en.wikipedia.org/wiki/Andrew_Johnson.
[172] Online: https://en.wikipedia.org/wiki/Pennsylvania_Avenue.

a very handsome man is going to follow them all the way to the Baltimore and Ohio Depot,[173] which is down there near where the Taft Monument[174] is now. He's going to seem very interested in them, but she doesn't really think much of it, and only after the assassination is this going to become 2 and 2 and get 4, *that's* John Wilkes Booth.

He's going to watch them get on the train and he's going to have another meeting at 8:30 that night. He's going to substitute Secretary [of State] Seward for General Grant. Since Powell isn't very bright, a killer, but not very bright, Davey Herold is going to guide him just as we said at our last stop. All the assassinations are to take place around 10:15, since Booth knows *Our American Cousin*[175] [the play Lincoln would see] very well and he knows when the most humorous scene in it will be and knows they'll be a lot of laughing.

I'm going to leave him in there in the theater, because they're going to tell you onsite when we go into the theater what happens when they go in the theater. The only thing I'm going to tell you is he'll be waiting by the Star Saloon, it's a reconstruction, it was next door to the Ford's Theater, immediately adjoining it on the south side. Booth looks at his watch and it's around 10 o'clock. He goes to the bar and calls to the bartender, "Taltavull,"[176] and says. "Set a bottle up, I'm going to pour myself a few drinks," cause he's waiting for about 10:15, waiting until the play get's closer to the most humorous words, has a few drinks of whiskey, pays for the bottle, leaves the bottle there. As he walks out, a barfly will say to him, "You'll never be the actor your brother was," and Booth will say, "When I leave here tonight, I'll be the most famous man in America." That becomes important later on. The barfly doesn't understand what he means.

So, when Booth has ridden up here, Edmund Spangler[177] was the stagehand. Booth had known Spangler, who's a general handyman for his father Julius Brutus Booth[178] since John Wilkes was seven years old, back in

---

[173] Online: https://en.wikipedia.org/wiki/New_Jersey_Avenue_Station.
[174] Online: https://en.wikipedia.org/wiki/Robert_A._Taft_Memorial.
[175] Online: https://en.wikipedia.org/wiki/Our_American_Cousin.
[176] Online: https://en.wikipedia.org/wiki/Peter_Taltavull.
[177] Online: https://en.wikipedia.org/wiki/Edmund_Spangler.
[178] Online: https://en.wikipedia.org/wiki/Junius_Brutus_Booth.

1845. As you know, John Wilkes Booth was born in 1838. Spangler works here as a stage hand. So, Booth will hand the reigns [of his rented horse] to Spangler and tell him, "Hold my horse for when I come out." So, Booth goes in, and after he assassinates the President, as you'll hear inside, badly wounds the 13th person he [Lincoln] asks to go to the theater. No one seems to want to go with him to the theater that night. The thirteenth one he's going to ask is Maj. Rathbone, whose fiancée is Clara Harris,[179] who's the daughter of the senior senator from New York, and they go to the theater that night and you'll hear more about that [from the NPS ranger] inside.

Break a Leg

After the assassination, Booth is going to leap out of the President's box, after shooting Lincoln, knifing Rathbone, landing on the stage in a crouch. You're going to notice they all used to tell it here that Booth broke his leg when he jumped to the stage. Most of the people that know more about it that anybody else do not think he broke his leg when he jumped to the stage. They're of the opinion he broke his leg when he's riding up Soper's Hill on the Brandywine Road near the beltway [today]. His horse fell with him. We'll go into more detail on that later as it's still somewhat controversial.

So, after brandishing his bloody knife at the audience, and shouting the Virginia State motto, "Sic Semper Tyrannus," thus always to tyrants. Shaking his bloody knife at them, he then comes off the stage, rushes by [actor] Harry Hawk,[180] the conductor, and comes out this door. [Police] Commissioner Burns has seen it, and he's following him, he's that guy you see in that drawing [near the front of the theater] as you see, following Booth.

Now, Booth is riding this horse from the Pumphrey Livery Stable. Spangler has had to do some work, he's a stagehand, so while Booth is in the building, he hands the reigns to [Joseph] "Peanuts" Burroughs,[181] not a very smart young man, he's 17, and tells him to have the horse ready when

---

[179] Online: https://en.wikipedia.org/wiki/Clara_Harris.
[180] Online: https://en.wikipedia.org/wiki/Harry_Hawk.
[181] Online: https://emergingcivilwar.com/2014/02/26/in-jumping-broke-my-leg-another-look-at-the-lincoln-assassination-legend/.

Mr. Booth comes out that door (behind me). So, Booth is in some hurry, because he can hear the pitty-pat of Commissioner Burns feet on his heels as he bursts out the door. Burroughs grabs for the reigns. Burroughs doesn't react very fast, As I say, Peanuts isn't very bright. When he holds the reigns a moment too long, Booth will take the bloody knife, which he still has in his hand, and brings the butt of the knife down on Peanut Burroughs point of his shoulder blade. Peanut Burroughs lets out a bellow and let's go of the reigns, and our tour almost ends right now, because as Booth throws his left foot in the stirrup – he's not used to this horse, it's a rental horse, [and] the Pumphrys are still owners[182] out in Chevy Chase [Maryland], out in that area. I've had some of them on my tour, so they're still in the area.

House where Lewis Powell stabbed, but failed to kill, Secretary of State Henry Seward

It almost ends because the horse spooks, it's shy, and for a brief second, Booth's right leg is pointing up at the stars. His left leg is in the stirrup as he's trying to get control of the horse, get his keyster in the saddle, and ride down the alley just like we walked in, turn left in the cutoff alley, and ride out into "F" Street. He'll ride through the District Government grounds, and then the next place they will know where he rides, and will pause, is when he reaches the Navy Yard Bridge. Any questions?

---

[182] Online: https://www.pumphreyfuneralhome.com/.

THE ESCAPE ROUTE

We then board a coach and visit each notable point as we travel the same route (or as close as we can) that Booth with his guide, David Herold, followed over the next 14 days. Booth sought to escape and hoped his actions would be praised in the press instead of vilified in the south as well as the north. He was finally tracked to Richard Garrett's farm in Virginia and the infamous tobacco barn.

Ed Bearss provides details enroute and provided an annotated map of the Booth route so we have awareness in advance of the important sites we will visit.

We stop for my interpretation at (1) the Surratt tavern; then (2) Take the route Booth and Herold took; to (3) the Pine Thicket in which he hid for a time; and then (4) the Port Royal Ferry to cross the Potomac River.

John Wilkes Booth Escape Tour

John Wilkes Booth's escape route. Public domain. https://en.wikipedia.org/wiki/John_Wilkes_Booth#/media/File:Booth_escape_route.svg.

Boston Corbett. Library of Congress description: "Sgt. Boston Corbett, U.S.A." Author: Matthew Brady. Public domain. https://upload.wikimedia.org/wikipedia/commons/a/a3/Boston_Corbett_-_Brady-Handy.jpg.

KILLING BOOTH

A Hanging Tree

Booth is tracked over 14 days to the Garrett farm,[183] and Union soldiers arrive.

Twenty yards [from where the bus can pull over] would be the Garrett house. It fronts north, two-and-a-half stories; 30 feet in length; 20 feet in depth, and has a swept yard.[184] The soldiers arrive there about 4 AM. They have with them [William Storke] "Willie" Jett,[185] who is handcuffed. They ride up to the Garrett House, approaching it from where we those temporary barriers, and they go up, walk through the gate, Everton Congor,[186] who is on his crutches, steps up to the door, backed by Lafayette Baker,[187] and they pound on the door.

Mr. Garrett answers the door. He's rather cadaverous. He's in his nightshirt, and he's very tired, and they ask him, "Where is John Wilkes Booth, is he here?" Now Mr. Garrett has a habit of stuttering when he has a gun poked in his stomach and asking him where John Wilkes Booth is. He starts stuttering and he's not answering them.

So, there's a tree in the yard. They go to the tree, throw a rope over the limb of the tree, and put the noose end of the rope around his neck, and they then lift him off the ground. The poor guy is struggling to get any breath, it's probably worse than waterboarding, and they let him down and they can't say anything. He's lost his breath, he's stuttering, and, well, we'll give it to him again. They lift him up. Let him down, and he's gasping for air. One of his sons is sleeping in, now the tobacco barn would be 30 yards west of the house, that's [pointing] west.

---

[183] Online: https://en.wikipedia.org/wiki/Port_Royal,_Virginia and http://wikimapia.org/9513670/Garrett-Farm-site-1865.
[184] Online: http://www.thegardeningdiva.com/swept-yards.html.
[185] Online: https://www.findagrave.com/memorial/6945683/william-storke-jett.
[186] Online: https://en.wikipedia.org/wiki/Everton_Conger.
[187] Online: https://en.wikipedia.org/wiki/Lafayette_C._Baker.

Photo of the Garrett Farm near Port Royal, Virginia, where John Wilkes Booth, the assassin of U.S. President Abraham Lincoln, died. Retrieved from https://upload.wikimedia.org/wikipedia/commons/5/58/Garrett_Farm.gif.

The sons are in the smokehouse, which is to the south of the tobacco barn. He comes over and says, "They're locked in the tobacco barn." So now, they shackle old man Garrett in his nightshirt. They take Jack Garrett with them and he leads them across. Booth has woken up; he can hear the noise that's around the tobacco barn. They're going to cuff the two Garrett boys, Jack and Willie, and they're going to say, "We know you're in there, John Wilkes Booth, we want you to come out with your hands up," because they [have] removed the pin from the door lock.

BANG

Booth is all defiance. He's up and shouting, and says, "No, we're not coming out, we're armed and we'll go down fighting. Well, Davey Herold [with Booth for days] doesn't go for any "last stand," and he tells Booth, "I'm going to surrender." Booth then calls Davey every foul name you can think of, generally focusing on courage and masculinity, and he finally says, "The son of a bitch is coming out. Don't shoot." So, before he comes out, he hands Booth the Spencer carbine. Now they have Herold up, he's joined Garrett, the two Garrett boys, Willy Jett, are all cuffed under the tree.

Boston Corbett

Ed Bearss describes the man who will play a key role in the Booth story.

Boston Corbett[1] is in his forties. His name was Thomas Corbett. He'd emigrated to the United States with his wife and two lovely daughters in the early 1850s from England. He is by trade a hatter. What comes up in Alice in Wonderland? Mad as a hatter. Why do they use that? Because when they make beaver hats, they use large amounts of mercury. If you inhale large amounts of mercury, you ain't quite with us after that.

So, he will come here, and a plague will visit Boston, and his wife and two children will die. He'll become a drunken derelict, wandering the streets of New England towns. He'll be saved by a female evangelist and change his name from Thomas Corbett to Boston Corbett. As a street corner evangelist, he will be tempted by a prostitute. He lusts for her but does not succumb, and then he punishes himself. Now remember, Jimmy Carter got in a lot of trouble and got an article published about him lusting for women, but he doesn't punish himself. Now, Boston Corbett is going to castrate himself with a rusty razor, it's not a vasectomy, almost dies, but that doesn't keep him out of the Union Army. He'll serve in the Union Army, be captured by [Col. John Singleton] Mosby[1] near Chantilly [Virginia], and spends nine months in Andersonville, then he's exchanged. He's in pretty good health.

Then Booth sends out a challenge, it is, "I'll come out [he's an actor to the end], I'll come out and I'll fight you one at a time." They said, "No, we don't play that game. You're going to come out or we're going to burn you out." They surround the tobacco barn. The door of the tobacco barn faces east, toward us. The back of the barn is west of us. Everton Conger is on his crutches, goes around to the back, gets a bunch of thatch, lights the thatch, sticks it through an interstice in the tobacco barn, and sets some bedding afire.

They have it surrounded. The senior NCO[188] is Boston Corbett ..., and he will be on the south side of the building, looking through an interstice [gap between vertical tobacco barn wall boards]. The Secretary of War has given orders, and if you thought Rumsfeld was tough, he's a patsy compared to Edwin McMaster Stanton. If they thought [Secretary of Defense Donald] Rumsfeld was tough, they must be weaklings in the Army now, because he was tough, and he said he wants Booth alive.

So, as they look through the interstices, as the fires build up, they can see Booth on his crutches. He has his carbine in his right hand and starts hopping, cause his left leg is broken, toward the door. He'll drop one crutch and then the other crutch, and hop forward, and BANG, Corbett has shot. The bullet, since he's going that way [east towards the bus], Corbett's on the south side, the bullet goes through [Booth's] No. 2 vertebrae. So, everything below No. 2 vertebra is paralyzed.

Two soldiers rush in. They grab Booth, carry him out, and lay him on the porch of the Garrett House with his legs, and he has no use in his legs, dangling over the porch. His butt on the porch, his back on the porch, and then the wait will set in. A little before 7 [AM}, Booth is going to speak. Booth cannot move his hands, and he's going to tell the people he's thirsty. So, they're going to wet a washcloth and rub his lips. Then he says, "I want to see my hands." But he's paralyzed from here [pointing at neck] down, so they have to pick up his hands so he can see them. When he looks at his hands, he will say, as the interpreter said this morning, "Useless, useless." Then he will say, "Tell Mother I died for my country." His head flops to one side, and Booth is now dead

Boston Corbett is now handcuffed and joined all those other guys under the tree. They had placed him under arrest because both Conger, Baker and [Edward Paul] Doherty[189] believe we may have a lot of trouble getting any money for this because Stanton said he wanted him alive. So, they decide

---

[188] Online: Noncommissioned officer.
[189] Online: https://en.wikipedia.org/wiki/Edward_P._Doherty.

they're going to sew Booth in a bed cover and throw the body across the back of a horse as they get ready to start for Washington, DC.

Conger and Baker decide we'd better get to Washington first. Before any newspaper men get a hold of it, we want to be the persons that report that Booth is dead and Boston Corbett shot him, because they are expecting an explosion that makes Mount Helena look like something out of the *Little Sisters of the Poor*.[190] So, they race on ahead, catch the *John S. Ide*, and will pick them up when they get to Washington, and head for the War Department. When they leave here, they're going to take as prisoners both Garrett boys, old man Garrett, Boston Corbett, Willy Jett, and Davey Herald, so they've got lots of prisoners here with them as they start to Washington.

Ed explained the irony that…

Lincoln's autopsy will be held on Sunday the 16th, and it will be held by Dr. [Joseph K.] Barnes,[191] the man who pronounced Lincoln dead.[192] He is the Surgeon General of the United States. On the 28th day of April, he'll perform another autopsy, on John Wilkes Booth.

Roadside sign along Virginia Route 301.

---

[190] Online: http://littlesistersofthepoor.org/.
[191] Online: https://en.wikipedia.org/wiki/Joseph_Barnes.
[192] Online: http://www.abrahamlincolnonline.org/lincoln/education/medical.htm.

BIBLIOGRAPHY

This reading list was recommended by Ed Bearss and provided by South Mountain Expeditions.

Alford, Terry. *Fortune's Fool: The Life of John Wilkes Booth*. New York: Oxford University Press, 2015.
Kauffman, Michael W. *American Brutus: John Wilkes Booth and the Lincoln Conspiracies*. New York: Random House, 2005.
Mark, Sarah. "Tracking an Assassin," The *Washington Post*, April 14, 1995. https://www.washingtonpost.com/wp-srv/local/longterm/tours/civilwar/booth.htm. (The article provides a comprehensive description of the various stops on the escape route tour.)
McAuliffe, Kieran. *John Wilkes Booth Escape Route History Map,* 2nd ed. Toronto, ON: Kieran McAuliffe History Maps, 2013.
Steers, Jr., Edward, *Blood on the Moon: The Assassination of Abraham Lincoln*. Lexington, KY: University Press of Kentucky, 2001.
Swanson, James L. *Manhunt: The 12-Day Chase for Lincoln's Killer*. New York: William Morrow, 2007.

Chapter 5

SIOUX[193] INDIAN WARS TOUR

Ed Bearss led the South Mountain Expeditions 2014 Sioux Indian Wars tour with Jerome A. Greene,[194] a noted Indian historian and retired NPS employee. The tour began at Ft. Phil Kearney,[195] where the Great Plains[196] and the Rocky Mountains[197] meld in the land of the Big Sky, along the Bozeman Trail.[198] After visiting the museum there, we walk inside the partially reconstructed or refurbished fort and its walls.[199]

---

[193] Online: https://en.wikipedia.org/wiki/Sioux.

[194] Greene wrote the second Foreword of the second Ed Bearss memoir book, *Walking the Ground: Making American History* and is pictured with Ed Bearss on the cover of this third memoir book.

[195] Online: http://enjoyyourparks.com/Fort-Phil-Kearny-Wyoming.html and https://en.wikipedia.org/wiki/Fort_Phil_Kearny.

[196] Online: https://en.wikipedia.org/wiki/Great_Plains.

[197] Online: https://www.nps.gov/romo/index.htm and https://en.wikipedia.org/wiki/Rocky_Mountains.

[198] Online: https://www.nps.gov/bica/learn/historyculture/bozeman-trail.htm and https://en.wikipedia.org/wiki/Bozeman_Trail.

[199] Online: https://www.fortphilkearny.com/fort-phil-kearny-history.

Ft. Phil Kearney

The tour began at the Ft. Phil Kearny Interpretive Center and Gift Shop,[200] where Ed Bearss described the construction of the fort and the string of forts along the Bozeman Trail as protection from the Plains Indians using their well-modeled diorama.

(1)

(2)

(1) One view from Ft. Phil Kearney, located where the Rocky Mountains rise out of the Great Plains. (2) Wagon ruts defining the Bozeman Trail near the Fetterman Fight.

---

[200] Online: https://www.fortphilkearny.com/.

The fort itself will be essentially completed in this form by the time the serious trouble starts with the Indians at the end of October 1866. The fort as you can see [outside], they have reconstructed the corners of the stockade. There are two separate compounds here. This is the post. The flagstaff will be the greatest day that [Gen. Henry B.] Carrington[201] will have here because it's going to be 120-feet tall. It's going to be stepped, and the flag is a garrison flag and is 40 feet by 30 feet. So, if you're traveling up the Bozeman Trail, you know where the fort is.

The fort will be burned, and I'll go into what happens in the fort later on. So, that [flagstaff] will be erected there when the band will play and the fort will be essentially completed by then. Now, the commanding officer's quarters will be that building there [pointing]. We divide the walkways here as a "T." The main entrance to the fort will be here, coming up from the piney. It will be on low ground. Out here is where the civilian employees live, Portugee Phillips[202] and these [employees]. This is the quartermaster corral. Here, they have a part of it fronting on water. This is the quartermaster corral, this is where they corral their animals, their teams, and their wagons go and the people supply it with hay. It's roughly four-and-a-half miles to the pinery [where they got timber]. The road going to the pinery, and their sawmill is right over there, so they're going to have both round logs and sawn timber, because they build the fort, this is all going on over there [pointing].

These will be the barracks. They have cavalry here. The infantry barracks will be there [pointing], the post hospital there, and ... here, and each corner would be a bastion [pointing out the four corner bastions]. We're going to see the corners of the stockade. [They] have been reconstructed. Archeologically, they know just where they are, and you can stand up on the firing step there.

---

[201] Online: https://en.wikipedia.org/wiki/Henry_B._Carrington. Ed Bearss says people believed he got his job because of "what he knows, not what he's done."

[202] Online: http://www.lrgaf.org/journeys/ride-help.htm and https://www.loc.gov/item/2017685695/.

(1) Ft. Phil Kearny Interpretive Center and Gift Shop. (2) Ft. Phil Kearny diorama. (3) The 120-foot flagstaff. (4) The quartermaster corral.

Now, it's going to be very isolated, so after being here and getting his troops here, he's going to send two companies eighty miles up the road, the Bozeman Trail, to establish Ft. C. F. Smith,[203] that is located where the Bozeman Trail crosses the Big Horn River. It is just about two-and-a-half miles below where the Big Horn River comes out of the Big Horn Mountains. They had planned another fort up further on between Ft. C. F. Smith and the Crow Agency, which was then near present day Livingston, Montana, but they decided not, so they're going to strengthen Ft. Reno, eighty miles down the road, Ft. Phil Kearny here, and then another eighty miles on up to Ft. C. F. Smith. C. F. Smith, since they don't have a good supply of stone, will be principally built of adobe,[204] so it's pretty well all melted away.

[Pointing at diorama] so this is the port. The [powder] magazine would be here. It's kind of important because after learning that he's lost 81 people, Carrington is very worried that they're going to attack the fort. When the go out to recover the bodies on the 22nd, they recover most of the bodies late on

---

[203] Online: https://www.nps.gov/bica/learn/historyculture/fort-cf-smith-part-1-the-establishment.htm and
https://en.wikipedia.org/wiki/Fort_C._F._Smith_(Fort_Smith,_Montana).
[204] Online: https://en.wikipedia.org/wiki/Adobe.

the 21st, they'll recover all the bodies by the 22nd. When he goes out, the orders he leaves behind to the officer in charge, "If the Indians attack and get over the wall, make sure all the woman and children are in the magazine. If they come over the wall, you'll light the fuse, so the women and children won't be "guests" [of the Indians] and suffer a fate "too terrible to mention" as they say then. Everybody knows what he means when he says that. But they don't do that.

(1) Ft. Phil Kearny diorama. (2) One of the fort's bastions. (3) The fort's magazine. (4) A reconstructed bastion less the roof.

When Portugee Phillips and another leave here on the night of the 21st, they're going to run into a blizzard, and Portugee Phillips will arrive at Ft. Laramie[205] on Christmas night, and they're having a big ball [with] dancing, pleasant conversation, when this man staggers in and collapses, and tells them what has happened, because that [Laramie] is the nearest telegraph out there. [Marty Gane adds] His horse dropped dead after it arrived there, having galloped for 236 miles ["it was frozen, both of them were," adds an employee of the center].

---

[205] Online: https://www.nps.gov/fola/index.htm and
https://en.wikipedia.org/wiki/Fort_Laramie_National_Historic_Site.

THE FETTERMAN FIGHT, 21 DECEMBER 1866[206]

Next, we drove to the nearby site of what has been called "the Fetterman Massacre" on the 21st day of December, 1866. On that day, infantry and cavalry were sent from the fort to chase retreating Indians, but this was a common decoy employed by hostile Plains Indians. Once outside the protection of the fort, hidden Indians attacked United States infantry and cavalry, killed and then mutilated the dead. We walked out along the route they took, and Ed Bearss described the Indian attacks on the infantry and cavalry as well as pointed out wagon ruts from the nearby Bozeman Trail.

We are at the Fetterman Fight right now. On your map, and I have the map oriented. This is a wonderful place to be because you can see Ft. Phil Kearny on the map. It's blacked out in the same format as Ft. Phil Kearny. You can see Big Piney [and] Little Piney. You can see Sullivant Hill, and I've already told you that's the place where I counted off those three Indians for you, that were watching us [cutouts of Indian Scouts installed there]. That's Sullivant Hill, named for Margaret Sullivant Carrington. ...

Now, what we have done since we left there, we have followed the Bozeman Trail, we have crossed Big Piney Creek, we've come up onto Lodge Trail Ridge, we've crossed Lodge Trail Ridge. We see the Interstate if we look off to the right, we see the traffic going, and we are parked very near the monument, and the road we came up here is the state highway that parallels the Bozeman Trail.

... Now, you notice where the pinery is. So, they have to send wagon trains out of the fort, up to the pinery near where the Wagon Box Fight[207] is [shown on the map]. They load up with the logs and bring them back. So, from up on Pilot Knob, the [Indian] lookouts up there see the wagon train going out, ... up the trail, going up to the pinery and they've come against the Indians, [who] attack them. They finally called, they bullied, cajoled, whatever you want, propagandized poor old Henry Carrington to send out an expedition, "Let's take some aggressive action."

---

[206] Online: https://en.wikipedia.org/wiki/Fetterman_Fight.
[207] Online: https://www.wyohistory.org/encyclopedia/wagon-box-fight-1867 and https://en.wikipedia.org/wiki/Wagon_Box_Fight.

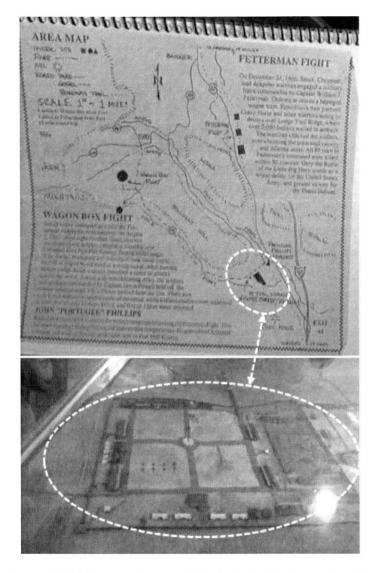

Map showing Ft. Phil Kearny and various Indian battles in the vicinity. Transformative fair use from owned image

He is going to order out Capt. [William J.] Fetterman,[208] and Fetterman is going to move up staying on the far side following Big Piney as he goes

---

[208] Online: https://www.wyohistory.org/encyclopedia/new-perspectives-fetterman-fight and https://en.wikipedia.org/wiki/William_J._Fetterman

up to pass around and cut off the Indians who are attacking the wagon train. Carrington is even going out himself, probably the first time he's ever been exposed to real danger in combat. He tries to cross Big Piney and it is frozen, rather lightly. He gets off [his horse] and tries to walk it in and he gets wet, then he has to kick, and he gets wet up to his crotch, and he's broken through the ice, so they're all going to ride across there and they're going to proceed up Big Piney.

As he does, [Lt. George W.] Grummond,[209] [Capt.] Horatio [Stowe] Bingham,[210] and 20 men disappear. Now, what they've done, they've disappeared, they're going over into the area where we are. The Indians have withdrawn from their attack on the wagon train as Fetterman is approaching, and they're over here in the area what is then called Pino Creek ..., but it's Prairie Dog Creek in here, and they're following an Indian. They run into an ambush, and they're in big trouble as a large number of Indians, 20 or 30 of them, come after them. They turn the horses about. Sergeant Brewer is soon dead and poor Lt. Horatio Bingham is dead, and Grummond escapes by sabering an Indian to death. Grummond has had a narrow escape.

Carrington arrives, and he is very upset for what Grummond has done, going out on his own. Fetterman shows up and they go back after collecting their four wounded soldiers. They killed six Indians and they've had Lt. Horatio Bingham is not with the living anymore or Sgt. Brewer. So, they go back to the fort.

Draw Them Out

This has registered on the Indians. Maybe if we use a decoy again at another time, and use a larger force of men, maybe we can draw them out and really do some damage to them.

So, naturally to say, Carrington is very shaken up by that and he will institute a rigorous training program, try to improve the discipline of his

---

[209] Online: https://www.findagrave.com/memorial/8997725/george-washington-grummond.
[210] Online: https://www.findagrave.com/memorial/20632424/horatio-stow-bingham.

men. His problem is going to be Fred [Capt. Frederick H.] Brown,[211] William Judd Fetterman, and most of all, George Washington Grummond. They're going to be talking about him, about what a coward he is, and such, and the Indians have taken a lesson in that, and they're assembling over in their villages.

Jim Bridger[212] is their [the Army's] scout. Jim Bridger is shocked. He finds out these guys have been fighting down south and don't know how to fight Indians. He's convinced that in fighting Indians, they're absolutely "babes in arms," although they have fought in big [Civil War] battles, and he is very concerned about what is happening.

On the 18th, Fred Brown and Fetterman go to Carrington and say, "We're gonna recruit 50 of the waggoneers here, civilians, and we're going over and make a preemptive strike on the Indian camps. Carrington refuses to allow it because that would weaken his command too much, because they would take a number of soldiers that as well as civilians over there and attack, and he scrubs it.

Well, Red Cloud[213] and his people leave their camps on the 17th and on the 19th, they're camped ten miles to the west of us [on the bus]. They've sent out Crazy Horse[214] and nine other warriors, and they're going to come over and draw them out [of the fort]. Early in the day, an Indian appears [in eyesight of the fort]. He sits down on his blanket, makes some signals and things, and when they send a couple of soldiers out to fire a cannon shot at him, to harass him, he gets up and leaves.

Well, at 10 o'clock, out goes the wagon train up the road going up to the pinery, which is about a mile and a half beyond the Wagon Box Fight[215] [location]. Again, the people on Pilot Knob holler, "Indians in sight! Indians in sight!" to the fort, and our friend Carrington says, "We'll, Capt. [James W.] Powell, I want you to take a detachment of men and go out and relieve

---

[211] Online: https://www.findagrave.com/memorial/14648652/frederick-h-brown.
[212] Online: https://en.wikipedia.org/wiki/Jim_Bridger.
[213] Online: https://en.wikipedia.org/wiki/Red_Cloud and
 https://www.pbs.org/weta/thewest/people/i_r/redcloud.htm.
[214] Online: https://en.wikipedia.org/wiki/Crazy_Horse.
[215] Online: https://www.hmdb.org/m.asp?m=86062.

the wagon train." Then, William Jedd Fetterman says, "I rank Powell, and on my privilege of rank, I rank him, I'm a brevet Colonel, ..., I want the command of the people going out." So, he's detailed 49 soldiers of the garrison armed with Harper's Ferry[216] caliber .68 muzzle-loading weapons. All the Indians know, if you're gonna fire a shot, you're gonna see your arm coming up as you have to ram in the new charge, the Indians aren't dumb.

Now, look at this land. Look at all the hollows. These are choke cherry bushes and the rest of it is in grassland. So, meanwhile, that first Indian with the blanket had been out, Crazy Horse with the nine warriors had gone out, the decoys, the Army is making their preparations, and he [Carrington] has ordered, since poor Lt. Bingham isn't around to command the cavalry any longer, George Washington Grummond will take 27 cavalrymen out of the 2nd US Cavalry, armed with carbines (single shot, breech loading), and he will leave the fort after Fetterman leaves, because it takes them longer to get their horses ready to go, about 11 o'clock.

Now, just what is said or not, because both Mrs. Grummond – after she becomes Mrs. Carrington [years later] -- will have some reason to take any owness from what goes wrong off of Henry Carrington. Just when Fetterman says, how close to his arrival here, does he boast in front of Jim

---

[216] Online: https://en.wikipedia.org/wiki/Harpers_Ferry_Armory.

Bridger, "With 70 members of the United States Army, I can ride through *the whole Sioux Nation*." Now, how many times does he say that. That's gossip been going around, picked up by Mrs. Grummond and Margaret [Carrington]. Mrs. Grummond says, "Everybody knows he said that, Margaret."

As he leaves with his 49 men, …, Fred Brown says, "I'm going to be relieved in two days, I haven't seen any real combat here, and I want Red Cloud's scalp." Fred, who's bald as I am, is going to lose whatever he would have for a scalp himself, and he volunteers to go out. So, he goes out, so they'll be three officers going out with Fred, Fetterman, Grummond and the cavalry.

Now, Grummond will leave about 20 minutes after the infantry does, and he will overtake them before they pass over Lodge Trail Ridge. Now, just what were the orders. Was it, "Do not cross Lodge Trail Ridge?" or "Do not pursue." I do not know, because that appears again only in the writings of Mrs. Carrington and emphasized by Mrs. Grummond, when no longer Mrs. Grummond, but Mrs. Carrington.

Meanwhile, the wagon train has turned back. They're coming back, and the warriors that have been harassing it returned to disappear. Now, in position on either side of the Bozeman Trail are Crazy Horse and his nine volunteers who are going to be the decoys this time, taunting the Army, everything from pulling up their breech belts and slapping their ass to other obscene gestures as they're going to drive them on. They disappear, but they've now gone over on Lodge Trail Ridge.

The cavalrymen have joined them [the infantry], counting Grummond, 28 cavalrymen, and they have two civilians with them, [James] Wheatley and [Isaac] Fisher. Wheatley and Fisher are armed – it holds a magazine – with 15-shot Henry weapons, or if you count the one shot in the chamber, 16 shot. So, when they come out here, and come over, out in front of them here going down this ridge as we [will] walk down it] toward Prairie Dog Creek, [where] they're going to be drawing them. The [tour] people that are going to take the walk, it's about a mile and a quarter, will see the rock where their furthest advance will be, and where Fisher, Wheatley and [Pvt. Adolph]

Metzger[217] [will be found]. Now, Metzger's a trumpeter, he's the only one that's not going to be terribly mutilated and he, according to Indian tradition, will be fighting to the last using his trumpet,[218] and his trumpet is saved and very battered, and they'll lay a buffalo robe[219] over him. Evidently, giving him a special tribute.

(1) Tour bus approaches Fetterman Fight Monument (2-3) Rocks around monument (inside and outside monument wall) where Fetterman and his infantry were killed and mutilated. (4) Ed Bearss starts his walk to where the cavalry was wiped out, several hundred yards behind Lodge Trail Ridge.

Now, Fetterman and most of the infantrymen are going to die right here among these rocks. Here is where they're going to die. When we get out of the site about 350 yards, most of the cavalrymen are going to die. Now, where are the warriors hiding? You won't know until you get out [of the bus]. I urge you, the people who are not going to take the short walk, that short walk will be down to that second fence line, I'm going to ask you to look and see if you could see any Indians there. You can see [into] these

---

[217] Online: https://www.findagrave.com/memorial/20715034/adolph-metzger.
[218] Online: http://www.buffalobulletin.com/article_6a18f6c0-7ab3-11e6-aa39-533499b42034.html.
[219] Online: https://en.wikipedia.org/wiki/Buffalo_robe.

ravines and who would be hiding in these ravines. There going to be somewhere about 1000 Indians hiding in these ravines. Over on this side [our right] are Arapaho[220] and Cheyenne.[221] Over on this side [to our left] people from three circles[222] of the Sioux, the Oglala,[223] the Miniconjou,[224] and Hunkpapa,[225] are over there hiding. That's what's going to happen. I'll give my final remarks here when I talk about the dedication of this monument on the 8th day of July, 1908, when two people are here, Col. Henry Carrington, who has three years to live, and the former Mrs. Grummond, who within a year of the death of Margaret, will marry Henry. Any questions?

We walk down the trail and Ed Bearss describes various markers along the Fetterman battle site.

Now if you're standing here, you're up high. They're in these ravines. The three circles from the Sioux Nation, the Lakota, Oglala, which Red Cloud is, which Crazy Horse is, Hunkpapa, which Sitting Bull is, but he's not here, and Miniconjou. Over here, Arapaho and Cheyenne. They're going to be in these ravines. As Chet Olsen said, there's about two inches of snow on the ground, and in the middle of the day, it's starting to melt, the snow is, and the sun has come out. So, there is snow cover.

Prairie Dog Creek is where that house is. When the decoys get there, half of them will go this way [right], half of them will go that way [to our left]. That's the signal to all the Indians that are hiding in these ravines to reveal yourself and come out and attack them. By this time, Fetterman's men are probably right in this area, that's the infantry. The cavalry will be down here about a half a mile in front of the infantry as they're moving down here, and where the sun doesn't get, there would be drifts. You can see to our right, there is evidence of the Bozeman Trail as we walk along here.

---

[220] Online: https://en.wikipedia.org/wiki/Arapaho.
[221] Online: http://www.sioux.org/ and https://en.wikipedia.org/wiki/Cheyenne.
[222] Online: http://thewildwest.org/nativeamericans/nativeamericanreligion/98-lakotaindiansthecircle and https://theschaefercenter.org/_documents/applause/study-guides/study-guide-2015-lakota-sioux.pdf.
[223] Online: http://oglalalakotanation.info/ and https://en.wikipedia.org/wiki/Oglala.
[224] Online: https://en.wikipedia.org/wiki/Miniconjou.
[225] Online: https://en.wikipedia.org/wiki/Hunkpapa.

Down at the fort, they'll start hearing gunfire at about 12:30, and the gunfire will be audible in the fort for about 45 minutes. That's what generally the Indians recollections are, [that] the fight will last about 45 minutes. When that 45 minutes are up, all the soldiers are dead. Any questions?

(1-2) To our left, warriors from the three circles of the Sioux Nation are hidden in these ravines. (3-4) On our right, Arapaho and Cheyenne warriors are hiding in these ravines.

Ed Bearss stopped at a plaque and pointed out the people depicted on it, "There of course is our three people. Here is George Washington Grummond, he's a younger boy, there's William Judd Fetterman, and there is Fred Brown. See, Fred has probably got a little more hair than I have. He doesn't have to come here; in two days he'd be on his way back to Ft. Laramie. So, the Indians are going to have a hard time scalping him."

Further down the site towards where the cavalry met their end, we pass a plaque about the type of weapons available to the Indians. Ed Bearss describes the typical Indian weapons on the plaque, saying,

This is the type of weapons. Most of the Indians are armed in the traditional way. Bows and arrows, lances, clubs, knives, scalping knives.

Only Wheatley and Fisher have Henrys[226] Some of the cavalry, remember the band had Spencers,[227] and they'll take the Spencers after that engagement on the 6th day of December in which Bingham and Brewer will lose their lives, take 40 carbines away from the band and at least 20 of the 27 cavalry [at the Fetterman Fight] are armed with Spencers, this one [pointing to the Spencer on plaque].. The rest of the Army was single-shot, muzzle-loading weapons, all 49 grunts were armed with that. The three officers undoubtedly have pistols.

(1) The key officers from the fort: Fetterman, Grummond, and Brown. (2) A plaque showing the weapons used by the soldiers and the Indians.

We walk on to a plaque and Ed Bearss says, "This tells us how the infantry is armed, bayonets. A Springfield rifle model 1863. Muzzle loading, effective range 200 yards, but the Indians know that if you're reloading, you have to be kneeling or standing up. So, what do you see, that ramrod, so you've in safe ground. The Army has bayonets, but they aren't going to get close enough to use them." As Grummond's cavalry went well beyond the infantry, they fought further along the trail we are following. Ed Bearss stops at the cavalry plaque and says, "They're going to fight dismounted. The cavalry will fight dismounted, but they're still mounted at this point. We're going down to where [they fought, beyond Lodge Trail Ridge.]

---

[226] Online: https://en.wikipedia.org/wiki/Henry_rifle.
[227] Online: https://en.wikipedia.org/wiki/Spencer_repeating_rifle.

(1) Plaque showing the infantry were equipped with muzzle-loading (single-shot) rifles with bayonets as from the Civil War. (2) Ed Bearss demonstrates use of the ramrod to load the infantry rifles – the Indians knew they had 20-30 seconds to strike during this loading time

We walk to a plaque further on, where the cavalrymen are attacked, and Ed Bearss says, "All right, we're running out of gas for them. Here, we're with the cavalry as far as they are going. Over here by this tree [turning and walking to the lone tree], is an important site, both for the Indians point of view and for the Federal view of what has happened. ... Probably most of the cavalry will do in this area where we are, and they will die after the infantry." He sees the "Big Nose" plaque and continues.

Now Big Nose, he is one of the decoy party. He's one of the ten people, counting himself, with Crazy Horse, and he's going to be one of the decoy party. [Reading from the plaque] 'He's riding a black horse belonging to Little Wolf, his brother, and is wearing Sweet Medicine Chief's scalp shirt. His horse, tired from decoying the soldiers, stumbles' [looking up] in this area here. [Reading again] 'Big Nose is hit, and two warriors place him in the depression' in front of you. His last request is that his head by placed uphill where he can breathe fresh air." That's the depression, right in front of you, where he can breathe fresh air. [Reading again] 'After the battle, he dies and is buried with the other warriors on the routes between here and the main camp.' The main camp is over on Tongue River, and he'll be buried like they generally bury them, in the tree. So, this is where we're going to have, right up here, this area, is where Big Nose is going to be killed – you can see the depression – coming up ahead of us there. See the depression, that's where the Indians will [place] his body.

(1) Plaque describing the wounding and last words of Big Nose. (2) The tree marking the depression in the ground where he was placed, with his head up.

We come to a point near the end of our walk, and Ed Bearss describes the scene.

Here's where Fisher and Wheatly and Metzger, they're going to find their bodies. It's in the rocks here. So, there you can see Prairie Dog Creek, and if you got this far, where Fisher, Wheatly and Metzger [and] several solders get this far, you would see the decoys move to the left and to the right. They'll be mounted. They'll come out, and the men who are on the left creek of us, which are then on the right, will move around to the left, and then the others cross over, ad that's the signal for [the Indians in] all these ravines you can see, where the Indians are going to come out of here. [Pointing to the other side of the ridge] all the ravines over there you can see.

The Indians will mutilate all bodies, except Metzger. They will especially mutilate the bodies of Fisher and Wheatly. The theory is they probably kill -- they're not many Indians killed in this battle – they'll probably be more dead Indians here than any place on the battlefield.

Some of the Indians have rifles, as I say, we don't identify what Indians have rifles, but all the Indians are going to have either rifles or carbines when the fight's over. All of them are going to have the soldier's weapons when the fight's over. So, the Indians are going to have 26 Spencer carbines when the fight's over. They undoubtedly will have Fisher and Wheatly's Henries. ... and they probably don't give a damn about the muzzle-loading rifles the Army's using.

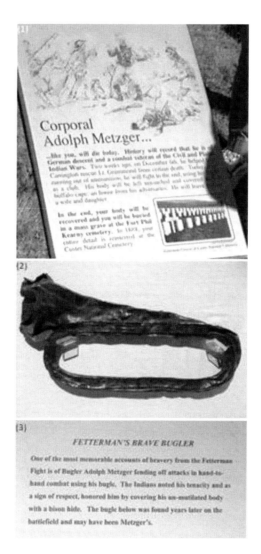

(1) Metzger plaque at the Fetterman Fight site. (2-3) Metzger's bugle was named the 2016 No. 1 artifact in Wyoming and is preserved on display. Courtesy of the Johnson County Jim Gatchell Memorial Museum, 100 Fort Street, Buffalo, Wyoming (URL: https://www.jimgatchell.com/).

(1) Fisher, Wheatly and Metzger fought and died here, the soldiers furthest advance. (2) Prairie Dog Creek, where half the Indian decoys (3) moved to our right and (4) half to our left signaled the Indians in the ravines to attack the dismounted cavalry where we're standing.

The first people that are wiped out is the Army [infantry], these [here] are probably the last to die, the next to last to die are going to be the cavalry. Asked whether their having the Henries made the difference here, Ed said, "Yes," and agreed as suggested by a tour goer that they could be protected in the rocks with a low silhouette, which is likely why more Indians were killed in this area.

(1-2) Ed Bearss points out Carrington and his wife, the former Mrs. Grummond, at the Fetterman Fight Monument in 1908, commemorating in part her first husband's death. (3) Ed Bearss explains Lt. Grummond had two wives, which his wife in the photo (2) found out when she went to collect his pension. (4) The editor at the Fetterman Fight Monument.

Listen, we're very lucky... we've just been able to come down here about the last five years ...[asked about who owns the land] That man right down there [pointing at nearest house], but the State of Wyoming has an easement that we can walk down here, but we can't walk down any further than here.

We walk back to the Fetterman Massacre Monument, where most of the infantry were killed, and Ed describes the monument and other details of the people, other than the Indians, affected by this day's battle with the Sioux.

(1-2) Ed Bearss points out Carrington and his wife, the former Mrs. Grummond, at the Fetterman Fight Monument in 1908, commemorating in part her first husband's death. (3) Ed Bearss explains Lt. Grummond had two wives, which his wife in the photo (2) found out when she went to collect his pension. (4) The editor at the Fetterman Fight Monument.

Here [pointing at the 1908 commemoration photo on the monument plaque] is Henry Carrington. He's then 77 years old. His bride, who he married in 1870, is the widow of Lt. Grummond. She doesn't learn until after he's dead, [when] she tries to collect his pension, that he already has a wife. Mrs. Carrington, Margaret Sullivant, and so they name that one ridge "Sullivant," will die in 1870. Hardly has she fallen in the grave, before he marries his second wife, who's a wife who's been a widow for four years. I don't know if their son, who is born, did he change his name to Carrington, or did he leave it as Grummond when he dies.

[Also pointing at the plaque] Pvt. Daley, who raised the first flag here, on October 22nd, that 40-foot by 30-foot flag, almost as big as that garrison flag at Ft. McHenry,[228] on that 120-foot tall pole, or staff, he is here to raise the flag here, on that day [in 1908].

On the bus leaving the Fetterman Fight site, Ed Bearss describes some of the units that served in his [Carrington's] unit and those he excluded, and why:

… These were Confederates that were serving time in the Union prison camps and they volunteer to serve against Indians, so they become such-and-such US volunteers, and they're there [Ft. Phil Kearney] and they want out. They've been out in the plains for two years. They want to get back. They've done their duty for the United States. Their Confederate neighbors might not like them as well as they used to because they [effectively] switched sides, and he [Carrington] has a company of Winnibegos.[229] Winnibegos are blood enemies of the Lakota, and they want to enlist with him, but poor Carrington believes that will exacerbate his problems up here, that having a company of Winnibego scouts with him. It wouldn't have made any difference as we know, and he tells the Winnibegos, "Return to Omaha, Nebraska, and be mustered out." So, that's why he has no scouts. He's made a terrible blunder on that.

He [Carrington] is very naïve and his scouts have really nothing to do. He has two scouts, the mulatto[230] [James] Beckwith,[231] or the "Black Crow," as he's known, because he's married to a Crow [Indian], and one of his four grandparents was a Crow Indian. They're going to rely on him and Jim Bridger. Now, there's very little trouble up at Ft. C. F. Smith because on the other side of the Big Horn River there, is Crow country, and the Sioux and the Cheyenne will be unlikely, unless they're in the presence of whites, to attack Ft. C. F. Smith, because there's a large number of the Crows hanging

---

[228] Online: https://www.nps.gov/fomc/index.htm and https://en.wikipedia.org/wiki/Fort_McHenry.
[229] Online: http://www.winnebagotribe.com/index.php/about-us/tribal-history and https://en.wikipedia.org/wiki/Winnebago_Tribe_of_Nebraska.
[230] Online: https://en.wikipedia.org/wiki/Mulatto.
[231] Online: https://en.wikipedia.org/wiki/James_Beckwourth.

around there and they would have to deal with them. So, they turn down the idea, so it's mainly a decision on the part of Carrington, showing he's naïve.

Yes, Jim Bridger is a good scout, but he's just one man and that again nullifies a large group of Indian scouts, who are blood enemies of the Lakota and the Cheyenne. I forgot to bring it up, what are the problems that Carrington is going to have with *no* Indian scouts?

HAYFIELD FIGHT[232]

Ed Bearss provides some background and describes the Hayfield Fight:

[After the Fetterman Fight] the new commander will arrive with lots of troops. They've re-designated the 18th US as the 27th US, and it will be commanded by John [E.] Smith.[233] He is an important player in the Civil War. He'd been a corps commander and a division commander. He is born in Switzerland, spells [his first name] John as a [Swiss] would [Johann], and his last name of course would be Schmitt, but he Anglicizes it to John Smith when he comes to the United States as an immigrant from Switzerland. He'll attend West Point and graduate from West Point and be a part of the Galena Mafia.

The Galena Mafia, of course, is headed by Elihu Washburn,[234] the local Senator, the local Member of the House of Representatives, who is very, very close to Abraham Lincoln, and the Chairman of the House Military Affairs Committee. The No. 2 man in the Galena Mafia is John Rollins.[235] John Rollins is a lawyer in Galena. His father was a lawyer before him, and his father had died as an alcoholic. Rollins will become [Gen. Ulysses S.] Grant's[236] Chief of Staff, and he knows Grant's problem with alcohol, and his principal, most important, mission is making sure that Grant doesn't run into evil companions like Benjamin Butler[237] and Nathanial Banks. They'll serve him drinks and Grant just can't … "one drink's too many, and a thousand not enough."

---

[232] Online: https://www.nps.gov/bica/learn/historyculture/hayfield-fight.htm and https://en.wikipedia.org/wiki/Hayfield_Fight.
[233] Online: https://en.wikipedia.org/wiki/John_E._Smith.
[234] Online: https://en.wikipedia.org/wiki/Elihu_B._Washburne.
[235] Online: https://en.wikipedia.org/wiki/John_Aaron_Rawlins.
[236] Online: https://en.wikipedia.org/wiki/Ulysses_S._Grant.
[237] Online: https://en.wikipedia.org/wiki/Benjamin_Butler.

The third member of the mafia, is, of course, U.S. Grant. Now, Grant has spent an unhappy period of his life between New Year's Day in 1854, the New Year's Day of '55. He goes for his meeting with Capt. [Robert C.] Buchanan,[238] a real martinet, he's going to tell Capt. Sam Grant that you have two choices, "Resign or be court martialed. I have irrefutable evidence that in a court martial, that you've been drunk on duty a considerable amount of time and that you've been gambling. You either resign or face court martial." Grant resigns. After not being very successful in business, I can go through the various businesses he's not successful in, in St. Louis County, so he moves to Galena. He's the third member, and he would probably never become the man he is but for the infamous Elihu Washburn and John Rollins keeping him on the straight and narrow most of the time.

So, John Smith is a member of that group, and he arrives here as a Colonel. He's been a brevet major general in the Army, and in mid-July, 1867, he arrives, and they bring with them the Allin alteration.[239] That is a firearm I've never seen fired before. That is the muzzle-loading caliber 0.63 Springfield and they convert it into a breech-loading caliber .50, and you saw how they did it by putting a sleeve in the bore and by milling out the breech and making it so they're able to load it by the breech, and they arrive here, and that means they now have the Allin alteration here. They also send on another Colonel, they send on Col. [Luther] Bradley,[240] who's a Lt. Col. In the 27th Infantry, has just arrived. He had been a brigadier general in the old army, and he goes up with two companies of reinforcements for C. F. Smith, and they're armed with the Allin alteration.

Now the hostiles, after a very cold winter, are ready to begin combat operations against Ft. C. F. Smith and Ft. Phil Kearny. So, mostly the Cheyenne will be sent to attack Ft. C. F. Smith, where the fort is built largely similar to Ft. Phil Kearny, except they use a lot of adobe, which was used in the southwest where you have less rainfall than you have in this part of Montana and Wyoming. They have established Ft. C. F. Smith in late August, 1866.

So, the Cheyenne are going to leave their base of operations on the Tongue River and go over an [attempt to] capture Ft. C. F. Smith. Red Cloud, with the Lakota, and a few Arapaho, intention is to attack Ft. Phil Kearny. On the 30th, the Cheyenne and the Arapaho sweep down on Ft. C. F. Smith and they're going to wipe out the Hay party. About three miles downstream from the Big Horn River, on the east side, they've erected a corral using cedar posts and then putting about two

---

[238] Online: https://en.wikipedia.org/wiki/Robert_C._Buchanan.
[239] Online: https://en.wikipedia.org/wiki/Springfield_Model_1866.
[240] Online: https://en.wikipedia.org/wiki/Hayfield_Fight.

feet of pipe between the bottom surface and the two-foot mark on the cedar posts. Above that, they're going to bring in very thick brambles. That's where they will camp out. Most of them are employees. The employees were mainly all armed with Spencers, you saw the Spencer shot [at an exhibition after the Fetterman walk] and Henry 15-shot. They've got a mowing machine the same way that anybody who grew up on a farm or a ranch in the early twentieth century [like Ed Bearss] knows how it works. You sit in a seat which was metal, you have a tongue [for the horses or other], and you have a sickle bar about eight feet in width, you let it down and you mow the grass, mow the hay, which you'll put up and use during the winter '67-'68.

It's [the corral] commanded by a good German boy, Lt. Sigismund Sternberg.[241] He's been in the Prussian Army. There's a handful of soldiers there, but most of his crew of some 30 men are going to be civilians that have been hired to mow the hay and put it up. Well, … the Indians sweep down. They see them coming. It's three miles to Ft. C. F. Smith. Ft. C. F. Smith is on a bench[242] just like Ft. Phil Kearny and the hayfields where there is hay are down in the Big Horn Valley. They sweep down. The first thing they see is the two guys on mowing machines putting the lash to their horses, driving them into the corral, the hayfield corral. There they'll take positions. They're armed with the Allin alteration.

Now, the Indians know that when you fire, a soldier fires, he has to be standing up or kneeling to reload, and when he does that the rifle has to be at about 90 degrees to the ground surface. That means you can always see the ramrod in the air as they're reloading, and the poor Indians don't realize that they're [defenders] are of course armed with Allin alterations, except for the officers.

Sigismund Sternberg, like the good Prussian he is, refuses to crouch, he stands in the entrance to the corral firing his pistol. He's a big fellow like a few Germans that have been in the Prussian Army, and of course, you don't stand up with no protection in the gate when they ride through, and you can just stand so long before you're going to get dinged and killed. Again, most of the Indians again are armed with bows and arrows as we heard, but they have more firearms now because they have all the firearms from Ft. Phil Kearny, from the massacre. They'll lay siege, ride around on their horses firing their bows and arrows, which is hard to do, but they can *ride like hell*, and they'll lay siege.

---

[241] Online: https://history.army.mil/books/AMH/AMH-14.htm and
https://www.findagrave.com/memorial/12887825/sigismund-sternberg.
[242] Online: https://en.wikipedia.org/wiki/Bench_(geology).

Finally, they'll hear the firing at Ft. C. F. Smith and order out a detachment with a mountain howitzer,[243] and it will be like the infantry to the rescue. They come down and the Indians skedaddle. So, the attach on the hayfield, the hay corral, has failed. Beyond Lt. Sternberg, there have been two soldiers killed and a couple of civilian contractors and a number of Indians killed. The Indians have even started a fire. The Lord isn't on the Indian side, because when the build the fires, the winds are blowing it toward the hay corral. Suddenly it changes just as it seems ready to engulf them [in the corral], and it stops.

WAGON BOX FIGHT[244]

Ed Bearss shifts to the Wagon Box Fight and describes events there:

The next day, Red Cloud will appear and he's going to attack the wagon box, and that is where they have thrown up a number of wagon boxes together. I believe you can count them and I believe there are about 12 wagon boxes, and the men in them are again armed with the Allin alterations, and again, it goes the same way. The commanding officer, Capt. Powell, doesn't stand up and his pistol, so he'll survive, and Indians will kill a couple of soldiers and a couple of the civilians, but they will not succeed. Of course, they heard the firing in Ft. Phil Kearny, just like they had down at the hayfield, and they order out a detachment with a cannon. The cannon approaches, boom, boom, boom, the howitzer fires, the Indians hear the firing, and they skedaddle. So, the Allin alteration, the advantage in technology, has given the Army two successes.

You saw the painting in the museum, and it shows they have an Army artiste made up a series of paintings to try to beat the Marine Corps as a propaganda agent, showing how good the Army can be. They're going to take the one they point for this operation will be the Wagon Box fight, and that was what was in that painting which you saw showing how the soldiers and the handful of civilians were able to hold off several hundred Indians using the new technology of the Allin alteration.

---

[243] Online: https://en.wikipedia.org/wiki/M1841_mountain_howitzer.
[244] Online: https://en.wikipedia.org/wiki/Wagon_Box_Fight.

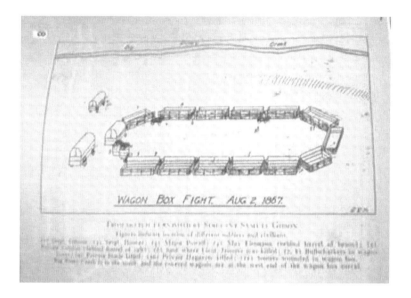

DEPRESSION

Ed Bearss explains that Indian conflicts were reduced over time, until a new wave of immigrants sought the American dream in the West. Arguably, they were not fully versed on the treaties protecting Indian lands.

Well, the Indian menace is beginning to pass. The railroad has reached Cheyenne, Wyoming. In two years, it will reach the Central Pacific at Promontory Point,[245] Utah, and we'll have a transcontinental railroad. The Government knows that, so they're [Army and Indians] going to meet at Ft. Laramie in 1868. Initially, Red Cloud will say in Indian, "Screw 'em, I'm not coming in to speak with them, because they've signed many treaties with us, but this is the only one they've kept. That's the one that will take our land.

So, they sit there and negotiate, have it out. Now, they're going to reduce the Sioux Reservation. The Sioux Reservation, as you look at the map, in the Gane Atlas, look at Map No. 2. So, the Sioux Reservation is reduced in size. It will now be that the eastern boundary of the Sioux Reservation, Great

---

[245] Online: https://en.wikipedia.org/wiki/Promontory,_Utah.

Sioux Reservation, will be the Missouri River. The south boundary of it will be the boundary of the present-day State of Nebraska, so the southern boundary of the Great Sioux Reservation will be the northern boundary of Nebraska. When it reaches western Nebraska, it enters Wyoming territory. Remember, Nebraska's now a state. They've got two Senators.

…The southern boundary of the Great Sioux Nation will then follow the Platte River all the way up to Platte River Bridge, then it will go north as far as the Yellowstone [River]. Then, north of that, this will be unceded land, and in the fine print, it will say that it will remain unceded land where the Indians can hunt and roam, and hunt Buffalo until the last of the Buffalo die, or they've been reduced to very few numbers. … it will extend northward, the unceded lands, all the way to the Missouri River. The Indians can roam into that area, from the Yellowstone River up to the Missouri River and continue to roam there and hunt, and live the traditional way of life, until the buffalo are [eliminated]. The Black Hills are within the Sioux reservation. The Sioux Reservation western boundary is the present western boundary of Wyoming and Dakota [territory]. That means that the Black Hills are Indian land, part of the Great Sioux Reservation.

There will not be any particular trouble until we have a great depression, just like you remember in 1908, 1929 and 2008, they have a big one in 1873.[246] It's into Grant's second term as President. The railroad has been building west. The Northern Pacific railroad, as you look at your map, …, has reached Bismarck, North Dakota by 1873, but they want to extend it on across western Dakota territory. It's all Dakota Territory, what is now present North and South Dakota, all the way across Montana, across the panhandle of Idaho, on to Spokane and on through Spokane to Seattle.

They've been harassed by the hostiles, that would be the winter roamers, during the nomadic season of 1872, but no important clashes. So, when they go west in 1873, they're going with the Seventh Cavalry, which is glad to be in the plains again. They're based in Ft. Abraham Lincoln,[247] you look on the map, just south of Bismarck, they're in Mandan, and [Lt. Col.] George

---

[246] Online: https://en.wikipedia.org/wiki/Panic_of_1873.
[247] Online: https://en.wikipedia.org/wiki/Fort_Abraham_Lincoln.

Armstrong Custer[248] is with the Seventh Cavalry, which are glad to cease policing the south and enforcing the rights of blacks during Reconstruction.[249]

So, the Seventh Cavalry will go west and Custer will not be in charge. [Gen.] David [Sloane] Stanley[250] is [in charge]. Now, David Stanley is a notorious drunk. He is a senior Colonel. In Custer's mind, he's a horrible drunk, and Custer should have command of the expedition, not David Stanley.

BATTLE OF THE ROSEBUD[251]

After the Fetterman Massacre site, we travel to the Battle of the Rosebud, and Ed Bearss explained which U.S. Army units were engaged and the sequence of action. He pointed out the Buffalo jump,[252] where Indians drove buffalo off a cliff in the days before horses enabled them to catch up to their prey. We debussed along an unpaved road and Ed Bearss gave us the background on the battle.

Rosebud Creek and New Plaques

There is the Rosebud [Creek],[253] where you can trace the timber, trace the disiduous trees. … Van Vliet's Hill is right up there [pointing], look right over that tallest telephone pole, that's Van Vliet's Hill. All right, the gap, see the gap on the map? Very obvious where the gap is. In the gap, closer to us, is going to be the Buffalo jump, that is circa 1300 BC.

---

[248] Online: https://en.wikipedia.org/wiki/George_Armstrong_Custer.
[249] Online: https://en.wikipedia.org/wiki/Reconstruction_era and
　　https://www.pbs.org/weta/reconstruction/.
[250] Online: https://en.wikipedia.org/wiki/David_S._Stanley.
[251] Online: https://en.wikipedia.org/wiki/Rosebud_Battlefield_State_Park and
　　https://en.wikipedia.org/wiki/Battle_of_the_Rosebud.
[252] Online: https://en.wikipedia.org/wiki/Buffalo_jump.
[253] Online: https://en.wikipedia.org/wiki/Rosebud_Creek_(Montana) and
　　http://www.pbs.org/weta/thewest/places/states/montana/mt_rosebud.htm.

Now what we're going to do, we will get off the bus up there by that single tree, and we'll not see the bus until we come back from the walk. The walk is about the same in distance as we had [at Fetterman], but its steeper, …, in a range from 1 to 10, I would put the grade at about a 5, and we'll go up as far as Crookshank Corners, which is right in this area here, you can see it on the map, where we'll interpret the battle. Now, since we've got the map oriented, let's see if these are all new interpretive markers since I've been here.

Rosebud Creek defined by tree line.

So, we'd better start right off here, and this of course, this is an overview, this is all the Plains Indian Wars[254] we have between 1854 and 1890. The last one is Wounded Knee,[255] two days before the end of the year, in 1890, and it's the most blatant massacre. We had the first one of these down near Ft. Laramie, where [2nd Lt. John Lawrence] Grattan[256] gets himself killed, and they're going to have the first war, Ash Hollow,[257] then we talk about Sand Creek[258] is November 29, '64. The Battle of 100 Slain,[259] that's of course what the Indians call the Fetterman massacre. Then we have the Battle of

---

[254] Online: https://en.wikipedia.org/wiki/Sioux_Wars#First_Sioux_War.
[255] Online: https://en.wikipedia.org/wiki/Wounded_Knee_Massacre and
　　　https://en.wikipedia.org/wiki/Wounded_Knee_Battlefield.
[256] Online: https://en.wikipedia.org/wiki/John_Lawrence_Grattan.
[257] Online: https://en.wikipedia.org/wiki/Battle_of_Ash_Hollow.
[258] Online: https://en.wikipedia.org/wiki/Sand_Creek_massacre.
[259] Online: https://en.wikipedia.org/wiki/Fetterman_Fight.

Powder River,[260] that's where poor old [Brevet Maj. Gen. Joseph Jones] Reynolds[261] gets to be fall guy for [Brig. Gen. l George] Crook[262] on the 17th day of November, St. Patty's Day. So, that is the battle they fight, and then what it does, it stirs up the Indians because they don't really gain any positive things from it, Crook doesn't get this start. The Indians here are Cheyenne and they flee to Crazy Horse's camp.

Ed Bearss reviews a plaque providing an overview of the Plains Indian Wars.

Crazy Horse is the beau ideal[263] of the Indians. If you ever find a picture of Crazy Horse, you can sell it for a lot of money, and those people who think they find it, are always discredited. He's a young warrior, and then of course we have Little Big Horn[264] on the 25th, Slim Buttes[265] over in South Dakota, and Wolf Mountain,[266] which is in this area here, but we won't have time to go there, and Wounded Knee. That's the series of Indian Wars.

[Asked about a new marker] Yes, that's a new one, it became a National Historic Landmark. Normally, it's impossible to get a National Historic Landmark because either the Indians don't like it or the property owners

---

[260] Online: https://en.wikipedia.org/wiki/Battle_of_Powder_River.
[261] Online: https://en.wikipedia.org/wiki/Joseph_J._Reynolds.
[262] Online: https://en.wikipedia.org/wiki/George_Crook.
[263] Online: https://www.merriam-webster.com/dictionary/beau%20ideal.
[264] Online: https://www.nps.gov/libi/index.htm and
   https://en.wikipedia.org/wiki/Battle_of_the_Little_Bighorn.
[265] Online: https://en.wikipedia.org/wiki/Battle_of_Slim_Buttes.
[266] Online: https://en.wikipedia.org/wiki/Battle_of_Wolf_Mountain.

don't like it. So, the two newest landmarks, and [Jerry] Greene is very delighted about it. Greene is responsible, because Greene, who's going to be joining us tonight, is an honorary Cheyenne and honorary Lakota. He's the only white historian that has that honor. So, he's the one that they dealt with the side of the white's and the property owner, Mr. Bailey. It also has to be his, and the Indians have to go [with it], the Crow and the Lakota have to go along with it. That's going to happen near the Buffalo jump. We'll point out where it is, we'll be very close to it.

Then, this [plaque] talks about the Indians, and these are talking about the whites. Total strength [combined fighting forces]: 978 Cavalry and Indians, 176 Crow, 86 Cheyenne, 65 Montana prospectors and 20 packers. Crook is unlike Custer, he welcomes correspondents. Custer does too, but he's got orders emanating from the President of the United States. Custer will not take any correspondents with him on this expedition he's going to lead on the 17th of May. Mark Kellogg[267] is probably going to say about 4 o'clock in the afternoon [at the Battle of the Little Bighorn], "Why in the hell did I let Custer talk me in to going with him." That's about an hour before Mark Kellogg is going to be killed and mutilated.

[Summarizing plaque] Here of course, it talks about them. Actually, they've scaled down the number of Indians here to about 750, fighting men. [Walking to the next plaque] Ok, we go over here, and these of course, talk about different ones, Plenty Coups,[268] I remember when he died well, because he died in 1932 when I was nine years old. [Pointing] Here's Counting Coups.[269] Now, you get more Brownie points for counting coups.[270] I touch you with my Coup stick. I get more Brownie points in the Indian hierarchy than if I killed you. So, that's very important in the Indian hierarchy.

---

[267] Online: https://en.wikipedia.org/wiki/Mark_Kellogg_(reporter).
[268] Online: https://www.nps.gov/bica/learn/historyculture/chief-plenty-coups.htm and https://en.wikipedia.org/wiki/Plenty_Coups and http://stateparks.mt.gov/chief-plenty-coups/.
[269] Online: https://opi.mt.gov/Portals/182/Page%20Files/Indian%20Education/Language%20Arts/Counting%20Coup.pdf.
[270] Online: https://en.wikipedia.org/wiki/Counting_coup.

Ed Bearss describes a New Historic Landmark here, for what the Cheyenne call this battle, "Where the Girl Saved Her Brother."

Plains Indians have a very high ratio of medals in the modern United States Army. To them, that's the traditional way by extension of counting coups. ... If you capture a couple of terrorists who went up against you, you would get more Brownie points than if you killed both of them. ... Now [Chief] Plenty Coups represents *all American Indians* when they dedicate in 1921 the Tomb of the Unknown Soldier,[271] he represents them all. So, what does he do? The senior Senator from Montana is Senator [Tom] Walsh,[272] so when he comes in, he's going to touch Walsh with his Coup stick. So, he is counting coups on the senior of the two Senators from Montana. So, that again is how it plays out into our time.

Ed Bearss reviews a plaque about Chief Plenty-Coups.

---

[271] Online: https://www.arlingtoncemetery.mil/Explore/Tomb-of-the-Unknown-Soldier and https://en.wikipedia.org/wiki/Tomb_of_the_Unknown_Soldier.
[272] Online: https://en.wikipedia.org/wiki/Thomas_J._Walsh.

[Flipping pages on plaque] Here, it talks about the various officers here. [Gen.] George Crook, I probably told you more than you want to know. I would not want to serve under George Crook. I definitely wouldn't want to be on his staff, or a junior officer under him, but you think of how shall I kill the dumb son of a bitch, you wouldn't say that, but how do you tell him, "You're on the wrong trail." I know you're supposed to meet the Indian Scouts at Goose Creek, but you're not going to Goose Creek, you're going to Prairie Dog Creek, and you're going to be 90 degrees off from where you want to be.

Crook's Hill and the Buffalo Jump

We drive to the start of our walk on the ground within the Rosebud Fight. Ed Bearss goes on to explain what we'll be seeing on the Battle of the Rosebud as we walk up Crook's Hill. On the way, we get a good view of the Buffalo Jump on our right.

Ed Bearss points out the Buffalo Jump from the bus headed towards the base of Crook's Hill.

Look to the right as far as you can. There it is. You're seeing the Buffalo jump, lots of sandstone. This is before they have the horse. See the Buffalo jump? That's where they'd drive them over. What they did, they would put Indians out with buffalo hides, what they used for blankets, behind rocks that would follow them into the jump, and when they went off the jump, a large number of them would break their necks or their legs. So, you're looking at the jump. This is the best view of the jump you'll have.

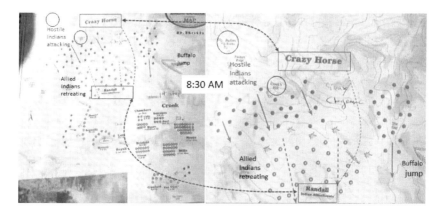

Hostile Indians under Crazy Horse charge (on horseback) down what will become Crook's Hill after the battle. Allied Crows and Shoshone scouts under Randall pushed back, but provide early warning to Crook's resting units, alerting them. Transformative fair use of owned image.

From the top of Crook's Hill, Ed Bearss describes the action at 8:30 AM that morning.

…. [Pointing at the crest of the hill] This is Crook's Hill, and this is where Crook eventually watches the battle. So, [looking back at the 8:30 AM map] this is at 8:30 and coming from that way [west] are the hostiles, they are the solid red circles. The guys falling back are Randall, who's in charge of the 182 Crow and the 84 Shoshone. These are the round circles as they're coming back. ….

Crook is now alerted …, if he had not had his Indian allied scouts, he would have been surprised. Remember, his men are taking a break. They've pulled the saddles off their horses and they're taking a break. They've been up since 5 in the morning, so they're taking a break. When he sees what is happening, [pointing at the red circles on the map these are all hostiles, coming in from that direction [pointing northwest on the map]. … All the way from here to here are hostiles, and this is at 9 AM. Crook is deploying.

We get out and walk up the Hiking Trail toward Crook's Hill, his eventual headquarters for the battle. We stop at a key point where we can see many of the prominent features on our map of the Battle of the Rosebud and Ed Bearss orients the group on our map and describes the battle as well as the "Girl Who Saved Her Brother" from the marker.

First Stand: 9 and 10 AM

Turn to Map 2, page 18 [in the Gane Atlas]. Hold your map about like this [orienting map with terrain features]. Hopefully, we'll get those pioneers up there [people who walked ahead], we can't wait any longer. Now, the river bottom, the furthest trees you see is the Rosebud. See, don't pay any attention to these trees [in the foreground], don't pay any attention to those [next set of] trees, but where you can see the watercourse next is the Rosebud, and it's leaving the area out there where it bends to the left.

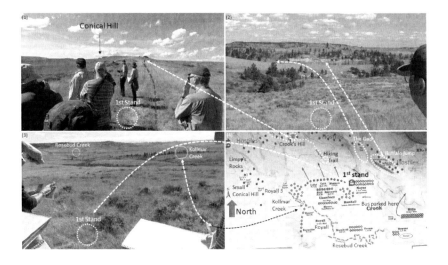

Positions Ed Bearss points out on the map and with his pointer [a riding crop] from part way up Crook's Hill: (1) Looking northwest to top of Crook's Hill; (2) Looking east to Buffalo Jump; (3) Looking southwest to confluence of Rosebud and Kollmar Creeks; (4) 9 AM time-sequenced tour=provided map of the Rosebud Battlefield. Transformative fair use of owned image.

Kollmar Creek, see the ravine in front of us and the trees, see going off in that direction, that's Kollmar Creek. That's where will point out Limpy's Rock. So, where you see those trees there, that's Kollmar Creek. It's only got water in it when it rains heavily. Conical Hill is left of the trees we see there [at the top of our trail]. Locate it on your map. You know more than I do, and then up ahead of us, just beyond where we see about halfway between those trees, and the next major rise where we're going to stop, will be Crook's Hill, that's where Crook runs the battle from [later in the day, after the Indians move off], from Crook's Hill. See Crook's Hill? It's marked. You've all located Kollmar Creek, you've all located the Rosebud, and when you turn this way [180 degrees around], you've all located the Buffalo Jump. That's the best view you're going to have of it.

Now, that is where they're going to drive [the buffalo]. The Indians are going to form a Vee, and the point of the Vee will be in the center of the jump. This is before they have horses. It's like a funnel. On the right, it flares out to the south and west and northeast on the other side [to our left]. Indians hide behind sage brush, rocks, and they're going to have buffalo hides, or anything like that, and the Indians are going to drive the buffalo down in this funnel shape, just like you're putting oil in your car, and they're going to drive them over that cliff. That's how they, before the horse, hunted buffalo.

Frontal view of the Buffalo Jump from the Rosebud Battle Hiking Trail from our 1st stand on the battlefield.

...As you go north of that, we're going into the gap, and the gap is very important, because that is the gap where Buffalo [Calf] Rode Woman[273] is going to ride in there and rescue one of their chiefs. His horse has been shot, he's been pinned by the horse, and right in that area is where she's going to

---

[273] Online: https://en.wikipedia.org/wiki/Buffalo_Calf_Road_Woman and montanawomenshistory.

rescue him, and that's what the Cheyenne call this area here [pointing at the gap on our map]. The "Girl Who Saved Her Brother," he's her brother, but her husband is somebody else, has another Indian name, and that's where he'll be rescued and she'll become a heroine.

Now, when the Cheyenne are taken down to the Indian territory, the hot place, down in western Oklahoma, they don't like it down there, and they're taken down there in 1878. They'd been promised that they would be staying in their native country, and they take them down there, and they're going to flee from there. They're going to try to go all the way from western Oklahoma, just where the Continental [Divide][274] begins, and they're going to go to the Spotted Tail[275] Reservation, Red Cloud Reservation, find friends there, and go the rest of the way on to the area around Lame Deer.[276] They're going to be pursued by the Army. She is going to be with them, this heroine of the Cheyenne, but she will only live a short time after they get back to Lame Deer because she's going to die of tuberculosis. She's going to die in 1879-1880.

Now, move to Map No. 3 [9 AM map]. Again, look at the Buffalo jump. Now, we are moving up the Hiking Trail, see the Hiking Trail? That's where we are, we're on the Hiking Trail, and here we have the Army advancing. Over here on our left, are Chamber's men, five companies drawn from the 4th and the 9th Regiments, and they've dismounted them, leaving men to hold them. We have sweeping down here to our left, between us and the gap, you have [Capt. Henry Erastus] Noyes[277] with his second cavalry battalion, they're dismounted. The Army people, Munson and Cain, are dismounted, and there coming up to where you can see the Hiking Trail is. We at this point are probably right here [on the map], where we have a distinct change in grade. We're right probably where my thumb is. The people that went on ahead, if you want to come back and see where we are now on the Hiking Trail.

---

[274] Online: https://en.wikipedia.org/wiki/Continental_Divide_of_the_Americas.
[275] Online: http://aktalakota.stjo.org/site/News2?page=NewsArticle&id=8692.
[276] Online: https://en.wikipedia.org/wiki/Lame_Deer,_Montana.
[277] Online: https://en.wikipedia.org/wiki/Henry_E._Noyes.

128 *Edwin Cole Bearss and Robert Irving Desourdis*

This gentleman [indicating one of the tour members nearby with our map] has where we are, we're there at the time of 9 AM. By 10 AM, we see the gap, we see the Hiking Trail, it is now [on our map] 10 o'clock, and the Indians are retreating through the gap. These are our Indians right here, at the end of the gap, that would be the Crows and the Shoshones, and over there on the other side of Kollmar ravine, you have lots of soldiers over there. You have Chambers over there, and we can see Royall moving up there. Royall is going to be in deep hockey by 11 o'clock.

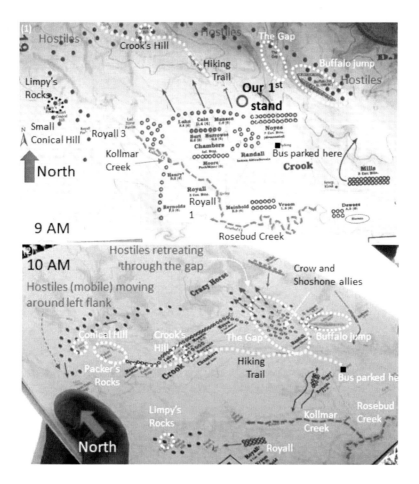

Evolving battlefield at 9 AM (Map 3 in the Gane Atlas) and 10 AM Map 4 on the Rosebud Battlefield. Transformative fair use of owned images. All locations approximate

Buffalo are on their way toward extinction. They had seen buffalo, remember, on the 16th, and the [Indian] scouts went out, bang, bang, bang, shooting buffalo, and poor old Crook is having a doodily about it, because he's certain they're giving him away [wind noise] … The Crows and the Shoshones are generally under Randall. They're intermixed, and they're wearing white on their headbands so the Army won't shoot at them. … They're saving Crook's bacon.

First off [at 10 AM], you can just barely see the Buffalo Jump. Everybody see the Buffalo jump? Who's in possession of it? Well, we have our friendly Indians. Who's in possession of the gap? The hostiles. Then, on our trail here, we can see Crook's Hill. Now, we are near where you can see Munson, M, is going like this, his men are dismounted, they've left their mules behind. Our next stop is going to be where you can see a fence on your right … about 10 yards from the fence, we're going to stop…. The Conical Hill is getting more and more visible to our left.

Second Stand: The Gap

We walk up Crook's Hill towards a fence line on the eastern side of the battlefield. On the way, Ed Bearss remarks that: "this is the most pristine battlefield in the United States." As he walks towards our second stop along the Hiking Trail by an old fence line, he explains why the hostile Indians (there were also Crow and Shoshone Indian allies) were able to move around the flanks faster than the infantry, "The hostiles are riding horseback, so they're much more mobile than the Army."

Now, hold your map like this and look for Crook's Hill. That's going to be our next stop. That's where he's going to run the battle from. [Looking southwest] down there, in the distance, you can see Rosebud Creek. If you look here [pointing] you can see what look like rimrocks[278] with the hills behind it. That's up beyond Busby.

---

[278] Online: https://en.wikipedia.org/wiki/Rimrocks.

(1) Looking toward Crook's Hill and eventual command headquarters – the Conical Hill is just visible. (2) Rosebud Battle 10:30 to 11:00 AM with hostiles moving around Crook's left flank; transformative fair use of owned image. (3) Rosebud Creek southwest of our position. (4) Rosebud Creek northeast of our position and beyond the Buffalo Jump.

So, what is Crook going to do? Crook believes the Indian village is down there near where you can see the narrows in the valley. Look, you can see the narrows down there just before you come out and it seems to widen. So, Crook is going to tell Anson Mills,[279] who'll be a big man in the United States Senate, and he's going to tell Mills and Noyes, "Take your men and get in the rear of the enemy. Turn to Map 11. All right, you can still see Crook on Crook's Hill. We can see where's Noyes going. He goes down Rosebud Creek, here's where we turn, and he heads down Rosebud Creek due north in that direction because he's heard that the Indian camp is there. Who's now going down there? Mills and Noyes. Mills and Noyes are thundering down there, when suddenly, Crook is in deep do do.

Now, if we look at our map here, when we get up to Crook's Headquarters, we'll get a better view of it. You can see where Crook's Headquarters are, you can see Kollmar Creek, and over there, you can see Royall is in deep. There you can see Royall, the Small Conical Hill, we'll

---

[279] Online: https://en.wikipedia.org/wiki/Anson_Mills.

see Limpy's rock, you're going to see Conical Hill, and you're going to see their subsequent positions.

If you flip the map over, the Map between 12:15 and 1:00, you're going to see that Royall is in deep trouble. You can see here he's retreated from his first position, which will appear on an earlier map, his second position to his third position and what are surrounding him there, these solid red dots. The Indians have got Royall pretty much moving to where the hair is short. So, that means that Crook has to get the word to Mills and Noyes, "Forget about the Indian village, forget about it, get your keysters up here to he can strike the Indians in the rear. So, coming across that flat there are Mills and Noyes so they can strike the Indians along here from that direction to take the pressure off Royall, because the time is running out for Royall.

We'll leave here and go back to the [dirt] road. When we get back up there, our friend from California, when he gets up when you're not climbing any more, the ground has leveled off, and you can see some trees over in that direction, that's where you're going to halt. The last time, the people out in front kept going, and I had to ruin my vocal cords when I told them to "get your asses back!" You're not supposed to go on, you're supposed to turn to the left. So, remember our friend from Visalia, when you get up there, where you're no longer climbing, the ground is level, and there are trees off to your left, halt there, or you'll find out how a man throws a temper tantrum.

Third Stand: Through 2 PM

We get to the top of Crook's Hill and Ed Bearss orients the group on the maps in the Gane Atlas. When he first arrives, he says, "There are usually a large number of medicine bundles[280] up here." He methodically goes through the battle maps again starting at 8:30 (which we will not repeat here) and eventually gets to the 2 PM timeframe, after Crook has sent men to save Randall's people.

---

[280] Online: https://en.wikipedia.org/wiki/Sacred_bundle.

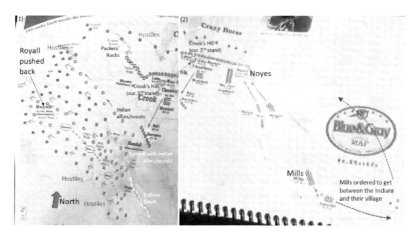

Now the 12:15 to 10:00 PM map: (1) Royall surrounded and pushed back by flanking hostiles. Transformative fair use from own photo. (2) Noyes and Mills ordered to get between the Indians and their village. Transformative fair use from own photo.

The Indians, here we come, there's the Buffalo Jump, they've scrubbed the mission of Noyes and Mills. "Tell them to get their asses up here to come in and get in our rear, because we're covering Royall's retreat." They pull [Capt. Frederick] Van Vliet off that hill [from across Rosebud Creek, now named for him], we're still holding here on Crook's Hill, and the hostiles are now withdrawing. They've now got Royall out of his pickle he's gotten into, and the hostiles decide, "We're going back to camp." We protected our village. We have held the initiative throughout the day.

Crook will put the best face on it he can, "I won. I held the ground." He decides he's short of rations, and on the morning of the 18th, he goes back to Goose Creek. He won't move his keyster out of there until the early weeks of August. There is no communication at all and there's no need, there's been no orders for them to communicate because [Gen. Philip Henry] Sheridan[281] is convinced that if they encounter the hostiles, [Maj. Gen. John] Gibbon[282] can handle them alone, [Gen. Alfred Howe] Terry[283] can handle them alone, or Crook can handle them alone. So, there's no orders for any

---

[281] Online: https://www.nps.gov/waba/learn/historyculture/general-philip-h-sheridan.htm and https://en.wikipedia.org/wiki/Philip_Sheridan.
[282] Online: https://en.wikipedia.org/wiki/John_Gibbon.
[283] Online: http://www.pbs.org/weta/thewest/people/s_z/terry.htm and https://en.wikipedia.org/wiki/Alfred_Terry.

concentration or any communication, and that would be Sheridan's fault. So, our friend Crook isn't going to know – they're going to know in Philadelphia – before Crook is going to learn down at Goose Creek what has happened on June 25th to June 27th to Gen. Custer. He knows nothing about it. In fact, he's out on a fishing trip when he learns about it, and his senior officers.

(1) The 2 PM map shows the Indians withdrawing. Transformative fair use of own image. (2) Crook says "I won. I held the ground."

The Indians will consider their losses. The Indian losses will range from 12 to 15 dead, 60 wounded, to as many as 25 dead, 50 wounded, [and] the Army dead will vary from who you're getting the report from, and those who died from their wounds, will range from 12 to 20 dead and about 50 wounded. Crook will say, "I don't want to leave my wounded yet. Regardless of being short of supplies, rations, ammunition, not leaving his wounded behind, that's going to be his excuse for falling back to Goose Creek on the 18th. Are there any questions? This is probably the most questioning group I've ever had up here.

We return to the bus and head for our hotel in Billings, Montana, where Ed Bearss spent some of his childhood.

BATTLE OF THE LITTLE BIGHORN[284]

Perhaps one of the visits closest to Ed Bearss's place of birth and boyhood, if not his heart for history, is the Little Big Horn and the battle

---

[284] Online: https://en.wikipedia.org/wiki/Battle_of_the_Little_Bighorn.

fought there. The tour spent the next two-and-a-half days moving to each of the locations related to the Battle of the Little Bighorn, ending close to Last Stand Hill. This is the spot where the bodies of General George Custer, two of his brothers, the Seventh Cavalry doctor, and many others were found. They had been surrounded, killed, then mutilated by warriors and revenging squaws. The Little Big Horn battlefield is only 40 miles from his family's Sarpy Ranch, a place he had visited many times with his friend Jerry Greene, who was an NPS Ranger-Historian at the Little Big Horn Battlefield National Monument Park.[285] He is now one of the leading authorities on the Plains Indian history and its clash with American "manifest destiny."

In the 1930s, Ed Bearss's mother and grandmother both performed services to benefit the Crow people on their reservation. Growing up in Montana, he had many Native Americans in his school and some were among the best athletes they had. He has a notable appreciation of the Indian people and civilization, understanding their treatment by settlers. Perhaps the settlers were unaware of the treaties protecting Indian lands or didn't care, or didn't think that the Indian reaction would happen to them. The avenging U.S. Cavalry, particularly people like George Armstrong Custer, a notable Civil War commander, helped us to understand the Indian response to U.S. Cavalry attacks. Growing up in Montana and serving as a Marine, Ed Bearss appreciated the culture and resilience of the Indian warriors and their families.

It's Kind of Sad

On our way to the Little Big Horn Battlefield, Jerry Greene described, at a high level, why the Indians were inevitably going to be defeated:

[When Indian camps were overrun, much of their materials were lost from] ... the troops piling it all up and then burning it. They even go around and destroy cups, spoons and any implement that was left, they would destroy, so that the Indians could not use it anymore. These were like guns,

---

[285] Online: https://www.nps.gov/libi/learn/historyculture/battle-story.htm.

the people lacked renewable resources, and that was really the reason why the Indian Wars ended, because they had no renewable resources, particularly guns and ammunition, and even more important, people. Warriors, especially when warriors were killed, they had no ready reserve to draw on. They couldn't draft warriors from another tribe. So, it's just a matter of time and constant barrages against these people. It's kind of sad to think about, but that's what the Government did as they tried to dominate the continent. I don't mean that in a critical way, that's just the way it happened.

Later, Jerry described an interesting exchange between Gen. Gibbon and Custer as the latter departed for what would be his undoing:

Actually, when he left, he pulled out and he [Custer] was mounting up and Gibbon--this is true--Gibbon said, "Now, Custer, don't be greedy, save some Indians for us." Custer kind of smiled and he said, "No, I won't," or "No I won't." You can interpret it two different ways." He went on to explain a marker along the road [following the path Custer took], Now, you will see a marker along here. I think it's going to be on our right. I'll try to point the marker out and you can pause. There's another one [marker] that I think is closer to the site. It's called the Nathan Short marker, and that's really a spurious marker. In August, 1876, after the Little Big Horn [fight] and the commands of Terry and Gibbon were camped down across the Yellowstone [River] from the Rosebud [Creek], from this route where we are. Okay, I think it's on the right, it's a fairly new marker. They found a dead cavalry horse with all its equipment, a carbine lying nearby, and they thought maybe it was a messenger or somebody from Custer's command, the horse was branded "Company C, Seventh Cavalry." I think it [the marker] was put up in the early 90's. Looking around, they never found a body associated with it, but the horse had been shot in the head and it was probably a deserter, somebody who deserted along here, but they don't know for sure who it was.

Now, the name Nathan Short became associated with it because one of Custer's messengers [Sgt. Daniel A.] Kanĭpē,[286] not Kanĭpe as some people like to refer to him, Kanĭpē is the way the family pronounces it. I can tell

---

[286] Online: https://www.ncdcr.gov/blog/2016/04/15/daniel-kanipe-of-marion-survivor-of-custers-last-stand.

you about that. But he's the one that in the early 1900's said that the markings on the equipment were No. 50, they stamped the equipment, and marked it, and that it belonged to Nathan Short, who was also in Co. C, as was Kanipe. There was no reason for him to say that, but ever since the name Nathan Short [has been associated with it]. Short most likely was killed at the Little Big Horn with the regiment, with Custer's battalion.

Later on in August, they found two dead bodies over on the Tongue River when Crook and Terry joined forces up here, and moved east trying to track the Indians, they found two bodies over on the Tongue River, which is the next major stream to the east, but these were not soldiers. They were most likely miners in the vicinity who had been killed by the Indians more than a year before. So, there's no connection with Nathan Short on this monument, other than the name that Kanipe gave it and one that stuck, because later on as the years passed, other soldiers said, "Well yeah, there was a body down there along with the horse, but most of the diary accounts talk about the horse and they never mention the body. The body is something that was curiously added to the story by men who couldn't remember or just wanted to…[bus noise]. The officers examined it and not the enlisted men.

We come up on the marker and Ed says, "I've never seen this one." Yes, this is the Nathan Short marker. Jerry says, "Yes, this is the Nathan Short marker, and I've seen a recent photo of it, so that's how I know, I've not seen it before now either. Further down the road, we came upon another marker identifying where Custer and his men had camped, and Jerry explains, "Another marker up here, this may be Custer's camp on June 22nd. Reading the plaque, "General Custer camped here June 22, 1876, … probably off to the right, near the stream."

Ed Bearss continues with the story, "Custer halts his men here and they're going to camp, this has been a short march, and he's going to tell them – because he hears rumors that some people are talking behind his back -- and he's going to insist on strict discipline, and that's when he gets off on this one about what Jerry said, the articles that [Maj. Frederick William] Benteen[287] wrote that appeared in the St. Louis paper. He [Custer] said, "If

---

[287] Online: https://home.nps.gov/libi/learn/historyculture/capt-frederick-benteen.htm and https://en.wikipedia.org/wiki/Frederick_Benteen.

you did that," he's probably standing with a ... in his hand, he says, "I'll horse whip him." Benteen got up and told him, "I wrote that letter," and Custer more or less drops the subject. It lets you see the feelings of Benteen. Now, Benteen is a Virginian. If you want to read some good books, see the letters of he [Benteen] and his wife. They definitely do not have a Victorian marriage. They have a very erotic [relationship].

Reno Attacks the Village

As our first stop in the National Monument, Ed Bearss and Jerry Greene explain the charge of [Major Marcus Albert] Reno's[288] men toward the Sioux village on the Little Bighorn, June 25, 1876, starting below the village and moving up [north]. Ed Bearss starts the talk, saying: "Jerry is like I was at Vicksburg. I used to walk Vicksburg on my days off, and Jerry did the same thing here at the Little Bighorn when he had his days off."

Ed Bearss begins his talk at our stand overlooking the Valley of the Little Bighorn, the current town of Garryowen, and the woods along the bank of the river where a massive Indian camp was present on June 25, 1876.

Indians Not Running

[Seeing] the teepees of the Indian camp you can see the advance of Reno, and this is going to be his advance from the river. So, Jerry and I are going to get up and down there in front of you folks, and I want you to get your maps oriented. Everybody has found Garryown, it's those buildings there. Now, the ground is as flat as a billiard table. From Garryowen, now remember, as you look at your map, the army, when Reno advances, will be in the area across the interstate [highway]. Find the interstate on the map, and you can locate where Reno's advance is coming. The Little Bighorn is in the trees over there. Now, almost all the area we can see to Garryowen is open ground, except, that heavy woods is there just like it is today.

---

[288] Online: https://en.wikipedia.org/wiki/Marcus_Reno and http://www.littlebighorn.info/Articles/renorep.htm.

I'll start in, and remember, Reno at 3:15 [PM] with his force of 130 men will cross the Little Bighorn, three companies of them, easy to figure, A, M and G. It takes them from 10 to 15 minutes to cross the Little Bighorn. Between the banks and the river, is a bank that is roughly three feet high. So, that means you ride up there, you'd better put your spurs to your horse, and drive it off. The water in the Little Big Horn can run anywhere as deep on me, and I've been wading in it, swimming in it, and everything you want. At this time of year, if I were as tall as this gentleman, it would be up to me [pointing to femur]. If I was short as our shortest man over there, it would be up to his crotch. They cross with their horses. They debauch from the timber out where we can see those hayfields, and we're going to form up ... in columns, we're going to be riding our horses, ... and about opposite us here, they are going to cross where the Interstate is [today].

(1-2) The flat plane along the Little Bighorn. (3) Draw down to Little Bighorn viewed from our stand. (4) The Little Bighorn River and its ~3-foot banks.

When they cross [what is today] the Interstate, he is going to deploy his men. Initially, G Company is in reserve, A and M are on the flanks. Jerry will point out now where the nearest part of the village is. It'll be the part of the village, as you can see on your map, those are Hunkpapas. The Hunkpapas are very close to present day Garryowen. You see Garryowen?

Probably within about 400 yards of Garryowen is where the nearest [Indian] village is of Hunkpapas. It [the Indian village] extends about two and a half miles north, as Jerry and the sign told you, and you can see the camp.

You can see the horse herd up on the bench, and the Rees [Arikara scouts][289] have been sent to run off the horses. That man looks like a Ree there, he's going to like it, because if he runs off the horses, he can keep them. But, most of them are going to see the Indians coming out and they're going to head back with the reservation as fast as the Rees can. The Indians are beginning to turn out, rather slowly at first, because they have scored strategic surprise on the Hunkpapas. I'll turn it over to my friend Jerry now, and he can go on as the Army boys, as you can see, and they're going to order "dismount," so the soldiers will dismount. This man is going to be lucky, because he's going to hold the horses for [pointing at three tour members] him, him, and him, and you're going to be spared with the horses, but you'd better not panic, you'd better be there when Reno begins to lose his nerve. Jerry, take over.

Jerry Greene picks up Ed Bearss speech from that point.

Well, as Ed pointed out, troops ford[290] the stream and then begin moving down in a column formation in the order of M and A and G, with G in reserve. As they advance and get closer, they begin to trot and eventually move into a gallop and bring G company up into line, so that they're scattered across the valley, say from where the highway is today. You can see the cars moving along there, and on the other side, approximately the three companies are, according to this map, beyond the highway, but where the highway is is a good indicator of the line of Reno's advance toward the village.

Now, where that building formation is today, that old museum, that's not the Garryowen museum. The Garryowen museum is a little further down, but that's about where Reno halts to a stop, because the Indians are not moving, they're not scattering, in fact there's evidence of them going to combat Reno's advance. Already, word has gone back to Custer by one trooper taking the word back, saying that the Indians don't appear to be

---

[289] Online: http://www.native-languages.org/definitions/ree.htm.
[290] Online: https://en.wikipedia.org/wiki/Ford_(crossing).

running. So, Custer gets that word. By then, he's already moved up in this general direction from Reno Creek apparently trying to find a place to ford and support Reno's charge on the village.

This is an enormous camp, and it must have been very frightening just to see all the smoke and rising dust around. The Hunkpapa on the south side of the camp began running their horses back and forth to stir up more dust, and the women and children behind them were running towards the north to get away from the approaching troops. The charge was continuing, but at one point the Sioux, and the numbers that keep growing and coming to the front to meet Reno, began increasing to Reno's left.

You see where the bench land is and where the pony herd is. Right over in that area they begin pressing against Reno's left flank, the left of his line.... Well, Reno dismounts his men and forms them as skirmishers[291] in company order, with every fourth man taking the horses of his colleagues to the rear. So, that cuts back on the number of effective forces meeting the Lakota advance, because they keep pressing on this flank. In fact, this line of M, A and G, turns gradually to a north-south alignment.

The Indians Strike Back

Ed breaks in and directs the group to a map, "Look on Map 29, they're falling back on the wooded area." Jerry continues…

and they keep pressing them back towards the woods, and at one point, Reno allows that they must get out of there or they're going to be overwhelmed, if they don't move into the wooded area. That's the only defensive area they see in front of them. There where you see the edge of the woods, that whole area was occupied by Reno's command eventually.

---

[291] Online: https://en.wikipedia.org/wiki/Skirmisher.

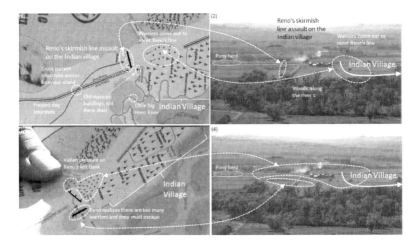

(1-2) Reno's companies M, A and G cross what is the present-day interstate and form a skirmish line to attack the village, achieving strategic surprise. Transformative fair use of owned images. (3-4) Large numbers of rifle-armed warriors push Reno's left flank east and the whole line parallel with the interstate as they head for the woods. Transformative fair use of owned images. All indicated locations approximate.

After, say, 15 or 20 minutes on the line, the next half hour takes place in the woods as they try to stem this attack on the flanks--both flanks and in front. So the troops are aligned more or less in a north-south configuration in this heavily wooded area in front of us, and over the next half an hour, 30 minutes or so, it [the attack] just increases and the Arikara Indian[292] scouts are attacking the camp and burning a lodge, and the smoke from that adds to the dust. It's a mass of confusion in the woods, and after about 30 minutes or so, Reno is standing in the woods with Custer's chief scout Bloody Knife,[293] as I

mentioned earlier. Bloody Knife [now] gets hit in the head with a bullet. His blood and brains splatter over Reno, who is standing next to him.

---

[292] Online: https://en.wikipedia.org/wiki/Arikara.
[293] Online: https://en.wikipedia.org/wiki/Bloody_Knife.

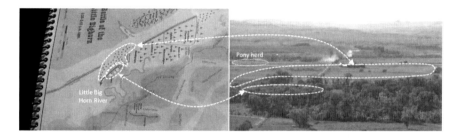

Indian pressure forces Reno's companies into the woods.

Reno is already under a lot of pressure, [and he] begins to lose it and calls on his men to "mount"-- they're on foot here in the woods-- to "mount," and then to "dismount, and then to "mount," and finally the men don't know what to do. Some of them are taking shelter behind the trees and Reno mounts his own horse and in effect leaves the underbrush. Many of the troops follow and some of them can't follow. Some of them are trapped down there. I think about 16 were trapped down there, could not get out or had no horses. The Sioux or Cheyennes were taking their mounts. They were clubbing them enroute, in the direction [of the bluffs below us on the east side of the river].

Jerry Greene and Ed Bearss take us through the Reno fight at the Little Bighorn Battlefield.

Pummeled by Sioux and Cheyenne

Reno is trying to get back to the initial ford, but again they keep pressing his flank over into this area, and finally the men begin running their horses into the Little Big Horn right down below us, jumping into the river. Some of the men lose their horses during that movement and some Indians are knocking them off their horses. It's quite a torment for those troops as they come across, and the Sioux are very successful in capturing the mounts, some men are crossing the Little Bighorn as best as they could and they get up into this area right below us.

You see that flat right by the river, they come across that area, and right in here is the heaviest flux [instability] of Reno's command, [in] these draws, coming up as best they can, but they're being pummeled by the Sioux and Cheyenne repeatedly. Many of them are killed, most by gunfire, but there were bows and arrows, too, and then the Sioux are such adept riders that they could beat on the troops with their war clubs. Many of those people died by virtue of the clubs that the Indians were using. So, that's about 3:30 p.m. It takes a long time for this all to materialize and by the time they get up to this point [atop the bluffs], and they're straggling up here, with the Indians shooting at them probably from the point where any shelter for them would end, right down over this little ridge in front of us, perhaps.

They get up here and Capt. [George Daniel] Wallace[294] reaches in his pocket and pulls out his watch and it's 4 o'clock. So, for 45 minutes, those troops have been through hell in the valley. They're up here, they're casting about, "What's going on?" and people are still straggling up here. Reno ends up losing 40 men, with many more wounded, in his withdrawal from the valley. They get up here, and they take a position behind any little hillock that they can, just to fire and establish a perimeter for a defense against the attacking Indians.

The Indians are very adept at taking advantage of the tortuous nature of this terrain to keep firing at the soldiers. They had plenty of ammunition. They had lots of guns, and they were very effective in that 45-minute period in disrupting Reno's attack on the camp. We know that they got up here and

---

[294] Online: https://www.findagrave.com/memorial/5816415/george-daniel-wallace.

they wondered after a brief time up here, where the support was coming from Custer that he had said would be there. Nobody knew exactly where Custer was. The last they'd seen of him was down in the Reno Creek area and they didn't know exactly what had happened to him, but we're going to get into that speculation tomorrow in great detail.

Asked about how drunk Reno was [a history rumor], Jerry said, "I don't know if he was that drunk. He certainly could have had a nip, but I've not heard of him having a nip down there, but I know up here he had a nip that night. He probably had several nips that night. I've not heard of him having anything. I have heard that there were charges that he was drunk the night of the 25th up here, but I've not heard of him [being drunk] during the charge or before the charge. Ed Bearss says, "He's more lost his cool from what has happened." Jerry says, "Well, he's completely disheveled."

Jerry Greene points out that Sharpshooter Ridge is just behind that high point, and some historians say Custer was seen up there.

Where's Custer?

Asked about whether Custer heard the firing from Reno's attack and retreat up the hill, Jerry responds.

A lot of things have happened while Reno is in the valley. Custer is in the vicinity, let's say. Some people down in the valley claim to have seen Custer up here on that ridge, up at that point, do you see where those markers are" He was going like this [waving his arm]. But they were still in the skirmish line at that time, that was before the withdrawal, the retreat, so Custer was either cheering them on or signaling, "Go back, go back." He was cheering them on, and then he disappears.

(1) Jerry Greene points to where some of Reno's men – when in the skirmish line -- say they last **saw** Custer, (2) waving his hat up on the ridge, (3) in the area of where those markers are today.

Some accounts say [and a lot of historians believe to this day], to right now, I mean, that he went up onto the Sharpshooter Ridge, which is right behind that high point right there. That leads toward Weir Point [named for Thomas Benton Weir[295]], but that's known as Sharpshooter Ridge. Some of the troops in the valley say they saw him up there, or at least historians today interpret that he was up there. When I was a seasonal up here, the only thing we heard about Sharpshooter Ridge was that the next day, when Reno was surrounded by Indians here, there were Indian sharpshooters up there shooting at his line and some of the troops of Company M, were hit by one individual up there, one Indian sharpshooter.[296] Now, some people say that's where Custer was seen, up on Sharpshooter's Ridge.

---

[295] Online: https://en.wikipedia.org/wiki/Thomas_Weir_(American_soldier).
[296] Ed Bearss related the following story along one of the trails, "The last surviving officer, who writes more than anyone we've been discussing, and he's the one that discusses the Indian sharpshooter that kills the fourth man to his right, kills the third man to his right, wounds the

I think he was seen over here where it says, "Custer last seen," or something like that, and that possibly the troops moved back and he went up higher, I don't know why he had to go higher to see how big that village was, because he could see it from up here. He could see the totality of it.

Ed Bearss explains Custer's probable tactical plans after seeing Reno's skirmish line and waving his hat to them, saying, "He's [Custer] looking for another crossing upstream to strike the village from… [wind noise]. He is going to end up trying to cross at the mouth the long draw. He is planning to cross at Medicine Tail Coulee, where there is a ford."

Beaten to a Pulp

Later, Ed Bearss talks about Isaiah Dorman,[297] who was in the Reno attack and wounded there, as well as others lost.

The man who'll be mutilated the worst of all will be Isaiah Dorman. He's with Reno. He's down in the bottom. Sitting Bull knows him. Sitting Bull is going to come to him and see that he is badly wounded. Sitting Bull, if he had his way and time and had it not been for the battle, he would have got some people to help him rescue Isaiah Dorman. He's black, he's married to a Sioux, and he is wounded badly. But, with Sitting Bull disappearing, he is going to be terribly mutilated. The Lakotas who get a hold of him are going to savagely beat [someone says "don't go into detail"]. …Isaiah Dorman is actually beaten to a pulp by the Indians, though Sitting Bull wanted him to be saved. I could tell you how horribly they disfigure him, mutilate him, but we have too many women on the bus to talk about it.

[Second] Lt. [Benjamin Hubert] Hodgson[298] will be knocked from his horse **while crossing the river**. He is Reno's adjutant. He'll grab the stirrup of one of his brother officers and hopefully, he is thinking, I will be pulled across the Little Big Horn, I can get my footing, but he is going to be dinged in the water before he reaches dry ground and Lt. Hodgson will be dead.

---

  second man to his right, and he decides he'd better get out and get digging." [I'm not sure that this statement is clear or even needs to be included here--Jerry]

[297] Online: https://en.wikipedia.org/wiki/Isaiah_Dorman.
[298] Online: https://www.findagrave.com/memorial/19726/benjamin-hubert-hodgson.

Also, there is 1st Lt. [Donald] Mackintosh,[299] one of the first, he's a Canadian, he is one of the first mixed bloods that's half Indian, to be graduated from West Point. He will be killed down there along with Hodgson and [Acting Assistant Surgeon] Dr. [James Madison] De Wolf,[300] [who] will be killed as he tries to scale the bluff.

There are going to be a number of people, including [Maj. Charles Camillo] DeRudio,[301] who are going to be able to hide out, because the Indians are going to shift their attention. They're only going to leave a handful of Indians down there firing at Reno's men as they retreat, as the Indians are beginning to move north to protect the village against the cavalrymen who are descending Medicine Tail Coulee. That is the most feasible ford across the Little Big Horn.

Jerry Greene then points out Medicine Tail Coulee on the right [east] of the bus as it begins to appear some distance from where it meets the Little Big Horn, "This is Medicine Tail Coulee on our right, this big draw, ravine,

---

[299] Online: http://www.arlingtoncemetery.net/donaldmc.htm and
https://en.wikipedia.org/wiki/Donald_McIntosh.
[300] Online: https://www.armyupress.army.mil/Journals/Military-Review/MR-Book-Reviews/november-2017/Book-Review-007/ and
https://en.wikipedia.org/wiki/James_Madison_DeWolf
[301] Online: https://en.wikipedia.org/wiki/Charles_DeRudio.

heading down towards – in a kind of a northwest direction– to the Little Big Horn, down where the trees are. This will factor very significantly tomorrow as we discuss what Custer's movements and then possible movements were.
…[wind noise] Custer's path, it was very clear to the troops--to Reno's troops--once they got on the hill [above the Little Bighorn], and particularly after their engagement was over and the Indians had left, you could see the way that Custer--the path through the grass where Custer advanced from [what is now called] Reno Creek.… That was a good indicator of Custer's route, at least at that point.

While driving to Weir Point[302] after visiting the Reno-Benteen siege site the day before, Ed Bearss describes the point of land where Custer was perhaps last seen by Reno's men in the valley. "We're now beyond where Custer, Martini,[303] and Mitch Bouyer[304] rode up and looked over onto the Little Big Horn Valley. At that time, Reno [and his] men are in line of battle. They're advancing dismounted, and that's the last time that we know of Custer going to see Reno's command."

Weir Point

Twin Peaks

Jerry Greene explains Reno's movement to Weir's Point his fight down on the Little Big Horn below the bluffs.

Once Reno gets up to the hill, and the troops are eventually wondering, "What the heck's going on, where is Custer?" and nobody was moving in his direction even though they heard gunfire coming from the north. Captain Thomas Weir then mounted his troop and decided he was going to march to the sound of the guns, and Reno didn't want to go. Reno did not come to Weir Point, but the rest of the troops at last did mount up and followed their commanders up to this area [that we're approaching].

---

[302] Online: https://www.hmdb.org/m.asp?m=21640.
[303] Online: https://en.wikipedia.org/wiki/Giovanni_Martino and
  http://www.littlebighorn.info/Articles/Martino.pdf.
[304] Online: https://en.wikipedia.org/wiki/Mitch_Bouyer.

As I mentioned, this area where the road runs through was a big gap that was cut in here in the 1930s that would not pass muster today under the terms of the Historic Preservation Act.... You see two ridges on either side of the road, that extend north in the direction of the Custer fight. The troops marched up on top, or they probably kept their horses down here, and ascended to the top, and through binoculars they could see what apparently were the last stages of Custer's fight, the dust from the distant Indians milling around, so, from here [bus stops] you can actually see where the Last Stand area is, and this is kind of the view that the troops with Weir and the other officers saw.

Dust and Indians on Horseback

At Weir Point, Jerry Greene describes what he believes Custer did after seeing Reno's command for the last time, movements that focused on his trying to strike at the Indian Village a few miles north of where Reno attacked. Custer's doing so caused many Indians to move north towards Custer's action, which likely saved a number of Reno's men, too. Ed Bearss sets up Jerry Greene's interpretation:

Now, Benteen arrives at Reno's position on the bluff at 5:15 [PM]. He finds Reno has lost command and control. Reno has already met Sgt. [Daniel] Kanipe, with his admonition to push on and support Custer, and twice (this is word of mouth), and twice will say, "Bring packs. Bring packs." He will also be cognizant of what is in writing, the one that [Custer's] adjutant gives [Trumpeter] Giovani Martini, which are a series of two-word [penciled] sentences. It is again, "Benteen, push on." "Big village." He'll repeat it twice, "Big village," and then off goes Giovani Martini.

Also, before Benteen arrives here, and before the pack train arrives here, . . . Boston Custer [one of Custer's brothers], has left the pack train and is hastening forward to join his brother. He is going to beat both the pack train, and he has this written message, even more stringent, "Big village, Benteen, big village, push on." In response to the pleas by Reno, Benteen will yield to Reno as his commanding officer, not Custer, and he will reorganize using his men, including the company commanded by Weir, [and will] begin to set up a perimeter of defense down where we just were, but they can still hear the firing.

Weir, in essence, who has the hots for Libby [Custer], says, "If you guys aren't going to move," he's [Weir] is going to tell Benteen and Reno, "I'm going up and find what has happened to Custer, where he is." They can hear them firing. So, he [Weir] will arrive up here [at Weir Point].

Evidently, realizing "Maybe I don't want to be called a wimp," Benteen, will then move up here with his men. Reno will stay where we just left, with half of his men. So, now, Jerry will pick up. Benteen has arrived, Weir is here, we have all of Benteen's men because they haven't been engaged yet, we have Weir's company, we have a handful, about 40 men, from Reno's command, because he stays back there. They'll surge forward, but they're not going to stay here. Now Jerry's going to pick up what they see and what is going on. And [pointing at the plaque] remember what they represent here, look at the smoke, over here the smoke represents dust and smoke clouds, and if you want to know where they are [turning towards Last Stand Hill], look at the trees. You can see the monument on Last Stand Hill, and Jerry's taking over.

Jerry Greene jumps in when Ed Bearss finished and says:

... and that's about it [group laugh], nothing more to say. That's [Last Stand Hill] about three miles from here, where Ed pointed out the monument is located, and you can see that that truly appears to have been the last vestige of Custer's movement there at the top of the hill, because the men were up here and they probably moved out on that point and they probably moved out on that point over there [pointing at two hilltops divided by the 1930's road]. These are kind of two ridges ... [Ed Bearss breaks in], "This will be the highest point, right where they put the road through." {Jerry continues] That could have been the highest point where they put the road through and destroyed historic property here in the 30's.

But anyway, Reno's men, the officers certainly, had binoculars with them and they could see through the binoculars the swirling dust in the area [of Last Stand Hill], they could see Indians on horseback, apparently, and as they watched them, they came to the realization that those Indians seemed to be getting closer, coming towards them. I'm not sure how long they were up there, maybe 30 to 40 minutes, watching all this, and when it was understood that the Indians were coming in their direction, it clicked, and they made a rather hasty retreat back to their position on the bluffs, where they had been before, a mile back. They actually threw out troops and there was some firing as the Indians approached them, within gunfire range, and were shooting at them. In fact, I believe one trooper was killed during the retreat. [Ed Bearss breaks in] "And he was killed very close to here."

[Jerry continues] Yes, and so, I think [1st Lt. Edward Settle] Godfrey[305] actually led them, or was the man who formed the line that kept everything in order as they pulled back to the defenses because they didn't just run back, but it was an orderly withdrawal, although with some impetus, let's say, because they didn't want to get surrounded by the Indians, who were arriving in larger numbers steadily.

So, they pulled back to the site that they had been at and where they knew that the bulk of the command could ride this thing out, quite possibly. It's really only when they get back there that they get to more formally consolidate that position, because really, they had no place else to go. So, they had to make do with what they had. They began throwing up earthworks in front of the assigned companies throughout that perimeter that we just walked around. From that time, as the afternoon passed, they were shooting at them.

The Indians again on the morning of the 26th took aim at Reno's command from the ridges over there to the east of the site, and they fairly peppered the command most for a good part of the day, until the afternoon, late afternoon. As Ed said, they packed up their truck and pulled out rather slowly to the south, towards the Big Horn Mountains.

The command did not know if this was going to be a ruse [and they'd send warriors back], there was a lot of debate over the state of the wounded. Reportedly, Reno, in a conversation with Benteen that Benteen repeated years later, came to him and proposed to leave the wounded and skedaddle and get out of there-- and that Benteen threw cold water on it and it never

---

[305] Online: https://www.nps.gov/waba/learn/historyculture/edward-s-godfrey.htm and
https://en.wikipedia.org/wiki/Edward_Settle_Godfrey.

happened, so they spent the entire night of the 26th ... [wind noise, words lost].

What Happened to Custer?

Tracing His Route

Jerry continues with the "big question."

So, in the meantime, the big question remained, "What happened to Custer?" Well, Custer, as Ed may have mentioned, had come up into this area and after seeing Reno's action in the valley ongoing, then – we neglected to point this out as we came along the road – but on the right there's a deep coulee going down [Ed Bearss breaks in], "Look on your maps, Cedar Coulee. Look on your maps, Cedar Coulee." [Jerry continues] Cedar coulee, and Custer diverts to the right after he comes down from the ridge with all those in his command, now apparently trying to find a place to ford the Little Big Horn, perhaps, and understandably, most likely to try to attack the village to take some flak off of Reno, who he last saw was engaged with the Indians down in the valley. The coulee, eventually, after about half a mile, empties into a much broader coulee called Medicine Tail Coulee. Now, it didn't have that name in '76 [1876], it's been named since by a Crow Indian family by the name of Medicine Tail, hence its name today, Medicine Tail Coulee.

They [Custer and his men] actually go out at kind of an angle, almost to the northeast. The mouth of Cedar Coulee enters Medicine Tail well beyond that point that the troops with Weir were on that we talked about moments ago. As I say it was a broad coulee, Custer could not see the Little Big Horn from where he debauched into that broader coulee [Medicine Tail], so he began sending some of his troops up on the ridges, and in the meantime, that's about where he has [1st Lt. William Winer] Cooke[306] send trumpeter Martini back with that message to Benteen. He still wants to get--make sure you know-- he sent Kanipe back, but he sends a second message with Martini

---

[306] Online: https://en.wikipedia.org/wiki/William_W._Cooke.

trying to get those packs sent forward as quickly as possible. He knew that something was imminent.

He knew that undoubtedly; he'd have reason to have those packs on hand. So that takes place ... around where we get into Medicine Tail, and then they begin moving down Medicine Tail, trying to see if they could see the mouth of it, see the Little Big Horn in front of them. As they do, they send riders up the hills beyond the ridges. All those ridges that are barely discernible right now, will become more discernible to us as we proceed.

(1) Jerry Greene pointing towards the Reno-Benteen position from Weir Point. (2) Map showing the confluence of Cedar Coulee and Medicine Tail Coulee; Luce Ridge and Deep Coulee shown. Transformative fair use from owned images.

There is one ridge called Luce Ridge over there, it had another name at one time, it's now called Luce Ridge, and some troops went up on that. I think from that point they could see the upcoming ford area, and as Custer's men advanced below them, the ford gradually came into view. So, he [Custer] saw and he knew that this was the place that he was going to cross and try and support Reno, at least that's **the** general understanding of this entire movement. Now, when we get down into that area, and as we drive along in the bus, Ed or I will point out Nye-Cartwright Ridge to you because that is a very important ... [wind noise] in this story of Custer's advance. Ed says, "On your maps, locate Luce Ridge and Nye-Cartright Ridge on your map. Can you all locate them? Calhoun Hill. ... That's where Custer and the cavalry are going, down that ridge line."

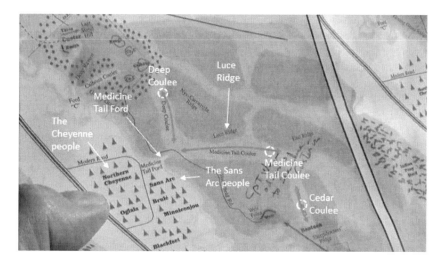

Annotated Little Big Horn Battlefield map. Transformative fair use of owned photo.

[Jerry continues over Ed] It moves in a northwest-going direction, in the direction of the Little Big Horn, and that's important to note, because there's another coulee beyond that big monolithic ridge in front of us there, and it's called Deep Coulee, and they kind of come down to a point of a Vee at the mouth of Medicine Tail ford. [Ed says] "Our next stop is going to be at Medicine Tail." [Jerry continues] So, keep all of this in mind if you can because all these landforms that I've mentioned are going to be significant in just a few minutes.

Ed Bearss adds, "And the Crows have told him that the best, the most feasible crossing is what's at the mouth of Medicine Tail Coulee, and right opposite the mouth of Medicine Tail Coulee are the village of the Sans Arc and of the Cheyenne. That's the upper end of the village." Jerry adds, "This is the northern end of the village, and Ed mentioned a good thing when he mentioned the Crow Scouts because their recollections are also going to be significant, they do not get involved in the engagement up here, but they are a witness to Custer's approach to the ford. [Ed breaks in] "All except one of them, the one that's wounded." [Jerry elaborates] Well White Swan,[307] you mean, he's wounded with Reno and is in the hospital area. But there are four of them, White Man Runs Him,[308] Hairy Moccasin,[309] Goes Ahead[310] and Curly,[311] and they're all together. Curly eventually becomes a well-known spokesman through several accounts, different accounts, … We'll get into more detail as we proceed.

[Answering a question] Yes, he's [Custer has] seen the extent of the village when he peered over the edge there at Reno's fight, and that was his first look, as I mentioned yesterday-- that was his "Oh, poop" moment, when he saw the huge nature of the Indian population that ultimately was going to greet him.

We visit Medicine Tail Coulee for Jerry and Ed's interpretation of what may have been Custer's last moments, as he may have died there and been brought to Last Stand Hill by his men, or perhaps he was "dinged" and killed later.[312] As we drive toward Medicine Tail Coulee and other sites, including Last Stand Hill, Ed Bearss and Jerry Greene describe Custer's sending two or three companies down Medicine Tail Coulee toward the Indian village

---

[307] Online: https://en.wikipedia.org/wiki/White_Swan.
[308] Online: https://en.wikipedia.org/wiki/White_Man_Runs_Him.
[309] Online: https://en.wikipedia.org/wiki/Hairy_Moccasin.
[310] Online: https://en.wikipedia.org/wiki/Goes_Ahead.
[311] Online: https://en.wikipedia.org/wiki/Curly_(scout).
[312] We leave it to the reader to learn what happens at Medicine Tail Coulee and visit the NPS trails, plaques and Visitors Center to experience the ground for themselves.

and the evidence found there. At a stop north of Medicine Tail, Jerry points out that:

It's believed based on the finds, the archeological finds, of shells and lead and devices that were thrown on to cavalry mounts that some action occurred down here. Particularly, I want to specify that Indian accounts were very important from this time forward, because they help us pinpoint with some degree of hopeful accuracy what happened to Custer's command. Incidentally, the Crow scouts that do not take part in the action are stationed up here at the hilltop [to the south] where I'm pointing, overlooking the river, and I would point out that Hairy Moccasin, in one of his accounts afterwards, said, "Custer went right to the river. I saw him go that far." That's pretty explicit, and he would have been with the command all this time, so he certainly knew who Custer was.

Medicine Tail Coulee (today) – Custer may have been "dinged" here and brought to Last Stand Hill by his men. Transformative fair use from owned image.

We drive to Last Stand Hill, where the bodies of Custer, his brothers and friends, as well as senior officers were found after the Indians -- perhaps many squaws -- had finished their mutilation of the dead.

Custer's Last Stand: The Remains

In the case of Custer's remains, he had been shot twice, once in the left forehead and once in the left breast, either of which could have been fatal. He was on Last Stand Hill. There are theories he was indeed killed as he attempted to cross the ford [at Medicine Tail Coulee] into the village, at least he was hit, and perhaps knocked off his horse, and his body was either wounded or dead and carried back up carried back up the hill with the troops as they retreated or withdrew from the ford area back to Last Stand Hill, or that he died on Last Stand Hill. That's the picture that most people like to view, and of course it's shown in a hundred or more different images of Custer's Last Stand or Custer's Last Fight.

After the fight, Custer and his brother Tom,[313] a captain of Company C, were first buried together, and my impression was that there was a blanket involved, they were wrapped in a blanket and put under a large Indian basket that would help keep wolves and other varmints from digging at the remains, but I don't think that necessarily succeeded. That was a factor in all of these burials, particularly of the enlisted men. They had to bury them and get out of there so quickly and get the wounded downstream that some of them scarcely got any covering at all in that kind of dry, ashy, sandy soil. They only had, I believe, four shovels with Gibbon's command, and that necessarily retarded the burials a great deal. Some of the men used their cups, and I'm sure other mess gear to help dig the graves. Much as we'll see this afternoon, they dug some trenches Reno's part of the field to keep the Indians from firing into the area, and especially covered the area of the hospital and you'll understand all of that this afternoon.

So far as the dead officers were concerned, they were all buried possibly at the place where they were found and the markers that you will see, the white markers, represent not necessarily where they fell, but where they

---

[313] Online: https://en.wikipedia.org/wiki/Thomas_Custer.

were found, and possibly even that is not true, because some of them were quite probably dragged around after death by the victorious Indians, who would throw lassos around them and pull them around. So, the stones represent *where they were found, rather than where each man fell.*

Terry couldn't carry the dead back with the command, so all the officers as well as the enlisted men were buried variously throughout the field. Custer's family members, his brother-in-law Capt. [James] Calhoun[314] and Capt. [Tom] Custer, his younger brother Boston[315] [Custer, a civilian contractor], his nephew [Henry Armstrong] "Autie" Reed, were all buried in the Last Stand area that we'll be seeing over the next couple days. They remained there until June of 1877, when an expedition came out to retrieve the officers remains, and at that time, many of the dead had been pulled out of their original shallow burial graves and had been dragged around by wolves, who knows, it's possible that Indians could have gone in and retrieved some of the remains. But it was a terrible site when they returned and found all those officers whose remains had deteriorated over the course of the year, and there was some difficulty in identifying the remains.

In regards to Custer's remains, there was a serious question as to whether or not they got Custer. Bones had been scattered around. My recollection is that the accounts said that a skull and a femur, and maybe part of a backbone was retrieved and was attributed to Custer. One sergeant's account of the reburials made the statement as regarding Custer that apparently they had identified tentatively one set of remains as Custer's, and then another set of remains looked like they could have been Custer's too, and the sergeant who wrote the record said, "I think we got the right set of remains the second time." So, if Custer is indeed, or what's left of him, is indeed at West Point in the cemetery, …, years ago I was researching at West Point, and I actually came within six feet, possibly at least, of George Armstrong Custer, in the cemetery.

All of the officers' remains were placed in boxes, individually marked boxes, and they were transported down to Ft. Custer, which was built in 1877 at the junction of the Big Horn and the Little Bighorn rivers. From there, a

---

[314] Online: https://en.wikipedia.org/wiki/James_Calhoun_(soldier).
[315] Online: https://en.wikipedia.org/wiki/Boston_Custer.

steamer carried them down to Bismarck, and then they were sent to various cemeteries, private and public, around the country.

The site at the battlefield on June 27th, when the soldiers of the Seventh and survivors came down to bury their comrades was such that the hot sun had swollen those remains, it was a terrible sight. There were just absolutely millions of flies all over and the stench was ungodly, especially in places like Deep Ravine where some of the dead were found.

Last Stand Hill

We get to Last Stand Hill and Jerry Greene points out some of the markers where bodies were found and first buried, whether or not they could be recognized.

[Pointing at markers on Last Stand Hill] These markers were put up I believe in 1891 for the individuals. There's Custer's in front of us, it's outlined, but his brother [Boston] and his nephew, Autie Reed, are the two down there towards the corner, and they're kind of together there. Dr. Lord's is in here, I think, it has his name on it. Tom Custer is in here. [Capt. George Yates[316] I believe is in here.

---

[316] Online: https://en.wikipedia.org/wiki/George_Yates.

Little-Known History

The Suicide Boys

Ed Bearss has Jerry speak about what Ed Bearss calls, "The Cheyenne equivalent of the [World War II Japanese] Kamikaze[317] pilots-- **the** "Suicide Boys."[318] They are underage, just like those **Kamikaze** pilots, and they're going to be Noisy Walking,[319] Closed Hand, Little Whirlbird, and Cut Belly, and Jerry's going to tell you all about them. They're very important and it's so obvious of a warrior society. The Japanese are a warrior society. The Plains Indians have a warrior society. Take over Jerry."

Ed's and my friend Margot Liberty[320] is the real proponent for this element of the interpretation at Little Bighorn, although she is a great friend of the Northern Cheyenne people and she deals with this notion of the Suicide Boys, as they were called, in her book *Cheyenne Memories*,[321] which is an excellent book and is based on the memories of John Stands in Timber,[322] who was kind of the unofficial historian of the northern Cheyenne Tribe. If there was any Indian account that I would put all my faith in, it was John Stands in Timber, because he was very, very careful.

The information that he jotted down and relayed to Margot Liberty in a series of tape interviews in the mid to late 1950s was the genesis of the book *Cheyenne Memories*. Please remember the name of that book because it's an outstanding book. Most recently, Margot has had published by the University of Oklahoma Press the entire transcript of all her tapes with John Stands in Timber. It's a huge book. It's about this thick [2-3 inches shown] and it's about this dimension [8 by 10 inches shown], so it's very substantive. I was fortunate to be asked to review the manuscript for it. Great book, but she deals with a lot of elements of Cheyenne history. Well, John Stands in Timber dealt with them, and presented them, and made the news

---

[317] Online: https://en.wikipedia.org/wiki/Kamikaze.
[318] Online: https://friendslittlebighorn.com/gazettsuicideboys.htm.
[319] Online: https://www.findagrave.com/memorial/60216233/noisy-walking.
[320] Online: http://www.friendslittlebighorn.com/interviewmliberty.htm.
[321] Online: https://www.goodreads.com/book/show/1610399.Cheyenne_Memories.
[322] Online: https://www.goodreads.com/book/show/1610399.Cheyenne_Memories.

with the accounts of the Suicide Boys, for example. We knew little about them before Margot's first book came out in 1967.

The Suicide Boys, their purpose was to lead a charge, they were young men, and to scatter horses, and drive the enemy away and confound the enemy in any way that they can. But we knew little or nothing about this element of Northern Cheyenne warrior, we were warrior dumb, I guess you'd call it, until her rendition came out in *Cheyenne Memories*, and now it's been added to by this transcript by John Stands In Timber.[323] He went to Haskell College down in Kansas and he worked on the Cheyenne Reservation the rest of his life. I don't know any Indian historian who was more trustworthy and accurate than his transcriptions of events that have affected the Northern Cheyenne. ... So, the Suicide Boys were a factor here, and it's simply an element, a little-known element of Cheyenne participation at the battle of the Little Bighorn.

Ed Bearss adds, "The only thing I can add after what Jerry has said is that I never knew about the Suicide Boys until sometime in the 1970s, when the book comes out. Jerry says, "I was behind the desk when she walked in **in** 1968 and I had her autograph my copy of *Cheyenne Memories*, which I still own. Margot lives in Sheridan today. She's in her 80s I believe or late eighties.

Body Markers

Seventh Cavalry Markers

The locations of the Seventh Cavalry bodies after the fight at Last Stand Hill could only be surmised by where they could find the most convincing remnants of a particular person as Ed Bearss explains. Walking to Deep Ravine, Ed Bearss[324] and Jerry Greene talk about the U.S. soldiers' markers and the impact of bureaucracy on battlefield interpretation. Ed begins:

---

[323] Online: https://muse.jhu.edu/article/724346/pdf.
[324] Ed Bearss was walking back from Deep Ravine when (relative to remaining well hydrated) he said, "...because I like to walk battlefields. I don't want to; I don't like battlefields so well that I want to die on one."

When they do the archeology, they mark one interment, not two, because they've got to use up 40-odd stones [more than they need] or they've got to send them back to the Quartermaster General. They made a map when they erected these stones in '91 [1891], but there's no map of where they buried the people on the 28th day of June. They marked the spots, but they made no map. They made no surveyed map. [Referring to the assumed graves,] On a number of these, they dug down where they have two stones, and there's only been one body there. Using up these 35 odd stones, because they're only going to mark four on Reno-Benteen. So, you've got 211 here, this makes 214, and they're going to have the four stones over there, they've got about 25 extras. Between 215 and 252 [--] that's bureaucracy and counting right, bureaucrats don't like to send things back.

We come to the marker for Asst. Surg. George E. Lord,[325] and Ed Bearss provides his story. "All right, his medical case is found here [in the Indian village]. There's contrary evidence that he died on Last Stand Hill." Jerry says, "But his body is found up there [pointing at an adjacent ridge with markers] and it was later identified by a couple of people who really knew him and knew what he looked like, knew what his hands looked like. He was a surgeon. George Lord. I'm serious, I don't know why this marker is here. There's an explanation, but I don't know what it is. I don't know if it's just a misplaced marker. But it's obvious it's an early marker.

---

[325] Online: https://en.wikipedia.org/wiki/George_Edwin_Lord.

Ed adds, "Again, I want to emphasize, when they have these monuments of two that close together, [they] are generally only one interment. When they dig down there, there are not two interments. They're going on what the archeologists on grave sites say about small bones, such as in the phalanges of the fingers and toes."

Indian[326]

Ed Bearss describes the introduction of the Indian death markers.[327]

Beginning about 20 years ago, or 25 years ago, they began to mark where tradition places the death sites of the Indians, and they're always of that color, so you know it's an Indian marker. Indian traditional history, where some of them have left mounds of stones where they had found their loved ones where they fell. That was started here about 25 years ago by Park Historian John Doerner[328] ... and the Indians like that.

Indian markers.

---

[326] Online: http://www.friendslittlebighorn.com/warriormarkershistory.htm.
[327] Online: http://littlebighorn.info/Articles/IndianCasualties.pdf.
[328] Online: https://friendslittlebighorn.com/arikaramarkers.htm.

Political Correctness

The next day, Jerry Greene and Ed Bearss discuss what might be called "political correctness" in the Park Service and their own sentiments. "[Pointing at two Indian markers in the distance] They're Indians. I like the term "Indians" because that's what they were known as in 1876, and I feel 'Native American' is an academically contrived [expression]." Ed Bearss brings in his experience.

Because I go and I asked the Crow, "What do you want to be called?" Do you want to be called a "Crow" or a "Native American." He said, "We're Crows." I've asked Oglala, "What do you want to be called, "Oglala" or "Native American"? We prefer "Oglala." Jerry adds, "They want to be known by their tribal names or tribal distinction or, a lot of them say, and I've heard them in conversations, "He's an Indian." They talk in terms of Indians and whites.

Ed Bearss describes his National Park Service experience with the expression.

Because I knew a female in the Park Service [who was] responsible for any Park Service publication, you have to refer to the Indians as "Native Americans," and I did not like her. Fortunately, I've outlived her a long time [she was in the Headquarters of the Park Service]. She retires, and as soon as she retires, I start saying that we will call them by their tribal names, and then I've become all the more convinced because I keep asking them. The Nez Perces, and particularly the Crows, where I have a very good relationship, because I went to school with them. I know some of the Oglalas, and I figured if anybody would be, and ... he told me this order, " Oglala, a branch of the Lakota people, in the suite we classify as Sioux, which is a pejorative, in the same way as being called a "Native American."

Archeology

Ed Bearss described **formal** archeological investigations **at** Little Bighorn Battlefield.

[The last body remnants found] were done here in 1958. It is going to be down in the Reno-Benteen area. There they recovered a set of human remains and they investigated and reinvestigated some of the earthworks up there. So, the earthworks that you're going to see, it's shaped like a frying pan, the Reno-Benteen [defensive area]. Where we were yesterday would be like the pan, and it is lower in one part in the center, and that's where they will take the wounded to better protect them. Then they will have the the handle of the pan going down the ridge that extends furthest to the south of any, and there they investigated and restored the rifle pits down there. Some of them they did not investigate, and those will be considerably more eroded than the one section they reconstructed in 1958. The next archeology will not occur until subsequent to the prairie fire of 1983. They knew from Ft. Custer, being established in 1877, that there's never been an extensive grass fire down at Little Bighorn, and as you notice in the area, it's a lot of sagebrush. Two factions, one of them for the archeology (they were subsequent to the fire) and others will be opposed.

Jerry Greene added his experience.

I don't know of any large-scale fire like the '83 one ever happening there. There were incidents of smaller fires, and I recall one while I was working one day at Reno-Benteen. I remember running along the side of a road trying to stomp it out. Somebody got a car back to headquarters to send out the big water tanker truck we had ready at all times. They had to bring that truck there to put out that fire. Fortunately, it wasn't a windy day. There were little incidents like those but nothing like that '83 blaze that just cleaned off the section north of the field.

Preserving the Battlefield

Jerry Greene explains the limited battlefield access allowed visitors during his time working at the battlefield.

Our instructions were to keep people off the battlefield. There's more access today to different parts of that field than I ever would have imagined in 1968. We had loudspeaker horns, and we'd go out onto that veranda and we'd tell people, "Please return to the Visitor Center." If we saw them wandering down in the direction of deep ravine, and there were signs placed all around, "Beware of rattlesnakes," that helped serve the purpose of keeping people off the pure, untrailed part of the engagement site. Maybe with that philosophy in mind, when Neil [Mangum][329] proposed the trail down to deep ravine, I was one of those who was not crazy about it.

However, when I went down the trail for the first time, I could very easily see the importance of the interpretive view of that trail because I think no place else on that site do you get the impression of how starkly tortuous that terrain is on that part of the battlefield. It's still a terrific asset today to be able to access that, to go down to that pivotal station at the end where those men died towards the end of the fight, apparently. To just see it, you get a visceral reaction that will stay with you. It's one of the most important interpretive sites on the field, and Neil was absolutely right and smart to pursue that. It just tells you how stubbornly held views have changed here through the years, and mine certainly have.

Ed Bearss and Jerry Greene in front of a Last Stand Hill painting in the National Park Service Visitors Center.

---

[329] Online: https://www.blueandgrayeducation.org/tours/on-sacred-grounds/.

BIBLIOGRAPHY

Greene, Jerome A. *Indian War Veterans: Memories of Army Life and Campaigns in the West, 1864-1898*, ed. Jerome A. Greene. El Dorado Hills, CA: Savas Beatie, 2007.

Greene, Jerome A. *Stricken Field, The Little Bighorn since 1876*, Norman, OK: University of Oklahoma Press, 2008.

Greene, Jerome A. *Finding Sand Creek: History, Archeology, and the 1864 Massacre Site*, Norman, OK: University of Oklahoma Press, 2006.

Greene, Jerome A. *Washita: The U.S. Army and the Southern Cheyennes, 1867–1869.* Norman, OK: University of Oklahoma Press, 2008.

Greene, Jerome A. *American Carnage: Wounded Knee, 1890.* Norman, OK: University of Oklahoma Press, 2014.

Greene, Jerome A. *Nez Perce Summer, 1877: The U.S. Army and the Nee-Me-Poo Crisis.* Helena, MT: Montana Historical Society Press, 2014.

Greene, Jerome A. *January Moon: The Northern Cheyenne Breakout from Fort Robinson, 1878-1879.* Norman, OK: University of Oklahoma Press, 2020.

Stands in Timber, John and Margot Liberty. *Cheyenne Memories*. New Haven, CT: Yale University Press, 1998.

Stands In Timber, John and Margot Liberty. *A Cheyenne Voice: The Complete John Stands in Timber Interviews.* Norman, OK: University of Oklahoma Press, 2019.

Addendum:
Bear River Massacre Conflict Resolution

By Harry Butowsky, April 2019[330]

In 1989, I traveled with Ed Bearss to visit the Bear River Massacre Site, near Preston, Idaho. This place is the site of the Bear River Massacre, in which a village of Shoshone Native Americans were attacked by the California Volunteers on January 29, 1863. Estimates of Shoshone casualties are as high as 384. It is also known as Bear River Battleground or Massacre at *Boa Ogoi*.

I was doing my Geology NHL (National Historic Landmark[331]) Study at the time and Ed came with me to Idaho to see the Bear River site, which was proposed as a National Historic Landmark. The support for the site was strong within the local community made up of the white population and the native American population of the area. The problem was in how to commemorate and interpret the site. The white population saw the site as a battlefield site while the Native Americans want it to be a massacre site.

We met everyone at a public meeting that was held at night. Tempers and opinions were running high Both sides held to their opinions. Ed got up to address the crowd and gave them the complete history of the site. He knew more about this history than anyone else in the room. He spoke for about one hour then took questions.

The end result of his talk was that both sides learned something of their history and when Ed proposed to write the nomination himself to reflect both sides of this history everyone was in agreement to support the National Historic Landmark proposal. As part of the compromise Ed told the crowd it would be called the Bear River Battlefield Massacre Site. The site is now a designated National Historic Landmark.

---

[330] Harry Butowsky was a senior member of Ed Bearss's History Program in the National Park Service. His biography and association with Ed Bearss are documented in the second book of Ed Bearss memoir entitled *Walking the Ground: Making American History*.

[331] Online: https://www.cr.nps.gov/nhl.

Historians call the Bear River Massacre[332] of 1863 the deadliest reported attack on Native Americans by the U.S. military—worse than Sand Creek in 1864, the Marias[333] in 1870 and Wounded Knee in 1890. I believe only someone of Ed's knowledge and speaking ability could have brought both sides of the community together. His talk was just a masterpiece.

---

[332] Online: https://en.wikipedia.org/wiki/Bear_River_Massacre.
[333] Online: https://en.wikipedia.org/wiki/Marias_Massacre.

Chapter 6

THE GREAT WAR TOUR

As a wounded Marine at Cape Gloucester, New Britain, Ed Bearss was part of – and familiar with – American World War II history, particularly in the Southwest Pacific, as he lived it. He is knowledgeable about the history of 20th Century European warfare, from his early life's reading and mapping study of the Italo-Ethiopian War,[334] Spanish Civil War,[335] and [Adolf] Hitler's evolution[336] as well as early conquests (Austria, Czechoslovakia, and Poland) until he got into the Marines and got busy. Learning about the importance of "a few inches of earth" at Suicide Creek,[337] and with Pete Shed's Shiloh walk[338] a decade later that you must "walk the ground" to really "get it," Ed Bearss already had an intense interest in walking the ground at key battle sites in Europe.

For his South Mountain Expeditions WWI tour, Ed Bearss with Marty Gane engaged a European historian familiar with World War I sites and events, few of which Ed Bearss had previously visited. Michael Kelly[339],

---

[334] Online: https://en.wikipedia.org/wiki/Second_Italo-Ethiopian_War.
[335] Online: https://en.wikipedia.org/wiki/Spanish_Civil_War.
[336] My Mother had read *Mein Kampf* and shared her thoughts and foreboding with me.
[337] See the first Ed Bearss memoir book, *Walking the ground: From Big Sky to Semper Fi*, Chapter 2.
[338] See the first Ed Bearss memoir book, *Walking the ground: From Big Sky to Semper Fi*, Chapter 4.
[339] Mike Kelly online: apollobattlefieldguide@gmail.com.

who is a Western Front expert and tour historian, was our guide and historian for the 2017 South Mountain Expeditions World War I (WWI) tour.

Pre-Tour Sightseeing

Brussels

Michael Kelly had us start our tour in Brussels. Brussels was captured early in the war by the Germans and served as an excellent place to spend a few days on the South Mountain Expeditions pre-tour activities. As had become the convention, Marty Gane had South Mountain Expeditions do a series of local tours a few days before the start of the official history tour. The logistics value of this approach was to offer people some buffer time to arrive and get adjusted to the time zone before we begin. When we did the World War I tour, we began in Brussels, and toured chocolate factories and a couple local breweries, some did a Segway tour of the city. It was a fast way to see the major sites in the city, and do so in an entertaining way - I didn't do it.

Brussels Segway tour.

Bruges

Bruges[340] is a preserved medieval town with many shops and restaurants, hotels and both passenger-boat and horse-drawn guided transport for tourists around the town. Many thousands of tourists do experience the town. Belgian waffle restaurants and chocolatiers can be found on many streets. The Church of Our Lady Bruges[341] is one of the most visited sites. It is known for displaying Michelangelo's "Madonna and Child" Statue.[342] I walked around the church, seeing the many spaces preserved by the church for centuries and saw the statue. It was one of the pieces of art stolen by the Nazis and hidden in Austria at the Altaussee Salt Mines[343] and found by the US Army Monuments Men.[344]

(1) Mike walks us into Bruges using a headset to communicate to our radio receivers; (2) horse-drawn tourist carriage in front of the Church of Our Lady Bruges; (3) tourist boat transport on Bruges waterways; (4-5) Michelangelo's "Madonna and Child."

---

[340] Online: https://en.wikipedia.org/wiki/Bruges.
[341] Online: https://en.wikipedia.org/wiki/Church_of_Our_Lady,_Bruges.
[342] Online: https://en.wikipedia.org/wiki/Madonna_of_Bruges.
[343] Online: https://www.salzwelten.at/en/altaussee/.
[344] Online: https://www.monumentsmenfoundation.org/the-heroes/the-monuments-men.

Dunkirk

In addition to Brussels, our World War I tour took us close enough to Dunkirk, where more than 330,000 Allied (mostly British) soldiers escaped to England after German successes is in the Spring of 1940.[345] We visited the museum, which sits within an earth-covered bunker that served as an Allied command post during the evacuation. We took a tour of the museum and then stood on an elevated platform to better view the east mole and the lighthouse at its end. I spoke to a part of the group on this platform about the events that took place in our view.

Dunkirk pre-WWI tour visit.

---

[345] Online: https://en.wikipedia.org/wiki/Dunkirk_evacuation.

MIKE KELLY'S TALK

Before starting the WWI tour, Mike Kelly gave us a talk about how the war got started. This was very useful for several in our tour group who had not read the bibliographic materials provided and knew little about the complex European political environment leading up to World War I.

Mike Kelly providing the tour goers with historical background to the causes of the Great War.

IEPER (YPRES)

As one of the battlefields that was active throughout the war, we started in the Belgian city of Ypres,[346] pronounced "Wipers" by the Tommies[347] (i.e., British soldiers). Ypres is the French spelling for Ieper. The present-day spelling is Ieper, but we'll be using Ypres here. Ypres was fought over and around beginning in the late autumn of 1914 until 1918.

---

[346] Online: https://en.wikipedia.org/wiki/Ypres.
[347] Online: https://en.wikipedia.org/wiki/Tommy_Atkins.

The Cloth Hall[348]

The Cloth Hall was a large building that housed thousands of looms in the Middle Ages. They brought in many cats to get rid of the mice and rats, but their number grew so great that the myth is they were thrown from the windows. The cat became a symbol used in the city for this reason. The clock tower in the building is accessible through a number of stairways accessible through the Flanders Fields Museum [349] From the roof walkway, there are extensive views of the city and surroundings. The Cloth Hall was devasted in WWI, as was every building in the city, and rebuilt to its original appearance as were the many other buildings over several decades.

The Cloth Hall was used to house 5,000 looms in medieval times, wool was sent from the English monasteries and woven in the Hall and then stored there. The word diaper means D'Ypre - cloth of Ypres. – Mike Kelly

---

[348] Online: https://en.wikipedia.org/wiki/Ypres_Cloth_Hall.
[349] Online: https://www.flandersfields.be/en/do/flanders-fields-museum and https://en.wikipedia.org/wiki/In_Flanders_Fields_Museum.

Flanders Fields Museum

This museum in Ypres is found on the main square, in a large building called Cloth Hall, that dates to the Middle Ages and once had been a place where cloth vendors sold their wares. The building was a target for German artillery from the surrounding ridges and was eventually reduced to a pile of rubble, but it has been rebuilt. This museum along the town's ramparts (medieval wall) includes a diorama of the city in its WWI destruction, blasted into rubble, dirt and brown dust covering all structural ruins. It is an important image to have in mind when you see the town today.

A bit of modern (restored) Ypres from roof of the Cloth Hall and model of Ypres after years of shelling during WWI.

(1-2) The Menin Gate is visible from the roof walkway of the Cloth Hall; (3) The Menin Gate approaching ceremony time; (4) The bystanders are in place for the daily ceremony to begin; (5) The buglers sound The Last Post; (6) Wreaths are placed on the stairs to the cemetery.

Today, the Flanders Fields WWI Museum has many displays from the Great War, a small amphitheater with video of actors portraying soldiers and nurses in uniform reading from soldiers' letters, a dynamic lighted relief map of the Ypres area, and a video to provide a quick understanding of the strategic and tactical plans and actions throughout the war. The rooftop is accessible from inside the museum if you buy the extended ticket. You climb stone spiral stairs into the bell tower, then go up again on a metal staircase to an exit on the roof. Plaques with color imagery from the rooftop identify the various buildings visible from that side of Cloth Hall.

Menin Gate[350]

The Menin Gate along the main thoroughfare into the center of Ypres is used for a major remembrance ceremony for the many thousands of Commonwealth soldiers killed in the Ypres Salient and whose names are carved into the stone walls. Every night of the year, of every year since 1929 and excluding the WWII years, a large crowd gathers on either side of rope guides so the main roadway is clear for the ceremony. Buglers and a bagpipe player in kilt enter one end of the gate and play the "Last Post" beginning at exactly 8 PM every night. When the music is over, several groups of two-to-three people place memorial wreaths in one of the gates stairways.

> The Menin Gate was opened in 1928 to commemorate 55,000 Commonwealth soldiers killed in the Ypres Salient in the Great War and who have no known grave. It is not medieval. – Mike Kelly

---

[350] Online: https://www.cwgc.org/find/find-cemeteries-and-memorials/91800/ypres-memorial and https://en.wikipedia.org/wiki/Menin_Gate..

The Wipers Times[351]

A fascinating true story turned into a recent black comedy film by the same name was the publication of a Trench newspaper[352] in Ypres called "the Wipers Times." Or since Ypres protruded into German lines forming a bulge or "salient," its secondary title was "Salient News." In such miserable death-defying existence in the trenches, officers of a unit in the British Army decided to publish a periodical newspaper using a printing press they had found. It was a "tongue in cheek" publication that poked fun at their plight, such as higher-level officers never in the front line and believed to get medals and leave far excess to their value. They included advertisements (though all businesses in Ypres had been destroyed or evacuated), soldiers might need.

(1) "The Wipers Times" front page of the first issue (February 12, 1916). Public Domain. Retrieved from https://upload.wikimedia.org/wikipedia/commons/2/22/The_Wipers_Times_1916-02-12_p1.jpg. (2) the Wipers Times was printed in a space within the cities rampart wall occupied by the *Casemates* restaurant as of Oct. 2018.

---

[351] "The Wipers Times: The Complete Series of the Famous Wartime Trench Newspaper.," Ian Hislop (Foreword), Malcolm Brown (Introduction), Patrick Beaver (Notes), Little Books Limited, London, 2006.
[352] Online: https://upload.wikimedia.org/wikipedia/commons/2/22/The_Wipers_Times_1916-02-12_p1.jpg

> TAXIS!   TAXIS!   TAXIS!
>
> OUR new consignment of highly decorated cars are [sic] now placed at the convenience of the public, These are handsomely appointed and can be easily known by the Red Cross painted on each side. Whistle three times or ring up.
>
> Telegraphic Address: **Ripped, Wipers**...   Telephone, 1. Central.

The military unit who published the trench paper, the Sherwood Foresters, were moved to different locations depending on the war needs and their titles tracked their location, such as:

- *The Wipers Times* (12 Feb. 1916 – 20 March 1916, four issues)
- *The "New Church" Times* with which is incorporated *The Wipers Times* (17 Apr. 1916 – 29 May 1916, four issues)
- *The Kemmel Times*. With which are incorporated *The Wipers Times* & *The "New Church" Times* (3 July 1916, one issue)
- *The Somme-Times*. With which are incorporated *The Wipers Times*, *The "New Church" Times* & *The Kemmel Times* (31 July 1916, one issue)
- *The B. E. F. Times*. With which are incorporated *The Wipers Times*, *The "New Church" Times*, *The Kemmel Times* & *The Somme-Times* (December 1, 1916 – 26 February 26, 1918, 11 issues)
- *Better Times* (1 Nov. 1918 – 1 Dec. 1918, two issues).

The value of The Wipers Times is that the subjects they wrote about, and the sarcasm with which they did so, demonstrate the pressing issues of living in the trenches, trying to survive the many German weapon systems and all degrading and depressing aspects of life managed by green (inexperienced and unsympathetic) British officers. Perhaps one of the most revealing advertisements was in the Somme-Times, appropriate given the environment in which the men in the trenches lived and died.

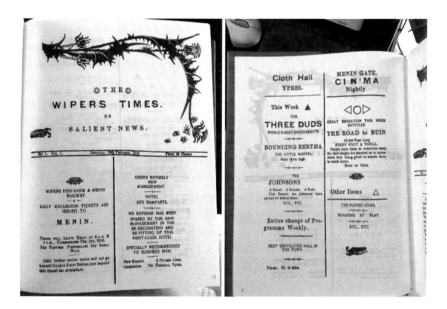

Are you a victim to Optimism?"
You don't know?
Then ask yourself the following questions.

– Do you suffer from cheerfulness?
– Do you wake up in a morning feeling that all is going well for the Allies?
– Do you sometimes think that the war will end within the next twelve months?
– Do you believe good news in preference to bad?
– Do you consider our leaders are competent to conduct the war to a successful issue?

If your answer is "Yes" to anyone of these questions then you are in the clutches of that dread disease.
WE CAN CURE YOU.
Two days spent at our establishment will effectually eradicate all traces of it from your system.
Do not hesitate – apply for terms at once to: –
Messrs. Walthorpe, Foxley, Nelmes and Co.
Telephone 72, "Grumblestones,"
Telegram: "Grous."

When you get a deep understanding of what soldiers experienced, you can easily understand why having "Optimism" on the Western Front, and correcting it by putting the victim of it into the WWI trenches, was easily a source for humor to those who read "The Wipers Times" while living in those trenches. There were other trench newspapers, but this one was associated with Ypres.

BATTLE OF VERDUN[353]

One cannot tour World War I battlefields without addressing what is arguably the greatest concentration of death and destruction in WWI, and that is near the historic French City of Verdun (21 February to 18 December 1916). So many French and German soldiers were killed in a relatively small area that remains are still occasionally found over 100 years later – as on all other battlefields used for agriculture or development – still in modern times.

(1) Observation portal and gun aperture on top of Fort Douaumont, seen in (2) and (6-7); (5) shows the high-caliber cannon turret whose nonoperational mechanism is shown in (4); Internal areas are shown in (3-4).

---

[353] Online: https://en.wikipedia.org/wiki/Battle_of_Verdun.

Fort Douaumont

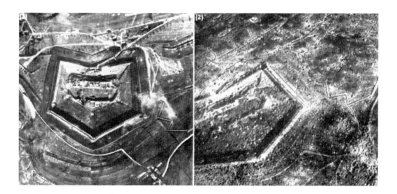

(1) Fort Douaumont before the battle (German aerial photograph.). Retrieved from https://upload.wikimedia.org/wikipedia/commons/0/0e/Fort_Douaumont_Anfang_1916.jpg. (2) Fort Douaumont Ende (after the 1916 battle), German Government, Department of photos and film. Retrieved from https://upload.wikimedia.org/wikipedia/commons/f/f5/Fort_Douaumont_Ende_1916.jpg.

One of the core targets of the German Army in this campaign was the capture of Fort Douaumont,[354] and a few other forts around the city. The fort exists today as a major tourist destination in this area and there is much to see in and around the fort, though areas are still dangerous due to likely unexploded ordnance. Our tour group entered the fort and its many multi-level corridors and special-purpose rooms as well as areas around and on top of the fort.

Fleury-Devant-Douaumont[355]

One of the tragedies of WWI was that it was fought in the civilized fabric of Western Europe, where French and Belgian civilians and their cities, towns, villages and farms and factories became tactical combat objectives. Much of this fabric of civilization was so thoroughly devastated that rebuilding there was considered dangerous (e.g., unexploded ordnance) and

---

[354] Online: https://en.wikipedia.org/wiki/Fort_Douaumont.
[355] Online: https://en.wikipedia.org/wiki/Fleury-devant-Douaumont.

futile. One such village, that was evacuated as the German artillery began hitting, was Fleury. All that remains of Fleury, besides a latter-day chapel and signs locating the purpose of the former building on each site, are shell holes and structure foundations all overgrown trees and vegetation as nature reclaims this destroyed village. Our tour – and many others – visit Fleury to see the remains of the buildings in the village.

The remains of Fleury. (1) Pictures on a site informational sign showing the original village; (2) Mike Kelly and I read a memorial sign to those lost in the battle; (3-5) Fleury landscape showing shell holes and town remnants; (6) a plumber's business; (7) a farm; (8) a wine-grower's business.

The human sacrifice in the WWI Battle of Verdun arguably represented the greatest density of human deaths short of Nazi death camps, probably the greatest concentration of soldier deaths. There were an estimated 714,231 French and German casualties,[356] or approximately 70,000 men a month or more than 2,000 dead every day. The French built a major human monument to this huge sacrifice planned and executed by generals who were not among the men as they moved forward on either side. The Douaumont Ossuary,[357] commemorating the Battle of Verdun, contains the bones of perhaps 130,000 men killed during the battle, many perhaps dismembered by artillery fire – which killed or wounded most soldiers in WWI. The lowest windows on the sides of the Ossuary provide a glimpse at some of these bones, and above the bone vault there are many memorials to these unknowns and the overall human sacrifice.

The Douaumont Ossuary and the windowed basement of "the bones," the unknown French and German soldiers who killed each other around Verdun.

---

[356] Online: https://en.wikipedia.org/wiki/Battle_of_Verdun.
[357] Online: https://en.wikipedia.org/wiki/Douaumont_Ossuary.

THE BATTLE OF THE SOMME[358]

In addition to the Douaumont Ossuary at Verdun, the Thiepval Memorial[359] on the Somme is another major WW1 tour site. The Somme battlefield (Battle of the Somme was 1 July – 18 November 1916) costs perhaps as many as around 300,000 on each side. The 1st July 1916, the first day of the Somme battle, British casualties were about 60,000, of which nearly 20,000 were fatal. Since many men were hit by shell fire and dismembered or eviscerated, or were buried as the stood, ate or slept in their current trench (soldiers changed trenches, including captured trenches), many men were never found. The Anglo-French Thiepval Memorial includes the names of over 72,000 men who have no known grave. There are 300 French and 300 Commonwealth burials behind the Memorial to signify the joint efforts of both nations. Most of the French graves behind the monument – in which only some part of a soldier was found to identify the nationality – are also "unknowns."

We approach the Thiepval Memorial and then see the names of the missing etched into the walls, over 72,000 of them, and then Mike Kelly describes the action as the Commonwealth troops and some French attacked the German positions located on the ground of the memorial, with over 25 lines of barbed wire in some places. I later walked down to see the French (left) and Commonwealth (right) graves.

---

[358] Online: https://en.wikipedia.org/wiki/Battle_of_the_Somme.
[359] Online: https://www.cwgc.org/find/find-cemeteries-and-memorials/80800/thiepval-memorial and https://en.wikipedia.org/wiki/Thiepval_Memorial.

Editor: The "Lost Lives" Project was in Thiepval when Mike Kelly's 2018 WWI tour was presented there in 2018, and the number of wrapped bodies for each of the 1,561 days of WWI were laid out in two rows in a large field facing the Thiepval Monument. The number of bodies varied greatly by the location and battle, so some days, like the first day of the Battle of the Somme, show many thousands of deaths.

All of us on this tour were from the United States, so it was natural for us to focus primarily – though far from exclusively – on American battle sites. Also, our co-historian guide, Mike Kelly, is British, so we saw many Commonwealth sites as well. We also visited several American battlefield memorials, all built on high ground. They are on high ground not because ease of tourist and visitor visibility, but because these monuments were built where the men fought and died, and the Germans had logically built their 1914-conquest fortifications on the high ground.

AMERICANS GET INTO THE FIGHT

The Marines at Belleau Wood[360]

Mike Kelly brought us to the small town from which the Marines headed towards Belleau Wood has almost a mythological value to me as a Marine. It was here in June 1918, long before my engagement at Suicide Creek, that Marines attacked a German stronghold in the woods near the French town

---

[360] Online: https://en.wikipedia.org/wiki/Battle_of_Belleau_Wood.

of Belleau. The Marines – at great sacrifice – took the wood and stopped the advance on Paris from the east. We walked through the heavily wooded area – now owned by the US – showing eroding trenches and many shell craters. Ed Bearss spoke about the attack on Belleau Wood by the 3rd Bn., 5th Marines, and 3rd Bn. 6th Marines, attacked at dawn on June 6, 1918. They came across open fields to the northeast toward German machine-gun positions on the edge of the wood, where we stood. Ed Bearss provided an interpretation of the action here:

(1) Georges Scott (1873-1943) illustration "American Marines in Belleau Wood (1918)" - originally published in the French Magazine "Illustrations" - retrieved from http://www.greatwardifferent.com/Great_War/Georges_Scott/Scott_Belleau_Wood_01.htm. Public domain. Retrieved from https://upload.wikimedia.org/wikipedia/commons/7/7a/Scott_Belleau_Wood.jpg. (2-3) Mike Kelly and I walking into Belleau Wood; (4) Remnant German artillery piece; (5) Marty Gane and I head to the edge of the wood where Ed speaks to our group about the Americans who attacked across the wheat field.

Now, everybody, get as close as you can. [Pointing at the map in Maj. Benjamin Berry's[361] book] we started from the village of Lucy la Bocage that's on that ridge. I'll let you people hold it. This is where we started our walk. We've come down this road here, and this is Bouresches, that [road we walked] connects this larger village with Bouresches. Now, this is Berry's four companies. They have left the area – remember the road that continued on where the bus went down to turn around – this is the road they go out. Berry runs into heavy resistance from the area ... alright, let me turn around ..., I don't want to fall on my ass. [Now turned with the Marine field of advance to Ed Bearss's right] That wood line sticks out like that then and now, so when he approaches through the woods into this large open field, [Colonel Berton W.] Sibley[362] is going in guiding on that road that led to the monument, remember, he goes then to the [future location of the] monument and he is going to be the only gyrenes[363] that is going to reach Bouresches.

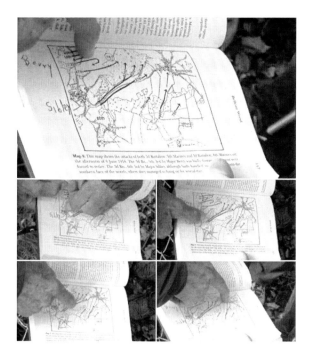

---

[361] Online: https://pennsylvaniamilitarycollege.org/major-berry-belleau-wood/.
[362] Online: http://bicentennial.norwich.edu/154-0/.
[363] Online: https://www.merriam-webster.com/dictionary/gyrene

Now, when Berry comes out into this field here, he takes heavy fire from the wooded area that we are in. He's going to be, he says he's suffering a "repulse," he's badly wounded, he's shot through the left arm, about a little bit further down than I am, and the bullet goes down [showing motion down left arm, then up] rather than up, and comes out the palm of his hand. He is now incapacitated. He sends his adjutant to meet with [Floyd] Gibbons.[364] Gibbons would be, he has probably the best description in a way, Gibbons would be within about 40 or 50 yards of the point of that woods there, because when he comes out of the woods, he is in the wheat field [in front of us], and there he is pinned down.

Sibley will be able to retain his gains; Berry will not be able to retain his gains. So, Sibley will have a toehold into Bouresches, and they will not get a complete possession of Bouresches for another ten days, the Marines will not. On this day they're going to lose 1,007 KIAs and wounded, more than the total number of Marines that fell in the Revolution, in the War of 1812, and the Civil War... [background talk].

---

[364] Online: https://en.wikipedia.org/wiki/Floyd_Gibbons.

Now, Gibbons is laying there, probably, he calculates when the adjutant comes up, about 30 to 40 yards from the upper edge of that wooded area. And, he is laying there and he's gonna take a series of wounds: one in the left arm; one in the right arm; and then a very bad wound, and one that is going to hit him in this area of the nose, tear his eyeball out of the socket, and with one of the optic nerves, he can rest it on the top of … [it's resting on the top of his bald head]. [Gasp from women in group.] He will lay there, he and the adjutant.

Along toward morning, they decide that they're going to try to get out of there. It has done some raining and the ground is rather slippery, and finally the Major (adjutant) is going to have to go to the rear to get help to get Gibbons out a here. They'll take Gibbons to the nearest sick bay. He's not with the German Army, he's with our army, and they're going to patch them up the best they can. He's going to write what they call a "stringer," describing very briefly and in abbreviated words, what has happened up to this date. He will then write it, because he's right handed, and he's going to say that the Marines, he'll use a verboten word, the Marines have taken possession of this area, but they don't know in Washington either at Army Headquarters or in the newspapers, they write "near Chateau Thierry," and that's when the shit is going to hit the fan, because it's going to come out that way.

First, he identified the Marines, now the Marines had done a good day of fighting, but the Germans ain't gonna be kicked outta here 'till we're into the first week of July, so the fighting at Belleau Wood is much more important except for the significance of the Marine Corps than what is happening. And when they write it up, the guy is going to say he can't figure out where Belleau Wood is, and he writes down "near Chateau Thierry." That's a bad word.

[Gen. John Joseph] "Black Jack" Pershing[365] [September 13, 1860 – July 15, 1948] is also wondering, "Isn't there an Army brigade in the 2nd Regiment of the Second Division? Why haven't we heard anything about them, outside of the word "infantry." No "Army" infantry or anything like that. So, Pershing has issued his order, "I do not want branches of the Service identified," Air Corps, Engineers, Infantry, whatever you want to have it, he doesn't want them identified, and they're going to say [a member of our group asks if that's because of security purposes.] No, he doesn't want the Marine Corps to get what they're going to inherit now. They're going to be viewed as victors not only of Belleau Wood, but of a more important battle, which is a turning-point battle, at Chateau Thierry.

So, Pershing decides, "No more Marines, no Marine Division, I can put up [with] Gen. [John Archer] Lejeune[366] commanding a Division, but that isn't a Division of Marines. And the wanna-be Marine Brigade, 2nd Brigade, which will give them a Division [that will] sit on their ass at Brest

---

[365] Online: https://en.wikipedia.org/wiki/John_J._Pershing.
[366] Online: https://www.lejeune.marines.mil/About/About-LtGen-Lejeune/ and https://en.wikipedia.org/wiki/John_A._Lejeune..

for keeping order in the landing base, and then it gets worse because Capt. Harry S Truman, he's a hard-boiled artilleryman, he's loyal to the Army, and he is [later] very upset at the United States Marine Corps and Admiral [John Geraerdt] Crommelin[367] of the Navy for opposing the unification of the Armed Services. That's when Truman's going to give his famous quotation, just like he did for [Paul Chandler] Hume,[368] the music critic of the *Washington Post*, who'd written a not-very-kind review of Margaret's debut on the stage, and it was, "If I go someplace and meet you, you'd better wear your jockstrap." In other words, he's gonna kick him in the balls. That's why Bill Perry [long-time tour goer] is such a proper man nowadays. So, this is going to play out in the Military Forces Unification: Equating the Marine Corps' propaganda machine to Adolf Hitler's or Joseph Stalin's. The Navy keeps their airplane carriers, the Marines keep their defined role in support of the Navy establishing bases and such.

---

[367] Online: https://en.wikipedia.org/wiki/John_G._Crommelin.
[368] Online: https://en.wikipedia.org/wiki/Paul_Hume.

The German 7th Army[369] Commander in 1918 is Generaloberst Max von Boehn,[370] who commands an elite German Division, and he says, "These guys [the Marines] are good. There at least as good as the best British and the French Divisions we fight, so we'd better watch out, 'cause right now over 8,000 American soldiers are arriving every day in France." The German commander of the 27th German Division actually says, "There as good as our best Divisions."

The Germans that the Marines are fighting are two substandard Divisions, but they also have two elite Divisions. You've got to also remember that a German Division at full strength is about the same as a Brit or a French Division at full strength, around 12 or 13 thousand men. Our Divisions are over 20,000 men. [Asked where the Germans were] They are on both sides of Belleau Wood. But as you look at the map, Sibley is able to handle the German resistance. The map in the one that was taken by this Marine Corps historian, who is a great believer in the Marine Corps, and I think Marty has that right now. Maj. Berton Sibley's Battalion gets a toehold in Bouresches. [Pointing at the Marines falling back] that is Berry, and he's falling back. Any questions?

---

[369] Online: https://en.wikipedia.org/wiki/7th_Army_(German_Empire).
[370] Online: https://en.wikipedia.org/wiki/Max_von_Boehn_(general).

Ed Bearss in front of the Marine Corps Monument in at Belleau Wood.

Now Mike Kelly, as I say, the Marine Corps have a bunch of lieutenant colonels and colonels, and they only have certain positions entitled to a full colonel. So, "Hiking Hiram" [Bearss][371] doesn't become a full Colonel until he goes to the 26th Yankee Division, and he's a Provost Marshall and then when the heavy fighting is over, he becomes colonel of the 102nd Connecticut Regt., but the glamor is over by that time. Any other questions? This site is much different than when I was here in 1999. I never got away from the monument. I never took the walk we just did.

We walked back to the Marine Corps monument in the center of the wood. Given Ed Bearss is a wounded Marine, this site and its monument have endearing and almost mythological importance to him and many other Marines.

AMERICAN MEUSE-ARGONNE OFFENSIVE

Pershing at General Headquarters in Chaumont, France, October 1918. Public domain. Retrieved from https://upload.wikimedia.org/wikipedia/commons/2/2a/John_Pershing.jpg.

---

[371] Online: https://en.wikipedia.org/wiki/Hiram_I._Bearss.

Marine action in Belleau Wood was conducted in coordination with the French Army, tactical operations to protect Paris from the major spring German offensive in 1918. "Black Jack" Pershing, the commander of the American Expeditionary Force (AEF) in Europe, had wanted – and President Thomas Woodrow Wilson (December 28, 1856 – February 3, 1924)[372] had the same desire – to operate as an American army with its own military objectives and officers. The American offensive in the Meuse-Argonne area of northeast France provided this opportunity.

The Lost Battalion[373]

Not too far away from Belleau Wood and a few months later in the historical chronology, Maj. Charles White Whittlesey[374] led his Battalion of the 77th Division into what became the famous "Lost Battalion" site in Charlevaux Ravine ahead of the units to its flanks.[375] He and his men were encircled for six days. When they were relieved, more than half his men were killed, wounded, or captured.

They had been attacked on all sides and were, at one point, shelled by their own artillery fire until called off by a wounded (famous) carrier pigeon[376] – a tremendous story of American heroism and sacrifice. Many more men, than lost by the Lost Battalion, were lost trying to save the battalion. About a score of the tour goers slid down the steep ravine wall off the access road to imagine what it must have been like to be surrounded in these woods and in this pocket. Again, my experience in the Marines at Suicide Creek and throughout my Civil War interpretation career, all emphasize the importance of terrain to understanding the details of the fight there and why the men became causalities or survived unscathed. No better example of this understanding of ground combat can be found than in the Charlevaux Ravine.

---

[372] Online: https://en.wikipedia.org/wiki/Woodrow_Wilson.
[373] Online: https://en.wikipedia.org/wiki/Lost_Battalion_(World_War_I).
[374] Online: https://en.wikipedia.org/wiki/Charles_White_Whittlesey.
[375] Online: https://en.wikipedia.org/wiki/Lost_Battalion_(World_War_I).
[376] Online: https://en.wikipedia.org/wiki/Cher_Ami.

(1) The Lost Battalion marker on the road above the Charlevaux Ravine; (2) Ed Bearss surveyed the ground above the Lost Battalion position, which was one of the positions occupied by the surrounding Germans; (3-4) Photos of some of the remaining foxholes (or shell holes) in the American held ground of the Lost Battalion battle.

> The wounded pigeon was called Cheri Ami, she was stuffed on her death and now resides in the Smithsonian. – Mike Kelly

Men from the "Lost Battalion" of 308. Inf., 77th division, near Apremont, Argonne Forest, France by War Department. Army War College. Historical Section. World War I Branch. ca. 1918-ca. 1948. Public domain. Retrieved from https://upload.wikimedia.org/wikipedia/commons/a/a8/111-SC-42759_-_NARA_-_55244719-cropped.jpg.

Hiram Bearss in WWI

Ed Bearss's third cousin (see Chapter 1 of *Walking the Ground: From Big Sky to Semper Fi*), the first Ed Bearss memoir book) Hiram Bearss served as a Marine Colonel in World War I. During the Meuse-Argonne offensive, he was moving forward with his adjutant ahead of his men of the

102nd Connecticut Regt., when they encountered a German battalion at Chateau d'Hattonchatel, near the village of Vigneulles. Although appearing to drop their arms on Col. Bearss's orders, one of the men (a senior officer) appeared to be preparing a grenade to throw at them. "Hiking" Hiram decked the fellow with a single punch to the jaw, adding further to his reputation.

Hiram "Hiking Hiram" Bearss and a Marine cartoon depicting the slugging of the German Colonel.

Tour-goer Craig Smith played the unlucky German slugged by Ed Bearss playing his relative "Hiking Hiram" Bearss.

Of course, this was a time when many German soldiers and their units were looking to surrender, as this submission by many more German soldiers to an American Battalion would have been possible.

Marty Gane of South Mountain Expeditions had arranged that some in the group with Ed Bearss to do a reenactment of the incident at Vigneulles, including Hiram's famous cigar smoking, so Craig Smith (a frequent history tour group member) pretended to be the unlucky capitulated German Colonel Ed Bearss pretended to slug. His brother Dave Smith kept suggesting he hit him again and again for more photos, and make contact "next time" (he didn't).

Finding the Sergeant York Site

Not far from Belleau Wood or the Lost Battalion is the site behind Chatel-Chehery[377] where Sgt. Alvin Cullum York,[378] Company G, 328th Infantry Regiment, 82nd Division, was acclaimed for heroic action (and using his superior sharpshooter skills) that earned[379] the U.S. Medal of Honor. Our guide Mike Kelly, who wrote a book called *Hero on The Western Front: Discovering Alvin York's WWI Battlefield*,[380] whose work Ed Bearss supported in an online video,[381] took us to a location several hundred yards from the actual site (see section addendum). Mike Kelly, our British WWI tour guide, described the background of the Sgt. York story that led to my tour of the site:

---

[377] Online: http://sgtyork.org/chatel-chehery.
[378] Online: https://en.wikipedia.org/wiki/Alvin_York.
[379] Many veterans complain about use of the term "awarded" or "won" a medal; it was "earned."
[380] Online: https://www.amazon.com/Hero-Western-Front-Discovering-Battlefield/dp/1526700751/ref=sr_1_1?ie=UTF8&qid=1548203602&sr=8-1&keywords=michael+kelly+Hero+on+the+Western+Front.
[381] Online: http://www.battlehistorianguy.com/.

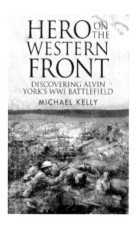

Cpl. Alvin Cullum York was awarded the Congressional Medal of Honor as a result of an action in a ravine near Chatel-Chehery. He, together with a 16-man patrol were detailed to infiltrate behind German machine guns that were holding up the advance of the 2nd Battalion, 328th Infantry on the morning of October 8, 1918. The patrol surprised a group of 90 or so Germans who were taking breakfast. After a short fire-fight, in which six of the patrol were killed and others wounded, York, single-handedly dispatched twenty-one of the enemy. The German officer surrendered his men and York and the patrol led off the prisoners to the American lines. He had captured 132 German soldiers. He was promoted to Sergeant and also received other awards from a grateful French nation.

Alvin C. York with his earned Medal of Honor. Public domain.

York's marksmanship was well known. Back in his home village of Pall Mall in the Valley of the Twin Forks, Tennessee, he had learned to shoot using 'black powder' weapons at the many turkey shoots that were held. His reputation for being a sharpshooter was well known. For many years, historians wondered where in the Argonne Forest in France, the action took place.

Early in 2000, an American army officer declared he had found the spot. Using unrecognized professional methodology, he found some expended ordnance and declared they were from York's weapon. It was unfortunate that his site was in the full face of the American 2nd Battalion attack and on an eastern facing slope when all American official records said it was facing west.

At a similar time, the Nolan Group, using historical records, and modern GIS technologies and archaeological survey, discovered the actual site in the forest. This was nearly a kilometer from the army officer's site.

Mike Kelly describes the action at the York site and the history, archeology and science that led to identification of the actual York-action site.

One of the most important records was the American Graves Registration Service (GRS) who's department officials buried the six dead where they fell. They were exhumed at the end of the war, and the coordinates of the burials were recorded. Using these records, the Nolan Group were able to locate where those burials took place. A large number of artefacts were recovered, many of them German and American, some of the latter were clearly marked with York's unit. '328 Co. G'. 328th Infantry, Company G. The Nolan Group were able to identify some American and German ammunition that could have been from York's weapons and from the German officer who was shooting at York.

This is an intriguing detective story of how the Nolan group[382] painstakingly pieced together evidence over a number of years. A book has been written by the British military historian and Battlefield Guide, Michael Kelly[383] in which all the relevant American official accounts and the German diaries, together with the patrol survivor affidavits are examined.[384] Nearly 200 color maps and photographs are produced to assist the reader to a better understanding. See the Addendum.

THE WAR ENDS

Armistice

On November 11, 1918, German emissaries came to Marshal Ferdinand Foch's[385] railway car in the woods of Compiegne to sign the Armistice document of surrender to the Allies and agree to turn over all weapons of war. Our tour went to the surrender site, which contains a museum that houses a replica of the original railway car, as the original was destroyed in World War II. That signature ended all fighting at the eleventh hour of the eleventh day of the eleventh month in 1918. This site became a vengeance

---

[382] Dr. Tom Nolan was the research and archeology team leader.
[383] Michael Kelly BA(Hons) Hist served in the Royal Navy and was a British police detective involved in many homicide and serious crime investigations over a 25-year period. He has guided groups from world-wide on the WW1 Battlefields and Normandy D-Day since 1999.
[384] Michael Kelly, *Hero on The Western Front: Discovering Alvin York's Battlefield*. ISBN 978-1-52670-075-9, Frontline Books. United Kingdom. Signed author copies available on: www.battlehistorianguy.com.
[385] Online: https://en.wikipedia.org/wiki/Ferdinand_Foch.

objective when Adolf Hitler forced France to sign its Armistice instrument in the same railway car in the identical location 22 years later.

(1) Compiegne Armistice site: (2) location of the railway car in famous clearing; (3) rebuilt monument showing German eagle impaled on sword; (4) WWII German guard on killed German eagle monument before it was blown up (Attribution: Bundesarchiv, B 145 Bild-P50288/Weinrother, Carl/CC-BY-SA 3.0, license available at https://creativecommons.org/licenses/by-sa/3.0/de/deed.en); (5) French Renault tank with a Hotchkiss machine gun, the same type that hit me on Suicide Creek – haunting me on this WWI tour; (6) replica Armistice-signature railway car in museum adjacent to the signature site; (7) Hitler (hand on hip at lower center of photo) eyeing General Foch's statue at the November 1918 signature site prior to Vichy France signing the 1940 Armistice with Germany – Hitler insisted on sitting in the same seat in the car that Foch had used 22 years earlier – Hitler's vengeance objective achieved; (8-9) General Foch's statue at the signature site; (10) I get a kick out of Mike Kelly's explaining that Hitler left the Foch statue untouched after he had the site destroyed to symbolically have him "see" it was now a site commemorating French defeat at the beginning of what would become WWII.

Versailles

Paris, the Palace of Versailles with its Hall of Mirrors, and the treaty. Public domain. Retrieved from https://upload.wikimedia.org/wikipedia/commons/b/b8/Treaty_of_Versailles%2C_English_version.jpg.

Following the Armistice, the Versailles Peace Treaty was developed over a six-month period (January to June, 1919) by the Allies political leadership from the America, Britain, France, Italy and Japan, eventually reduced to the "Big Three" of America, Britain and France. The Allied negotiations – no Germans present – led to a treaty with 440 articles intended to punish Germany for WWI, including its requirement to admit war guilt to justify massive reparation payments, which sought to capture payments to best make up for all the death and destruction beginning with the German invasion of Belgium in 1914. The treaty was developed in the French Ministry of Foreign Affairs located on the Quai d'Orsay, but signed at the

Palace of Versailles.[386] We visited the palace and the room in which the treaty was signed, the Wall of Mirrors, and then walked out into the palace gardens.

AMERICAN MONUMENTS

Mike Kelly planned our visits to several major American monuments[387] that are built on the high ground taken from the Germans in 1918.

Chateau-Thierry American Monument[388]

We visited the American Chateau-Thierry Monument on "Hill 204", which commemorates the American Army 3rd Division's support to the French in stemming the German tide during its Michael Offensive in May 1918. This last German offensive of the war was planned to overwhelm the Allies before the Americans could participate in great numbers, using a million German troops freed from the eastern front following the German-supported Bolshevik Revolution[389] that took Russia out of the war. The monument is also associated with the nearby Aisne-Marne[390] and Oise-Aisne American Cemeteries.[391] The Aisne-Marne Cemetery sits at the base of the hill containing Belleau Wood.

---

[386] Online: http://en.chateauversailles.fr/ and https://en.wikipedia.org/wiki/Palace_of_Versailles.
[387] Online: https://www.abmc.gov/ and https://en.wikipedia.org/wiki/American_Battle_Monuments_Commission.
[388] Online: https://abmc.gov/cemeteries-memorials/europe/chateau-thierry-monument.
[389] Online: https://en.wikipedia.org/wiki/October_Revolution.
[390] Online: https://www.abmc.gov/cemeteries-memorials/europe/aisne-marne-american-cemetery and https://en.wikipedia.org/wiki/Aisne-Marne_American_Cemetery_and_Memorial.
[391] Online: https://www.abmc.gov/cemeteries-memorials/europe/oise-aisne-american-cemetery and https://en.wikipedia.org/wiki/Oise-Aisne_American_Cemetery_and_Memorial.

The Chateau-Thierry American Monument. I walked up to see the view from Hill 204 and listen to Mike Kelly describe the American actions in the area. As with the other battle monuments, a compass engraving and map are provided, making it easy to place oneself in the terrain. More recently, a museum was opened below the monument, and it contains many displays of WWI scenes and equipment as well as the French Hotchkiss machine gun. This is the antecedent of the "Woodpecker" machine gun that shot me down at Suicide Creek at Cape Gloucester on New Britain 26 years later.

Montsec American Monument[392]

We visited the Montsec American Monument, which commemorates the American First Army attack and overrun of the German St. Mihiel Salient (September 12-26, 1918). The monument – as many do – includes engraved map directions with the names of towns and their distance from the

---

[392] Online: https://abmc.gov/cemeteries-memorials/europe/montsec-american-monument.

monument. This feature helps us understand where we are located relative to the salient and terrain features, towns, waterways, etc. The center of the monument – which has carved emblems for the divisions involved in these actions – includes an embossed map identifying these map features oriented from the monument. Given its height above the surrounding terrain, it provides an ideal location to get the "lay of the land," which matches well with my "lessons learned" at Suicide Creek.

The Montsec American Monument.

Montfaucon American Monument [393]

The third major American battle monument we visited was Montfaucon, which commemorates General Perishing's American Meuse-Argonne offensive from September 26, 1918 to November 11, 1918 (Armistice Day). It incorporates the American actions of the Lost Battalion and Sergeant York, and hundreds of other engagements up to the last day of the war.

---

[393] Online: https://abmc.gov/cemeteries-memorials/europe/montfaucon-american-monument.

The Montfaucon American Monument.

Mountfaucon (Mount Falcon) includes a climbable (via stairs) monument that dominates the surrounding countryside and with compass directions and distances at the top. In addition, the remains of German fortifications overcome by the Americans are still extant near the monument. There are Roman and medieval ruins behind the monument as well; clearly people have seen this prominent site as a critical location for hundreds of years.

German, Roman and Medieval ruins, the high ground here has long been valued.

HALLMARKS OF WORLD WAR I

The Trenches

One cannot tour World War I sites without seeing the trenches, either those protected and left to the elements or those restored and preserved (and maintained). The technology of the trench, the different tactical functions of each type of trench, and their zig-zag construction to prevent the enemy being able to shoot down the trench if breeched, are all apparent. We visited the famous Canadian Newfoundland trenches on Vimy Ridge,[394] part of the Somme battlefield, as well as the trenches evident at Belleau Wood. As many WWI soldiers have emphasized, the trench may be muddy, smelly, rat and flea infested, but it was the safest place to be during concentrated shell and machine-gun fire. There is no better example of the importance of the terrain in warfare, including man-modified terrain in the form of a trench system, than a WWI trench. Note the zig-zag in the trench, meant to prevent the enemy from shooting down the length of the trench.

(1-3) Vimy Ridge trenches – the Vimy Battle of April 1917 was a Canadian affair and part of a wider offensive known as the Battle of Arras.; (4-6) Eroded remnants of trenchworks at Belleau Wood. (7-8) Restored trenches at the Memorial Museum Passchendaele 1917 from a Mike Kelly WWI tour in 2018.

---

[394] Online: https://www.warmuseum.ca/the-battle-of-vimy-ridge/ and
https://en.wikipedia.org/wiki/Battle_of_Vimy_Ridge.

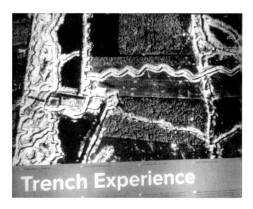

Airborne view of German trench complex in excellent Memorial Museum Passchendaele 1917, from a Mike Kelly WWI tour in 2018.

Tunneling and Underground Mines

(1) Mike Kelly describes the role and extent of the (2-3) Lochnagar Crater size and impact on the front line when it was detonated, and the consequences for the British attackers against the German stronghold that had been there. (4) Mike Kelly describes the (5) Spanbroekmolen crater at the "Pool of Peace" and its tunnel starting point in the (6) Distant clump of trees where mine was started.

Major trenchworks and fortifications had been built by the Germans on high ground along the Western Front after the German Schlieffen Plan attack in August 1914. These fortifications were proven impregnable to attack with the weapons at the time, so all sides – but mostly the British – used Welsh miners to tunnel underneath these German works, build a large gallery, on a bigger scale than we saw at Vicksburg, and install tens of thousands of pounds of high explosive, then detonate these mines as part of the next attack, or "push." As German countermines were dug, seeking to find and disrupt or destroy mining under their own fortifications, miners fought each other underground with a wide variety of weapons. The huge Lochnagar[395] and Spanbroekmolen[396] mine craters we saw demonstrate the massive explosions that eviscerated the German positions that had once dominated the fighting in these areas.

Tanks

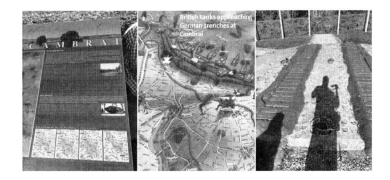

The Cambrai memorial site, where tanks were first used in their hundreds.

The British invented and developed a means of movement with armored protection. The committee working on the project first used the code name "Water Carrier," until they became irritated being known as the "WC" committee, so the adopted a new codename, "Tank." A knocked-out (hit by

---

[395] Online: https://lochnagarcrater.org/ and https://en.wikipedia.org/wiki/Lochnagar_mine.
[396] Online: http://www.greatwar.co.uk/ypres-salient/memorial-spanbroekmolen-pool-of-peace.htm.

an artillery shell) WWI tank was located underground many decades later and had it excavated. Today, it sits in a museum adjacent to a Commonwealth Cemetery where several of its crew are buried.

The tank is dark rust brown and appears to be deteriorating as it sits in the museum now exposed to the air. Although first employed in small numbers on the Somme, it was at Cambrai where the first mass use of tanks by the British against the Germans occurred. The tanks moved just behind the artillery fire and the infantry came behind them. The infantry casualties were much smaller than in earlier battles, the Germans had been routed, and the tanks proved themselves. Of course, it taught the German military the horror of being attacked by tanks as well as their effectiveness, a technology they employed "to the hilt" in their blitzkrieg tactics in World War II. These tactics – as shown in Cambrai in WWI[397] – would mostly remove the effectiveness of trenches, as well as the time to create them, in the continuous mobile warfare brought about by the tank and airplane.

(1-3) Tank "Deborah" dug up and put into a museum,[398] possibly the only remaining WWI tank in near-complete condition; (4) German shell entered "tank; (5) Result of shell detonation inside tank; (6) Some of the deceased crew; (7) Poppy wreaths with Remember crosses.

---

[397] Online: https://en.wikipedia.org/wiki/Battle_of_Cambrai_(1917).
[398] Online: http://www.tank-cambrai.com/english/home.php

Poisonous Gas[399]

The Germans experimented with poisonous gas, chlorine gas, against the Russians, releasing it from transportable tanks, when the wind would take it over the Russian trenches, then used on a mass scale on the Western Front, first at Ypres. They advanced the technology to counter the use of gas masks, using chemicals that caused you to vomit in your gas mask, causing you to remove the mask and then be killed by the chlorine. Gas was very effective at complicating the battlefield, particularly when the wind shifted. Hitler forbade the German Army using gas against soldiers (plenty was used against civilians in the Death Camps[400]) during World War II – perhaps because he had been injured by gas near Ypres.

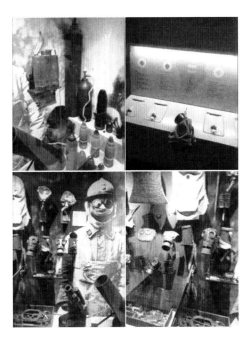

Gas delivery and protection technology and gas-smell experience on display in 2018 at the Memorial Museum Passchendaele 1917.

---

[399] Online: https://en.wikipedia.org/wiki/Chemical_weapons_in_World_War_I.
[400] Online: https://en.wikipedia.org/wiki/Extermination_camp.

A visit to the Memorial Museum Passchendaele[401] 1917 includes their extensive artifact museum and restored trench complex, including a safe smell station to get a scent of the different gases used during the war, so you get a sense of what soldiers would smell before its effects took them over.

Balloons, Zeppelins and Aircraft

The view from above was used since the Civil War to provide reconnaissance and perform artillery spotting (guide indirect fire to enemy targets) Although lighter-than-air craft in the form of hot-air balloons had been envisioned, if not tried, to attack enemy cities and positions since the late 1700s,[402] both lighter-and-heavier-than-air aircraft became a permanent part of war during World War I. Zeppelins[403] and heavier-than-air biplane bombers first hit London and other sites in England in World War I,[404] returning in far greater numbers with more advanced technology and lethality, and eventually using the first cruise and ballistic missiles, a generation later in World War II.

Nieuport 17 at the Thiepval Museum on the Somme Battlefield.

---

[401] Online: https://www.passchendaele.be/en/.
[402] Online: https://en.wikipedia.org/wiki/Incendiary_balloon.
[403] Online: https://en.wikipedia.org/wiki/Zeppelin.
[404] Online: https://en.wikipedia.org/wiki/German_strategic_bombing_during_World_War_I.

MONUMENTS TO THE DEAD: AMERICAN WWI CEMETERIES

American Cemeteries in Europe hold those Americans who made the ultimate sacrifice, to save the lives and future of France and Belgium. They are among the most important sites to visit and are all important in capturing my intent to speak for these guys, as I do at Antietam and other Civil War cemeteries in the United States. Our tour visited many American, British and German Cemeteries. The five American Cemeteries we visited are:

- Oise-Aisne American Cemetery[405] and Memorial in France, holding 6,012 American war dead, most of whom lost their lives while fighting near the cemetery in 1918. Our tour had a couple with us who had an ancestor buried there. The Cemetery Supervisor, Mike Kelly, the family and I conducted a ceremony at the site and the family received the American flag, brought down every day at 4 PM (and as a veteran, I participated in the flag-folding ceremony). The Supervisor showed us the grave of Joyce Kilmer, the American poet who wrote "Trees," killed by a German sniper only a few hundred yards from the cemetery.
- The Aisne-Marne American Cemetery[406] holds 2,289 war dead, most of whom fought in the vicinity and in the Marne Valley in the summer of 1918. It is the only cemetery in which the graves and their markers are concentric around one end of the hill containing Belleau Wood. I learned this from the Cemetery Supervisor, who met with me at the end of our visit.

---

[405] Online: https://abmc.gov/cemeteries-memorials/europe/oise-aisne-american-cemetery, particularly the introductory video on their website.

[406] Online: https://abmc.gov/cemeteries-memorials/europe/aisne-marne-american-cemetery, particularly the introductory video on their website.

American WWI Cemeteries managed by the American Battlefield Monuments Commission (ABMC). (1-2) Oise-Aisne; (3-4) Aisne-Marne; (5-6) Somme; (7-8) Flanders Fields; (9-10) Meuse-Argonne.

- The Somme American Cemetery[407] and Memorial in France contains the graves of 1,844 American military dead. From the Cemetery Supervisor we heard stories of particular soldiers interred here, and she showed us photographs and gave personal stories, as we had heard at other cemeteries.

---

[407] Online: https://abmc.gov/cemeteries-memorials/europe/somme-american-cemetery.

- The Flanders Field American Cemetery[408] and Memorial in Belgium contains 368 American military dead, most of whom fought in Belgium. Every one of the war dead, including the few unknowns, has been "adopted" by a Belgian citizen, who attempt to contact descendants and otherwise attempt to learn something about their war dead.
- The Meuse-Argonne American Cemetery[409] and Memorial in France contains 14,246 American military dead, the largest number of American war dead burials in Europe. Included are the names of 954 names of the missing.

BIBLIOGRAPHY

This bibliography is thanks to Geoffrey Blaha, an experience Ed Bearss tour-goer:

Davenport, Matthew J., *First Over There: The Attack on Cantigny*. New York: Thomas Dunne Books, 2015.

Keegan, John, *An Illustrated History of The First World War*. New York: Knopf, 2001.

Kelly, Michael, *Hero on the Western Front: Discovering Alvin York's WWI Battlefield*. Barnsley, UK: Frontline Books, 2018.

Libby, Frederick. *Horses Don't Fly: A Memoir of World War I*. New York: Arcade Publishing 2002.

Remarque, Erich Maria. *All Quiet on The Western Front*. New York: Ballantine Books, 1987.

Strachan, Hew, *The First World War*. New York, Penguin, 2005.

Tuchman, Barbara W. *The Guns of August*, New York: Presidio, 2004.

---

[408] Online: https://abmc.gov/cemeteries-memorials/europe/flanders-field-american-cemetery.
[409] Online: https://abmc.gov/cemeteries-memorials/europe/meuse-argonne-american-cemetery.

Videos

Videos on World War I include:

- *World War I*. DVD. New York: CBS News. 1964.
- *The First World War: The Complete Series*. DVD. Chatsworth, CA: RLJ Entertainment, 2005.

ADDENDUM:
SERGEANT YORK: WHERE WAS HIS FIGHT?

Robert Irving Desourdis

Dedication

This addendum is dedicated to the memory of Harry Rupert, who I met and appreciated as an enthusiastic supporter of Mike Kelly's engagement with the Nolan Group in finding and verifying the true Sgt. York action site.

The editor, Bob Desourdis (left), with the late Harry Rupert in Chatel-Chéhéry, France, October 2018.

Walking the Ground at the York Action Site

A York Site controversy has emerged because an earlier effort to locate and memorialize the York action site. Mike Kelly, from the UK, was part of the current "Nolan Team" from Tennessee who found what I believe they proved scientifically – based on Ed Bearss's National Park Service career – to be the actual site (in all probability) about 600 meters away from the a second memorial with markers. The Nolan Group of professionals used metal detectors and scientific archeology methods that found York's 328 Co. G artifacts (among other relevant items), GPS technology for artifact logging (the other amateur group did not) and German and American historical records (including burial records).

Ed explained an online video for Mike Kelly that the Nolan Group's best-practices combining history and archeology to get to truth matched what he would have accepted in a National Park Service report when he was Chief Historian, whereas the other approach would have been colloquialized, when he was in the Government, as "pot hunting."

Nolan versus amateur results – interviewed on Ed Bearss's front porch.

2018 Visit to the Actual York Action Site[410]

Background

As the editor (Desourdis) of the Ed Bearss memoir, and given Ed Bearss peripheral involvement in the Sgt. York story (see above) and his expertise in historical interpretation for the US Government, I was strongly motivated to go on a 2018 WWI tour with Mike Kelly, David Curry, Dr. Michael Birdwell and others from the State of Tennessee in October 2018. I also had been well versed through many tours with the importance of *walking the ground* as well as the use of professional tools in making history, not "pot hunting."

One of the important sites we visited was the York-action site, where Kelly, Curry and Birdwell were among the professional researchers, archeologists (American and French), and technical experts that did the necessary historical reference and data correlation from multiple historic sources, authorized metal detection and site digs. This addendum provides a narrative description of my education and experience at what I believe from the professional research performed and artifact evidence found *is* the true York Action site, 600 meters from a constructed (earth disturbed) memorial site. We visited both the actual site and the built memorial site. Detailed history of the York fight, American and German historical records, period maps and recovered (telling) artifacts, and much more, are fully documented in Michael Kelly's book, which I read before my trip to the actual site.

The narrative that follows contains many images extracted from video I took on the tour. Each photograph is numbered to indicate what was happening at the moment that image was captured, particularly when those experts present pointed at a particular land feature. These images are consecutively numbered and presented in the order they were taken.

---

[410] Online: https://ezinearticles.com/?The-Discovery-of-Alvin-C-Yorks-Firing-Position-in-the-Argonne-Forest-France-2006&id=1231565.

Trip to the Site

We left the Logis Hôtel, le Cheval Rouge Hotel in Sainte-Menehould,[411] and drove to the Commune of Chatel-Chéhéry, where we met with (the late) Mr. Harry Rupert, who provided a lecture on the 2017 South Mountain Expeditions WWI tour with Mike Kelly and Ed Bearss, covering the American attack through the town and the hills behind it – a preamble to the York Medal of Honor action. He has since been active in validating and verifying the true Sgt. York action site, monitoring its gradual destruction by a French logging company, and served as our guide to the actual site.

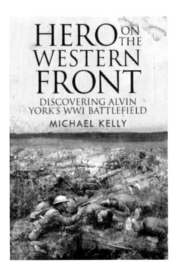

We drove to a field adjacent to a remote building and started down a logging road, and the York site team identified one of the machine-gun positions captured following the York action. We walked off the road led by Harry Rupert to an area behind the medieval dam used by a local monastery (recently damaged, they believed, by French logging activity), and Mike Kelly, began to point out what was believed to be the sequence of action of York's patrol to get behind German machine-gun positions.

---

[411] Online: https://www.logishotels.com/en/hotel/logis-hotel-le-cheval-rouge-2143.

On the way, I was told that when they first arrived here in 2006, tree branches had American memorials affixed, and the hill to our left was – for the last century – called "York's Hill."[412] We cut across the valley to our right and Mike Kelly points out where they believe York's men came down from the hill and passed by where we were standing up to the road, we had left some tens of yards back. Pointing to the crest of York's Hill, Mike Kelly described the movement of York's patrol ordered to try to outflank machine guns threatening his commands direction of attack.

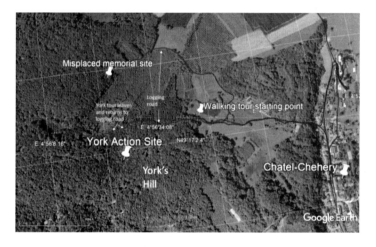

Location of the York Medal-of-Honor action site and the misplaced monument. The track is from the MotionX GPS[413] tracking software I had on my iPhone. Transformative fair use.

Ninety Prisoners

They infiltrated over York's Hill. They follow the line along until they got to a point [(1)], we think, you can't be exact, but just over here [he points to the right side of York's Hill], and they decided to come down [(2)], and they got we think somewhere where the road is [(3) Mike Kelly points to the road [(4)] we had been travelling until cutting left towards York's Hill], and they saw the two German's with Red Cross brassards on their arm [5], and they [the Germans] turned and ran in this direction [(6) where Mike Kelly and I were standing].

---

[412] Kelly, Michael. *Ibid.*, p. 117.
[413] Online: http://gps.motionx.com/.

The Americans formed a skirmish line across [(7) he motions a line across the direction of the Germans flight] and attacked in this direction [he points towards the stream (8)] and they go as far as this stream. They talk about it being a lot of foliage and a lot of undergrowth at that time, so it's probably thicker than it is now.

(1) Mike Kelly pointed to the right side of York's Hill and said they believe York's unit came down the right side of this hill towards our direction. (2) York's men moved through here and to the right of the image. (3) Mike Kelly points to the road (4) opposite York's Hill the historians they then moved. (5) Mike Kelly said York's men then spotted two Germans, indicating the red cross brassards on their arms. (6) The Germans ran through where we were standing beyond us toward a stream. (7) Mike Kelly motions the skirmish line athwart the direction of the Germans, then moving towards the stream (8) following the German's escape path. (9) Once at the stream, they saw Germans on the others side, fired some rounds, and about 90 Germans put their hands up.

But when they got to that stream, they looked over the other side, and there was something like 90 Germans sitting having breakfast. There were a few shots fired by the Americans. Immediately they capitulated [the Germans], held their hands up [(9)], surrendered, and they preceded then to round up the prisoners. It was then that the German machine gun opened fire on them.

The German Machine Guns Open Fire

Harry pointed out that the machine gun that opened fire on the Americans was just above the base of York's Hill behind the dam (8). Mike Kelly then said "That's the one that did the business, Harry." David Curry said "We dug it" and Dr. Birdwell responded "We sure did." We then walked towards the stream and Mike Kelly started to talk about their earlier search expedition.

> I can't be precise without the coordinates, but myself and Jim Deppen were digging, if you remember, there's a photograph of us digging this bloody great hole. All of a sudden, I got this little "ping," so I thought it [was] something very, very small, and so we carried on going through this clay substance, it was all ... and eventually found this disk. Jim went down to the stream to wash it, and do you remember the holler?

Dr. Birdwell, replicating Jim Deppen, yelled out "328, 328!" Mike Kelly said "That came back 328, Company G, and that was the first indication we had of the unit being in this direction."[414] Dr. Birdwell then walked to what he said was the little "spit of land" into the stream where the hole was dug. Mike Kelly explained the likely events at this location.

> So, what we think happened here is that this [the soldier ID disk marked with "328G"] was from one of the casualties, one of the American casualties, who stood this side of the stream while the others went over, and when the machine gun opened fire, whether it be that one [pointing up York's Hill where there was a second machine gun] or whether it be that one [pointing in the direction of the machine gun low on the hill behind the dam], whatever, he became a casualty.

From the edge of the stream, Mike Kelly pointed out where (10) machine-gun fire likely opened fire on this casualty, then pointed to the other side of the stream where the 90 German prisoners surrendered, and explained that he had wanted to take us through the events on Oct. 8, 1918,

---

[414] Kelly, Michael. *Ibid.*, p. 149.

while pointing out where he found the prisoner-discarded and burial artifacts.[415] We crossed the stream (14-15) and I captured the burial site (16) and stream (17) before crossing over and noting an overgrown tree stump (18) that Dr. Birdwell pointed out was likely there when the York action occurred.

(10) We move through the dense undergrowth toward the stream (11), where they encountered 90 Germans on the other side, who had surrendered. (12) When the prisoners were being handled, that's when a German machine gun at the base of York's Hill behind the dam opened fire on Americans away from the prisoners. (13) Mike Kelly recounts digging a large hole where he got a small metal-detector signal, and they found a small disc (14) covered with clay. His cohort digging the hole took it to the stream to wash it off (15), and it was a 328th Regiment, Company G, ID disc. Proving York's unit was here and they were digging at what they had read was likely an American first-burial grave site. (16) Mike Kelly explains that what had happened there was that a man had stayed on this side (our side at this point) of the stream and he was killed when the machine gun at (17) opened fire. (18) Dr. Birdwell had walked to where Mike Kelly and Jim Deppen dug the hole and found the disc.

---

[415] Kelly, Michael. Chapter 20 "The Artefacts from the Third Phase" and Chapter 24 "The Archaeologists and the Science." *Ibid.*, pp 186-203 and pp. 235-241.

(19) Mike Kelly at edge of stream pointing our direction of fire from the machine gun that may have hit the casualty yielding the 328G ID disc. (20) Mike Kelly points out where the prisoners were located in 1918 and where they found a large amount of discarded German-infantry equipment. (21) Mike Kelly indicates they found no remains of a wooden shack that York and others mention as being located within the prisoners, and it was not found anywhere else. (22) Harry Rupert reiterates the direction York and the rest of his 17-man patrol took form York's Hill into the ravine. (23) Mike Kelly emphasizes our effort to track events chronologically in our York-site tour. (24) Mike Kelly crosses the stream reported to be at the action site, and I captured the digging site producing the "328G" disk (25), the shallow stream October 2018 (26), and the likely 1918-period-tree stump (27) pointed out by Dr. Birdwell.

Sgt. York's Location

Dr. Birdwell and Harry Rupert walked to where all believe York was protected by the terrain (a few inches of earth) from German fire that day. He described and pointed out a concavity in the base of the hill, that likely protected York because it meant Germans firing at York had to raise up to see him in this depression. Mike Kelly summarizes the reason York survived:

> See where there's the depression in the hillside, and the picture of him shows him standing next to the depression, and as he said, the Germans couldn't see him, but they had to put their heads up over the gun to depress the barrel, then he could see their heads but they could not see him, because he's in that depression.

The Great War Tour 233

(28) Harry Rupert (foreground) follows Dr. Birdwell toward the York firing position, he stops and points it out to us (29). (30) Dr. Birdwell depicts the concavity of the ground in the depression believed to be the terrain feature that protected him. (31) Dr. Birdwell shows the area behind him that was likely where York was stationed for his Medal-of-Honor fight, and emphasized the depression in the base of York's Hill (32). (33) Dr. Birdwell explains that the depression meant that the machine gunners could not depress the gun low enough to get York hidden in the depression, but they had to expose their heads to York to see him – and his superior sharpshooting ability meant they would be picked off. (34) Mike Kelly is pointing to a German 08 m/g position at the top of the hill where we located German cartridges, both live and expended. He believes this is the gun that was in transit at the time of the capture of the German prisoners. The diagram on page 228 by Dr Nolan in Mike Kelly's book clearly demonstrates that this gun's field of fire would have been able to hit the patrol. See page 226 of the book for the explanations. (35) Mike Kelly said the machine gun with which York had his first dual therefore had to be the one he is pointing at behind me, so I turned and imaged the direction Mike Kelly was pointing behind Harry Rupert, where they found other vestiges of a machine-gun position. This image shows brightness which is the open area in the direction of York's command's eventual attack, so it is likely the gunners had to turn their machine gun around to deal with York's group coming in from behind them.

He demonstrated how York was protected by the depression, and could not have been hit, much less seen, from high up on York's Hill.

(37) I climbed York's Hill and looked down at the people below, where possibly a few of the American casualties were located – note that period images show far fewer trees. (38) Turning to the west I am looking in the direction where York's men had come down what became York's Hill and got behind the front German line.

I climbed York's Hill to see the view from where they found vestiges of a light German machine gun. Although American soldiers farther from the base of the hill could have been hit from up there, it was unlikely to be engaged with York located in the depression area (32) as illustrated in a line-of-sight terrain map in Mike Kelly's book.[416] Mike Kelly clarified the role of the machine gun traces found there:

> The upper placed m/g would not be the one that York charged (if ever he did charge one), the slope was too steep, the distance too great; he would have been shot long before he got up the slope, and he would have been running with Lt Vollmer chasing him!! Extremely unlikely. My comments on page 227 [of his book] encompass all this.

---

[416] Kelly, Michael. *Ibid.*, p. 228.

The Great War Tour

(39-41) Mike Kelly crosses the stream to take a photo where four of our tour group stood where the burial artifacts were found for Swanson, Wareing, Weiler and Dymowski. (42-45) We walk the half-mile or so (quarter mile "as the crow flies") to the invented York site where the misplaced site was installed. (46-48) The historic plaque at the site with the erred identification photo of York and Vollmer – discovered originally in our group earlier by Harry Ruppert (note the AM sunshine in the clearing as the hill faces the wrong direction). The plaque states that the actual York site is located 70-m downhill from the memorial, another error, it is actually about 400-m south (49) Just behind the misplaced memorial site, Mike Kelly points out where the 77-m German artillery was located – not part of the York action site, but documented in German and American histories (another "bug"). (50) Mike Kelly, Harry and Dr. Birdwell review the "bugs" in the invented site that either failed to research and prove, through history and archeology, or perhaps ignored when findings did not match the inventor's hopes.

The 1918 Photo

I came back down the hill and saw Mike Kelly make a photograph of the location where a 1918 photo shows the initial burials of Pvt. Wareing,

Pvt. Dymowski, Pvt. Swanson and Pvt. Weiler.[417] We positioned two of the group where they appeared to best match the ground from the 1918 photo.

Sergeant Alvin C. York at the hill where his actions earned him the Medal of Honor (February 7, 1919). Public domain. Retrieved from https://upload.wikimedia.org/wikipedia/commons/0/03/Alvin_C._York_shows_hill_on_which_raid_took_place_HD-SN-99-02157.JPEG. The late Harry Ruppert standing where the group believed York stood for his site photo in October 2018. Harry, in his retirement, had become an excellent onsite historian and guide regarding American history at the York site.

The Built Memorial

We then got back on the logging road we had left to go to the true York site, and continued along the pseudo-prepared trail to the distant memorial site. Once there, we looked at the bulldozed area and installed plaques, and Harry Rupert pointed out a fallacy in the identification of people in a photo on the memorial plaque. The text on the plaque states that the photo shows York and one of his prisoners, Lt. Paul Jurgen Vollmer, in the photo. According to the US Army Signal Corps, the photo was taken September 26, 1918, 12 days before the York action and the capture of Lt. Vollmer and other soldiers. In addition, the faces are dissimilar when looking more closely than the casual tourist would do, and those who would assume, "If it's on a monument, it must be correct."

---

[417] Kelly, Michael. *Ibid.*, p. 171.

Are these people actually these soldiers identified on the memorial plaque? Harry Ruppert discovered this apparent discrepancy.

We walked the installed path to the misplaced memorial site, where its creators (addressed in Mike Kelly's book[418]) have bulldozed the site after a "pot-hunting" effort, far less effort was spent scientifically verifying the find. Mike Kelly showed us where they found 77-mm artillery artifacts immediately behind and to one side of the memorial site. Apparently, this material was not collocated historically with the true York site, and Mike Kelly pointed out it had been found and he believed hidden by the creators of the misplaced site for that reason.

For me, the evidence for the Nolan Groups find of the true York Medal-of-Honor site is indisputable:

1. The Nolan site shows real artifact evidence of all six temporary burials from the York action, including a 328G (York's unit) ID disk, the other site produced no such positive proof at all of York's unit's presence. Had the men died near the built memorial, they would have been buried there and not brought a quarter-mile away and buried where the Nolan Group found them.

---

[418] Kelly, Michael. "Chapter 25 The SYDE Claims," *Ibid.*, pp. 242-257.

2. In 1919, a group of army officers visited the site to learn the facts of the encounter and to substantiate the award of the Medal of Honor. The group included Capt. Danforth and Maj. Gonzalo Edward Buxton Jr.,[419] so they knew where the site was. The map was annotated separately by Danforth and Buxton in 1929 for use at a re-enaction of the battle during an Army War Carnival. (See the Mike Kelly book.) They subsequently produced their own map of where it was located, which were used by the Nolan Group and proven accurate given the artifacts found and the historic literature, photographs and descriptions. Presumably, the creators of the misplaced monument site discounted these maps, or decided they were in error, much like their claim that the Signal Corps made an error in documenting the date of the photos of the erroneously identified Vollmer and York images. It is surprising the Americans helped win the war given their apparently error-prone nature.
3. Independent recall of the event and subsequent investigation and period maps state that the action site was on the side of a west-facing hill. While at the misplaced memorial site, the bright sunshine and compass directions show that hillside faces east – more American military errors? No.

There are many other more detailed deviations from fact-toward-fancy reflected by an analysis of the misplaced memorial site.[420] In the end, I endorse the conclusions of the Kelly book, reporting on the work of the Nolan Group.

---

[419] Online: https://en.wikipedia.org/wiki/G._Edward_Buxton_Jr..
[420] Kelly, Michael. Chapter 28 "The Analysis of the SYDE Claims," *Ibid.*, pp. 269-282.

The Great War Tour

York and his unit fought, and six of them died and were initially buried, in this location. The current memorial marker is about a quarter mile from the actual action site.

I had set out to live vicariously in the excitement the Nolan Group had in discovering the true York Medal of Honor site. I hope in this addendum to have at least furthered the Nolan Group efforts, if for no other reason, to properly commemorate where six men died and will be forever in the shadow of Sgt. York's gallant efforts. His efforts were to protect himself and his men, for which he used his supreme sharpshooting skills. York was also blessed (York might say "by God") to have been protected by the terrain, as Ed Bearss was at Suicide Creek, by **"a few inches of earth."** You have to walk the terrain, as these gentlemen and, luckily, I was able to do because of them. I thank them for making my visit possible. I was able to apply what I have learned from Ed Bearss in *walking the ground* to understand the action at the true York site.

Chapter 7

THE BEARSS IN HISTORY

NATIONAL PARK SERVICE RELATIONSHIPS

One of the greatest contributions Ed Bearss brought to the Park Service was the collaboration of several key people to build American history for Americans in a shorter time than any other History Program in the NPS. This collaboration between Chief Historian Ed Bearss and Sen. Dale L. Bumpers,[421] Sec. Manuel A. Lujan[422] of Interior, George B. Hartzog[423] as National Park Service Director, his immediate boss Jerry Rogers, achieved this success "making American history" nationwide.

NATIONAL PARK SERVICE PUBLICATIONS

The Chapter 8 Addendum in *Walking the Ground: Making American History* (the second book of the Ed Bearss memoir series) presented a summary of 90 publications he has authored or coauthored since joining the Park Service. He started in Vicksburg in September, 1955, and his first

---

[421] Online: https://en.wikipedia.org/wiki/Dale_Bumpers.
[422] Online: https://en.wikipedia.org/wiki/Manuel_Lujan_Jr.
[423] Online: https://en.wikipedia.org/wiki/George_B._Hartzog_Jr..

report digitized so far came out in 1957, titled Do*cumented Narrative to Support Historical Features and Vegetative cover Shown on the Pea Ridge Historical Base Map Part of the Master Plan Pea Ridge National Military Park, Rogers, Arkansas*, and the last one so far digitized from 1993, "Delivering a Powerful Interpretive Message." *Cultural Resources Management.*

History Tours

Chapter 1 lists the tours he has done for South Mountain Expeditions, a small portion of the overall Civil War and other tours he's done during and after his National Park Service career.

Publications and Awards

Ed Bearss has written, edited, or contributed to 19 books and more than 100 articles in his long and productive career as follows:

Though Ed Bearss didn't know what it meant, here's his daughter Ginny's "pic stitch" for Father's Day on her Facebook page.

AUTHORED BOOKS

1. *Decision in Mississippi* (Little Rock, Arkansas, 1962).
2. *Rebel Victory at Vicksburg* (Little Rock, Arkansas, 1963).
3. *Hardluck Ironclad: The Sinking and Salvage of the Cairo* (Baton Rouge, Louisiana, 1966).
4. *Battle of Cowpens: A Documented Narrative and Troop Movement Maps* (Washington, DC, 1967).
5. *Steele's Retreat from Camden and the Battle of Jenkins' Ferry* (Little Rock, Arkansas, 1967).
6. *Fort Smith: Little Gibraltar on the Arkansas* (Norman, Oklahoma, 1969), with A. M. Gibson.
7. *Protecting Sherman's Lifeline: The Battles of Brice's Cross Roads and Tupelo*, 1864 (Washington, DC, 1971).
8. *The Battle of Wilson's Creek* (Bozeman, Montana, 1975).
9. *Forrest at Brice's Cross Roads and in North Mississippi in 1864* (Dayton, Ohio, 1979).
10. *Battle of Five Forks* (Lynchburg, Virginia, 1985), with Chris Calkins.
11. *Campaign for Vicksburg*, 3 vols. (Dayton, Ohio, 1986).
12. *First Manassas Battlefield Study* (Lynchburg, Virginia, 1990).
13. *The Campaign for Vicksburg: I Vicksburg Is the Key, II Grant Strikes a Fatal Blow, III Unvexed to the Sea* (Payson, Arizona, 1991).
14. *River of Lost Opportunities: The Civil War on the James River* (Lynchburg, Virginia, 1995).
15. *Smithsonian's Great Battles and Battlefields of the Civil War* (New York, New York, 1997), with Jay Wertz.
16. *Fields of Honor: Pivotal Battles of the Civil War* (Washington, D.C. 2007), Introduction by James M. McPherson.
17. *Receding Tide: Vicksburg and Gettysburg: The Campaigns That Changed the Civil War* (Washington, D.C., 2010), with J. Parker Hills.

18. *The Petersburg Campaign. Volume 1: The Eastern Front Battles, June - August 1864*, (El Dorado Hills, California, 2012), with Bryce Suderow.

Other citations can be found online, including my television commentary in addition to the Ken Burns series.[424]

Edited Books

1. *A Southern Record: History of the Third Louisiana Regiment*, by Willie Tunnard (Dayton, Ohio, 1970).
2. *A Louisiana Confederate: Diary of Felix Pierre Poché* (Natchitoches, Louisiana, 1972).
3. *Memoirs of a Confederate, Historic and Personal: Campaigns of the First Missouri Confederate Brigade* (Dayton, Ohio, 1972).
4. *Your Affectionate Husband, J. F. Culver: Letters Written during the Civil War* (Iowa City, Iowa, 1978), with Leslie W Dunlap.

Contributors

1. *The Civil War Battlefield Guide* (New York, New York, 1998), edited by Frances H. Kennedy.
2. *Human Collaboration in Homeland Security*, 1st Foreword, by Robert Irving Desourdis and Kuan Hengameh Collins, (NOVA Science Publishers, 2017).

---

[424] Online: https://en.wikipedia.org/wiki/Ed_Bearss.

AWARDS

A partial list of awards – there have been many others, but no record-keeping about them – is provided below building on those listed in John C. Waugh's 2003 *Edwin Cole Bearss: History's Pied Piper* book.

1. Chicago Civil War Round Table $1,000 award to the individual or group that has done most to preserve Civil War battlefields.
2. Civil War Preservation Trust, Edwin C. Bearss Award for Leadership in the Preservation of Civil War Sites; Ed Bearss was its first recipient.
3. National Park Service Edwin C, Bearss Fellowship Award, established on his retirement to fund advance studies for NPS employees.
4. Letter of Commendation from the Secretary of the Army for his Key Role in Efforts to Resume Army Staff Rides.
5. Department of the Interior's Distinguished Service Award, its highest honor, rarely given prior to someone's retirement; Ed got his 12 years before he retired.
6. Elected a member (1964), then a Fellow, in the Company of Military Historians (1966).
7. First Annual Harry S Truman Award for meritorious service in the field of Civil War History.
8. Virginius Dabney Award from the Museum of the Confederacy for outstanding contributions to public understanding of the Confederacy and the American Civil War.
9. *Man of the Year* at Vicksburg in 1963.
10. B. L. C. Wailes Award for 1998-99, the State of Mississippi's highest historical award.
11. First award of the Pat Cleburne Sword by the Coalition of Arkansas Round Tables.
12. Bell I. Wiley Award from the New York Civil War Round Table.
13. Honorary Doctorate Lincoln College, 2005.

14. Honorary Doctorate of Humane Letters from Gettysburg College, 2010.
15. Nevins-Freeman Award for work in Civil War History from the Civil War Round Table of Chicago.
16. First Annual T. Harry Williams Award, from the Baton Rouge Civil War Round Table.

And the enduring gratitude of countless other Civil War Round Tables to which he has cheerfully spoken, pacing their rostrums, without a single note, without a microphone, without honoraria, and without a single dull moment.

James Lighthizer, President, American Battlefield Trust, Ed Bearss & William W. Vodra, Trustee, American Battlefield Trust. With permission, retrieved from http://www.battleofchampionhill.org/images/img_9179.jpg.

Recently, and it is fitting given the Ed Bearss's long-time Vicksburg connections, he received his first monument, a brass plaque mounted on granite at Champion Hill.[425] He has seen many monuments since he joined

---

[425] Online: http://www.battleofchampionhill.org/.

the Park Service in 1955, it is fitting for him to now be one of them and at Champion Hill, certainly one of the best places for it.

MY FAMILY IN HISTORY

It's been over 25 years since John C. Waugh's *Edwin Cole Bearss: History's Pied Piper* book was published and things have changed. Since then, Ed Bearss's wife and oldest daughter Sara, have passed away, the "lay of the land" when your 96 years old. The family interviews reported by John Waugh will not be repeated here and some are still available online, but instead, we present their contributions to history and Ed Bearss's descendants, his true legacy.

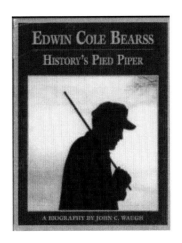

It was difficult being Ed Bearss's wife and kids when his work for the National Park Service was his No. 1 focus, morning, noon and night. Anything or anyone keeping him from that devotion had to make do without his presence, mentally and emotionally, if not physically. He is driven to his life's passion every waking hour, and had trouble with anything that prevented him from doing so, particularly when he was Chief Historian. However, beyond Ed Bearss, his wife and eldest daughter also made their contribution to the public knowledge of their American heritage.

MARGIE RIDDLE BEARSS

Ed Bearss's wife, Margie Riddle Bearss,[426] was interested in Civil War history, particularly personalities, and that led to his meeting her and following up for other dates, and eventually, marriage. Margie wrote

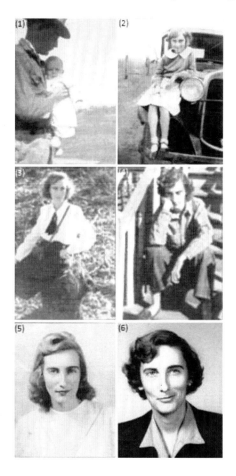

(1) Margie as a baby; (2) a girl in Mississippi; (3-5) when Ed Bearss met her; (6) As Ed Bearss's wife.

---

[426] Online: https://www.nps.gov/vick/learn/news/mbearssday.htm, http://opac2.mdah.state.ms.us/phpmanuscripts/z2022.php and http://battleofchampionhill.org/vignettes/margie.htm.

Sherman's Forgotten Campaign: The Meridian Expedition[427] and worked with Elizabeth Joyner[428] on the *Cairo* artifacts and co-wrote a book[429] on the subject. She went on to work with Rebecca Blackwell Drake[430] on several books, and the two of them were very close.

> **How I Met My Wife Margie**
>
> ... and I said we have this diary from the 72nd Ohio, ... and she wrote back and said, "I'd like to see it," so I said "All right, it's available, you can come look at it." Now, this is my day off. So, I'm home and the junior historian calls me up. By this time, I've been transferred to the Regional Office, but assigned to ... Vicksburg. He calls me up and says, "There's a young lady here. Wants to see the diary that we have."
>
> All right, we're gonna interrupt, at the diary. Well, the diary is ...then I live about four miles from the park and I show up and I go in and the schoolteacher [Margie Riddle] is there, who had been corresponding with me, with a friend of hers who's come over with her. So, I find that she's rather interesting and that's where I met my wife.
>
> What Marty wants me to talk about is on our first date. I go up to see her, and we'll pick that up later on. [tour group laughs.] ... and that's what Marty wants me [to talk about].

In their book *Collected Stories of the Vicksburg Campaign*,[431] published after Margie's passing, Rebecca wrote a biography on the book cover flaps to honor Margie and her accomplishments as follows:

> Margie's eighty years of life were remarkable - but then Margie was a remarkable woman. She was born in Brandon, Mississippi, in 1925 and, during her early childhood years, developed a love for reading. One of her

---

[427] Online: https://www.amazon.com/Shermans-Forgotten-Campaign-Meridian-Expedition/dp/B002AVZMZ0.
[428] Online: https://www.federalpay.org/employees/national-park-service/joyner-elizabeth-h.
[429] Online: https://www.amazon.com/USS-Cairo-History-Artifacts-Gunboat/dp/0786422572/ref=sr_1_1?keywords=joyner+cairo+artifacts&qid=1581966473&s=books&sr=1-1.
[430] Online: http://battleofchampionhill.org/annex.htm
[431] Online: http://battleofchampionhill.org/collected_stories.htm.

fondest memories was sitting on the front porch with her father -- each with their head buried in a book. For the Riddle family, hardworking people who lived in rural Rankin County, books were hard to come by. Often, Margie would read whatever was available, included the family Bible. After high-school, she attended Hinds Junior College[432] and Blue Mountain College for Women[433] where she pursued her passion for literature, poetry, and history, most especially history related to the Civil War. These passions would remain with her for life.

In 1958, when Margie married Ed Bearss, Vicksburg National Military Park Historian, she embarked on the journey of a life time. The historic journey began in 1962 when she was awarded a contract to create the museum at Grand Gulf Military Park,[434] located along the banks of the Mississippi River north of Port Gibson. Together, Ed and Margie worked to help establish the park which officially opened in May 1962.

Margie's work at the fledgling museum was challenging and time consuming. Using her artistic talents, she created the diorama, maps, and many of the exhibits. She also sought to obtain Civil War artifacts from local families who lived in the area. Many of the items obtained by Margie remain on display today. As she and Ed worked to develop Grand Gulf Military Park, Ed was also involved in the planning stage to raise the USS *Cairo*, a Union iron-clad gunboat sunk by the Confederates in the Yazoo River in 1862. Passionate about accomplishing both projects, the couple constantly blazed a trail between Grand Gulf and the site of the *Cairo* north of Vicksburg.

The years 1962 - 1964 were banner years not only for Ed and Margie but also for the preservation of Mississippi history. In 1962, low water in the Big Black River near Bovina exposed the [wreckage] of the CSS *Charm* and portions of the CSS *Paul Jones*. Both vessels were torched by the Confederates on May 17, 1863, following the retreat from the Battle of the Big Black. As Margie explored the century-old [wreckage], she photographed and cleaned many of the relics. Her photography and research were placed in a hardbound scrapbook entitled *Charm, Paul Jones* and *Dot*. The scrapbook is invaluable in that it documents a major portion of Mississippi [River] history.

---

[432] Online: https://www.hindscc.edu/.
[433] Online: https://bmc.edu/.
[434] Online: http://battleofchampionhill.org/history/vignettes.htm.

Rebecca worked closely with Margie on several books and they became close friends. Margie died from heart failure in 2006, but left her own legacy of work even beyond the books she did with Rebecca Drake and Elizabeth Joyner.

(1) Margie Bearss and Rebecca Drake; (2) *Sherman's Forgotten Campaign: The Meridian Expedition* by Margie Riddle Bearss; (3) *Collected Stories of the Vicksburg Campaign*, Margie Riddle Bearss and Rebecca Blackwell Drake; (4) *Darvina's Diary: A View of Champion Hill ~ 1865*, edited by Margie R. Bearss & Rebecca B. Drake; (5) *My Dear Wife: The Civil War Letters of Sid and Matilda Champion* of Champion Hill.

In 2007, Rebecca Drake wrote a letter to the Civil War Preservation Trust[435] (CWPT) to emphasize Margie's contribution to their efforts, particularly in preserving the memory of the critical battle that was to determine the outcome of the Vicksburg Campaign. The letter is a tribute to Margie and all she did for the Champion Hill site. It points out that Margie's engagement with history was like mine, not just reading and writing books, but getting as close to it as one can. Hold and feeling the artifacts from the past helped draw her closer to the people she wrote about, much like my walking a battlefield draws me closer to those who fought and died there. Quoting key passages from the letter:

> During the last three years of her life, Margie Riddle Bearss helped to found Champion Heritage Trust and worked tirelessly to preserve the history of Mississippi's most precious and forgotten battlefields: Champion Hill and the Big Black River Bridge. Margie learned to love Champion Hill where she played as a child and the Big Black where Margie and Ed discovered the sunken remains of the *Paul Jones* and *Charm*.
>
> Margie was not content to read history; she had to touch and feel it. With the Champion Heritage Trust, she helped to bring history alive at Champion Hill so others could touch and feel it as well. She co-authored three books with Rebecca Drake on Champion Hill and the Vicksburg Campaign, and sponsored living history events on the hallowed grounds of the Champion Hill Battlefield. Hundreds filled Sid and Matilda Champion's lawn to participate in living history events, book signings, and of course, Matilda's favorite recipe for buttermilk pies. Funds for preserving the history and allow others to also touch and feel it as Margie loved to do were raised by sale of the three books dedicated to Champion Hill Heritage Trust which have raised over $10,000 since founding of the Trust three years ago.
>
> Although wheelchair bound, Margie was at the 2005 dedication of *My Dear Wife ~ Letters to Matilda, the Civil War Letters of Sid and Matilda Champion at Champion Hill*, an event in which, for the first time since 1863, the public was invited to be on the hallowed grounds of the

---

[435] Online: https://www.battlefields.org/about/civil-war-trust.

battlefield. When introduced, Margie received a thunderous standing ovation.

Margie Riddle Bearss and Rebecca Drake dedicate "My Dear Wife: Letters to Matilda ~ The Civil War Letters of Sid and Matilda Champion" in 2005 on the grounds of Matilda Champion's home. Also shown is Sid Champion (Sid V) with the honor guard and the table used for amputations recovered from the Champion house before it was burned in July 1863.

In 2006, Margie returned to Champion Hill when we dedicated *Darwina's Diary: A View of Champion Hill ~ 1865*. The crowd was huge and again Margie received a well-deserved standing ovation. That would be her last appearance on the battlefield. She passed away in 2006 before we could dedicate our third and final book, *Collected Stories of the Vicksburg Campaign*. Margie would have been very proud to see the historic marker that we erected on the site of the original Champion House. The marker, the first of its kind at Champion Hill was placed there using the money raised through the sale of our books.

While failing in health, Margie continued to contribute to expand on the history of Champion Hill by writing articles and vignettes for www.BattleofChampionHill, the official website for the Battle of Champion Hill. A wonderful collection of Margie's vignettes based upon her memories stemming from her childhood spent there as well as memories of walking and studying the battlefield with Ed. Some of the vignettes were recorded and placed on the website where visitors will be held spellbound as they hear Margie read her memories of Champion Hill.

In her memory the Champion Heritage Foundation placed a large memorial stone in her memory, on the grounds of Sid and Matilda's second house (circa 1865) beneath the crepe myrtle tree where we held all of our book signings.

Our work will continue on in the future. Margie's youngest daughter, Ginny Bearss, has filled Margie's seat on the board of the Champion Heritage Foundation with the other board members Sid Champion, Jim Drake, Terry Brantley, and me [Rebecca Drake]. We continue to work with Sid Johnson Champion to help others to touch and feel history as Margie did by hosting large annual events on the Champion property.

Sid Johnson Champion (Sid V) proudly standing beside the first historic marker placed at Champion Hill. The marker honors the lives of his great-great grandparents, Sid and Matilda Champion, whose house was used as a Union hospital during and after the Battle of Champion Hill, then, after the Siege of Vicksburg, was burned by the Union.

Since Margie played such a prominent role in the opening of Champion Hill to the public, I think the CWPT might want to recognize her efforts and applaud the final three years of her life. In spite of living in the face of death, Margie never quit working and was always anxious to do everything possible to promote living history Champion Hill.

It was my honor to be her friend and her co-editor during the final three years of her life. With Sid Champion and my husband, Jim, at my side, I will continue to promote Champion Hill as well as her memory – she was without doubt the Matriarch of Mississippi History.

Ed Bearss's love for history was apparently passed to their eldest daughter, Sara.

SARA BEARSS

The Library of Virginia[436] has done an excellent job in summarizing her respected work for them. John Deal, Public Services and Outreach, submitted notification of Sara's passing in the library's March 2012 edition of their e-newsletter:[437]

Library Mourns Passing of Sara Bearss

The Library of Virginia remembers our esteemed colleague Sara B. Bearss, who passed away on February 13, 2012, following a brief battle with cancer. Born in Vicksburg, Mississippi, she was raised in Arlington. She

---

[436] Online: https://www.lva.virginia.gov/.
[437] Library of Virginia, e-newsletter, March 2012, Online: http://www.lva.virginia.gov/news/newsletter/stories/2012_03-march.asp#sara.

received a B.A. from Mary Baldwin College in 1982 and an M.A. from the University of Virginia in 1984. A gifted writer and historian, from 1984 to 2000 she was managing editor of the *Virginia Magazine of History and Biography*[438] at the Virginia Historical Society.[439] During this time, she authored *The Story of Virginia: An American Experience* (1995) and cowrote *Foster's Richmond* (1991). From 1997 to 2001 she was president of the Conference of Historical Journals.[440]

Sara came to the Library of Virginia in 2000 as senior editor of the Dictionary of Virginia Biography.[441] Her able hand guided the production of volume two (which includes surnames Bland-Cannon) and volume three (Caperton-Daniels) of the DVB, as well as current work on volume four (Darden-Fiveash). In addition to the DVB, Sara's expert writing and editing skills were felt on a host of Library projects, including Union or Secession and other exhibitions; annual African American Trailblazers and Virginia Women in History programs; *Broadside*,[442] the Library's quarterly magazine; and the forthcoming *Changing History: Virginia Women Through Four Centuries*.[443] She was also a driving force behind the recently announced partnership between the Library of Virginia and the Virginia Foundation for the Humanities[444] to publish historical content from the Dictionary of Virginia Biography and other Library collections on Encyclopedia Virginia.[445]

A Latin scholar of uncommon intellect, she loved film, literature, theater, opera, and classical music. Those who worked with Sara quickly understood her devotion to proper grammar and fondly recall her e-mail tagline "Friends don't let friends split infinitives." She leaves many friends in the public history and academic community throughout Virginia. A fund

---

[438] Online: https://www.virginiahistory.org/collections/virginia-magazine-history-biography.
[439] Online: https://www.virginiahistory.org/.
[440] Online: https://www.historians.org/about-aha-and-membership/affiliated-societies/conference-of-historical-journals.
[441] Online: https://www.lva.virginia.gov/public/dvb/.
[442] Online: https://www.lva.virginia.gov/news/broadside/.
[443] Online: https://www.lva.virginia.gov/news/press/ChangingHistory.pdf.
[444] Online: https://dh.virginia.edu/organization/virginia-foundation-humanities-vfh.
[445] Online: https://www.encyclopediavirginia.org/.

to assist the Library's efforts to conserve rare books is being established in Sara's honor. Contributions may be made to the Library of Virginia Foundation, 800 E. Broad Street, Richmond, Virginia, 23219.

The Library of Virginia also established the Virginiana Conservation Fund in Sara's name, announcing its creation in their Spring 2012 edition of their quarterly magazine.[446]

> The Library of Virginia knows of no greater champion of Virginia history than the late Sara Bearss, a gifted writer, editor, and historian who had served as senior editor of the Library's Dictionary of Virginia Biography since 2000. Bearss passed away on February 13, 2012, following a brief battle with cancer. In response to the extraordinary outpouring of support from the historical community (and Bearss friends and colleagues from across the country), the Library of Virginia Foundation has established the Sara Bearss Virginiana Conservation Fund.[447] Proceeds from this fund will provide ongoing support for the conservation and preservation of items in our collection that make an indelible mark on Virginia's history and culture. Preservation of our shared history was Bearss's passion, and we are grateful for the opportunity to continue her legacy in this way.
>
> The Library has also adopted a rare book for conservation to honor Bearss. Among the many historical figures of interest to her, Henry Clay was near the top of the list. In an attempt to find a rare title in need of conservation that related to Clay, we surveyed our Special Collections holdings for just the right item. An 1837 Philadelphia imprint with a lengthy title (which we will abbreviate here), *The Speeches of Henry Clay*, delivered in the Congress of the United States, seemed to be the perfect selection because the cover bore a gilded, stamped inscription to "The Library of Virginia presented by Judge Francis T. Brooke, who was Clay's close friend, is included in the Dictionary of Virginian Biography, and his entry was written by Sara Bearss. The original red leather binding will be

---

[446] In Memoriam: "Sara Bearss Virginiana Conservation Fund: New Fund Established and Rare Book Adopted in Honor of our Late Colleague," Broadside: The Magazine of the Library of Virginia (March 2012): 12. Online: http://www.lva.virginia.gov/news/broadside/2012-Spring.pdf, p. 13.

[447] Online: http://www.cwrtgb.com/images/Bearss_Memorial_Fund.pdf.

restored; the text block will be cleaned, deacidified, and guarded with Japanese paper; and the book will receive a custom clamshell box.

To contribute to the Sara Bearss Virginiana Conservation Fund, please send your gift to: Library of Virginia Foundation, Sara Bearss Virginiana Conservation Fund, 800 E. Broad St., Richmond, VA 23219. For more information, or to make a gift, contact Dan Stackhouse at dan.stackhouse@lva.virginia.gov or (804) 692-3813.[448]

Ed Bearss appreciates the Library of Virginia's memorializing his daughter in this way for her commitment to them and Virginia history.

COLE BEARSS

Ed Bearss's son joined the Marines and has served his country for 13 years in the African Contingency Operations Training and Assistance (ACOTA).[449] He has a wife and one son, Edwin Michael Bearss, but his duties keep him fully engaged. He also now has a grandson, Edwin Michael Bearss, Jr.

GINNY BEARSS

Ginny joined the Marines and later worked for the State of Mississippi, still living in the Brandon area. Not only has she been a great help to the life needs of her 96-year-old father, including "walking the ground" on his current tours around the world, but she was a great comfort to both Ed Bearss's wife and his daughter Sara in their final days. She stayed with each of them when he *could not*, helpless to deal with it, perhaps the only time in his life – and she made sure they wanted for nothing at the end. Ed Bearss

---

[448] In Memoriam: "Sara Bearss Virginiana Conservation Fund: New Fund Established and Rare Book Adopted in Honor of our Late Colleague," *Broadside: The Magazine of the Library of Virginia* (March 2012): 12.
[449] Online: https://en.wikipedia.org/wiki/African_Contingency_Operations_Training_and_Assistance.

appreciates the role she played then and now and am forever indebted to her. Her job was far harder than his, and it can be likened to the pain he felt for his comrades at Suicide Creek.

Ginny as a Marine and with me on Omaha Beach in 2018.

ANDY AND TODD

Marine Corps Museum, Quantico, Virginia.

In addition to that role, Ginny's two sons, Andy and Todd, have made Ed Bearss proud, have been close to them for many years, and they have visited him more recently as they have long had their own cars. They have been with me at different parks and monuments. They have Thanksgivings together, Todd and Andy, when they can get together with their grandfather.

My Grandson Andy.

COMPUTERS AGAIN

Todd with his wife Danielle and their two kids. I hadn't held them much when Ginny's kids were little, but I am enjoying it now.

Andy is an Information Technology (IT) guru in Raleigh, North Carolina. Although, as Harry will say, Ed was not computer-friendly when they worked together, yet now he has a flip phone and an Ipad. He never typed a key on a computer keyboard in his life. Andy has taken his grandfather to a number of Washington Nationals[450] games, and he is a Braves fan.

ANOTHER MARINE

Todd is in the Marines. Attacjed to the 6th Marine Regiment as a Staff Sergeant at Camp LeJeune. He has currently served over nine years with one combat deployment. Todd's family has produced two children, making them Ed Bearss's great grandchildren. It's been a long time since Ed Bearss was near babies, his own or anyone else's, and he enjoys their visits with them and their father, Ed Bearss's grandson Todd. They are a great legacy for him and he hopes they will soon be able to understand his historical interpretation when he takes them out on a battlefield somewhere.

CLOSE PEOPLE

The following reminiscences are unique and representative of the many stories we did not have the space to include in this edition, so each story

---

[450] Online: https://www.mlb.com/nationals.

CHARLES IKINS, COL. USMC (RET.)
"THE NIGHT HISTORY CAME TO DINNER"

I well remember five nights in September 1990 when I was enthralled by Ken Burns' series "The Civil War." As we know, it set the standard (and still does) for historical documentary filmmaking. No one had seen anything like it before.

As I watched the series I was introduced to historians, both famous and not-so-famous (to me). One that stuck in my mind was a man that spoke slowly and in measured tones punctuated by gestures which emphasized his points. I remember thinking to myself "Who is this Ed Bearss?" While he was the Historian for the National Park Service, I was unfamiliar with him. After that series, no one was unfamiliar with Ed Bearss. He became part of popular culture.

It was in part because of that series and Ed Bearss that my interest in my family's participation in the Civil War was kindled. Little did I know that roughly 14 years later it would lead to Ed Bearss coming to my house for dinner.

So, I began investigating the family mystery of an ancestor rumored to have fallen at Gettysburg. Although spoken of in my childhood, no one knew if it was true, or if so, the name. After years of research and through an amazing coincidence I discovered the name, enlistment and discharge records, and even the hospital records from Letterman Hospital at Gettysburg, where my great-great-great uncle, Private Simeon Ikins of Company K of the 136th New York Volunteer Infantry, died of his wounds and gangrene after six weeks of suffering.

Unfortunately, due to a transcription error in burial records, he was buried at Gettysburg National Cemetery under the wrong name – J. C. Kent - for the next 130 years and thus was lost to history. I discovered this in the original Letterman cemetery burial log at the National Archives and the transcription error between two separate burial records was clearly evident. But I was leaving in three days, having been activated from the Marine Corps reserves for deployment to Kuwait and then the liberation of Iraq. So just before I left, I dropped in the mail to the Superintendent of Gettysburg National Military Park my evidence as to who was really buried under the name J.C. Kent. Six months later in Iraq, I received a letter from the Superintendent; he agreed with me and steps were taken to honor and recognize Private Ikins' memory.

After my return home in mid-2003, the story came to the attention of the Washington Post, which sent one of its star reporters to interview me. The paper also covered (and brought a photographer as well) the family memorial service I arranged for Private Ikins at Gettysburg National Cemetery in July 2003.

Imagine my surprise when a week later and walking down my front steps to get the paper, I found a photograph of myself in full dress uniform saluting at my ancestor's grave on the front page (and above the fold!) of the Sunday *Washington Post*. The entire journey I had made in search of my ancestor was recounted. Uncle Simeon finally had the recognition he'd been denied for 130 years.

Enter Ed Bearss. It so happened that my neighbor John Sprinkle across the street managed historical structures for the National Park Service and as he recounts it:

"I vividly recall Ed coming into the office on Eye Street one day with a copy of the Washington Post in hand. On the front page … was a picture of Charles in uniform saluting a grave at Gettysburg. Ed declared, "Now there's a Marine that I'd like to meet." You can imagine my elation when I got to reply, "Well Ed, it just so happens that I can arrange it."

So, when John came to my door and asked "How would you like to meet Ed Bearss?" I was a bit dumbfounded, but said something to the effect of "Hell, yes!" and extended a proxy invitation to dinner. It took a few months, but eventually in March 2004 there stood Ed Bearss – the Ed Bearss - in my living room. In researching Ed in advance of the evening I found that he had been a Marine in WWII and not just that but wounded (severely) in action on Cape Gloucester. I couldn't believe I somehow didn't already know that. So, this was a great honor as well as a historic (pun intended) opportunity for me.

My wife Debbie had prepared a special meal and Ed was clearly charmed by her (and she by him) as I peppered him with questions about WWII, his wounding, and his recovery. We discussed his participation in the making of the [Ken] Burns' series and his writing on the Civil War. He told stories about the Marines he had served with and I could tell he deeply loved the Corps as he asked me many questions about how it had done in Iraq. I wish I had known he had once met Gary Cooper because I would have asked about that as well. I had never met someone who shared my level of interest and love for both history and the Marine Corps. He was warm, funny, and fascinating and that dinner is remembered as one of the highlights in my life to date.

I had set aside a gift for Ed, something I thought he would appreciate from a historical perspective. All Marines in war love souvenirs; in Ed's war it was samurai swords, personal flags, and weapons. In Iraq, we weren't allowed to have any of those things, but I did have something unusual. My last posting in Iraq was at Saddam's palace at Babylon. When the First Marine Expeditionary Force headquarters arrived there, the palace had already been completely and thoroughly looted by an angry local citizenry. What wasn't hauled off was smashed. Broken pieces of French porcelain bidets and toilets were scattered everywhere, chandeliers pulled down from the ceilings and pieces of marble ornamentation ripped from the walls and smashed on the floor. I kept a chunk of marble from Saddam's bathtub as well as a piece of marble lying on the floor of his office (and which broke in two later in my baggage).

I took one of those two pieces and wrote on the back the place and date I picked it up and that it was presented to Ed Bearss as a souvenir of the latest war in which his beloved Marines were involved. He seemed touched by the gesture. We took pictures and I'm so glad we did as there is my late beautiful wife between Ed and I. You can tell from her face how happy she was that Ed was there (Ed looks happy too, standing next to a beautiful redhead).

I'm glad Ed is writing his memoir. They need to be written and they need to be read by anyone who wants to better understand history and the collective individual stories that weave its tapestry. If you want to understand the Civil War, you must read Ed Bearss.

And I can only hope that somewhere in Ed's office sits a small broken piece of marble as a reminder of the night the Civil War (and Marine Corps history) in the form of Ed Bearss, came to my house for dinner.

Semper Fi, Ed.

REBECCA BLACKWELL DRAKE

After Margie's death in October, 2006, his daughter, Jenny, and grandson, Andy, occasionally brought Ed to visit with Jim and me in Raymond. During one of the visits, he discovered a new historic marker in our garage that had been placed upside down for storage. The marker featured Brig Gen Alvin P. Hovey's famous quote on the "Hill of Death." Ed stopped for a moment to admire the marker then stood back and read the quote upside down - word-for-word. Jim recorded the reading on his cell phone and featured it on the homepage of the Battle of Champion Hill Website. I'll never forget Ed reading Hovey's chilling words describing the death and carnage that took place at Champion Hill in 1863. Now, every time I see the marker atop the Hill of Death, I think of Ed. America will never see another historian as gifted as Ed Bearss. Even at the age of 96, he is still giving tours of America's Civil War battlefields and continues to hold the reputation as being "The Pied Piper" of American History.

WENDY SWANSON

I met Ed through his history tours with the Smithsonian. Signing up for my first tour of this sort (The Defenses of Washington) truly changed my life, for doing so opened up so many new worlds for me: participation in various history groups, writing, researching and meeting a whole new circle of friends. Ed's generosity stands out among his notable traits. Through our conversations, Ed learned that my home town had plans to erect a statue to a frequently forgotten Civil War hero, Strong Vincent. Ed took the occasion to laud Vincent's efforts in "Gettysburg Magazine." He also agreed to speak at the statue dedication. The commemoration committee was "over the moon" that a historian of Ed's caliber was their keynote speaker. My friendship with Ed made that possible.

Meanwhile, a comradery developed among those of us taking Ed's Civil War tours with Ed becoming more than a mentor -- he joined in on the fun and adventures as our leader. Having learned about military structure on the tours, we soon dubbed ourselves the "Bearss Brigade" (we did like the alliteration). Soon we designed and wore white hats identifying ourselves as such. One year some members of the "Brigade" learned that Ed would be celebrating a birthday while we were on a weekend tour. So, a small birthday party was planned ... complete with a cake brought along on the bus.

Little did we know at the time but a tradition was born. That small gathering became an annual "birthday bash" for Ed. The event has had several venues over the years but has always involved gifts for Ed, these appreciations transitioned from modest personal items to a fundraising agenda wherein each year Ed picks a worthy historic site to receive his birthday gift. Bash attendees donate monies to the selected cause in honor of Ed and his special day. As a result, over the years, Ed's followers -- now known collectively as his brigade -- have donated thousands of dollars to sites throughout the country, ranging from Gettysburg to the Trans-Mississippi and just about everywhere in between. Through this approach, the Brigade's affection for Ed has contributed to his life's work and to historic preservation.

Wendy at podium with Ed wearing flag, 2019 Ed Bearss Birthday Bash for Ed's 96th birthday.

JAY WERTZ

I first met Edwin Cole Bearss in Amarillo, Texas, in January 1992. Ed had just agreed to be one of the on-camera historical experts for my documentary series, *Smithsonian's Great Battles of the Civil War*,[451] (along with Dr. James B. McPherson,[452] the late Edward Ezell of the Smithsonian and historians from the four military schools – U. S. Military Academy at West Point,[453] U.S. Naval Academy,[454] the Citadel[455] and the Virginia Military Institute[456]). I had never met Ed in person until that time, but

---

[451] Online: https://www.amazon.com/Smithsonians-Great-Battles-Civil-1861-1865/dp/B000G0O5GY.
[452] Online: https://en.wikipedia.org/wiki/James_M._McPherson.
[453] Online: https://westpoint.edu/.
[454] Online: https://www.usna.edu/homepage.php.
[455] Online: http://www.citadel.edu/root/.
[456] Online: https://www.vmi.edu/.

executive producer Richard Stadin, who first contacted Ed, and I were in awe of his work and stature. We had seen him in that other Civil War documentary, which was begun about the same time as the Smithsonian project, but made it to the airways first.

Ed was in Amarillo to consult with local and regional National Park Service officials on the Alibates Flint Quarries National Monument[457] and other Native American historical sites in the area. Ed's knowledge of Native American History stands alongside his knowledge of other topics of American history in general. Those who assume his expertise to be only in military history will marvel at his knowledge of many subjects and periods. Of course, those of us who are students of American History also know that the history of conflict and military response are key elements of America's rich historical past. We sat down for a meal; Ed was warm and engaging. Though I was filmmaker with an interest in history and not a trained historian, Ed trusted in me and what I was intending to do. We agree to a shooting schedule to begin the following summer.

I next saw Ed on our first shooting day in Gettysburg, in July 1993. Ed was already waiting at Cemetery Hill[458] when my small crew and I arrived to set up. As soon as we began rolling film, and Ed began to describe the actions on Cemetery Hill that ended the first day's fighting at Gettysburg, I noticed people making their way toward us from all directions. I learned then that Ed gathers a crowd whenever he speaks publicly. His voice and style of delivery are a signature draw to those who have heard him before and a point of curiosity to those who are experiencing him live for the first time. Combined with his knowledge, it is easy to see why he is often considered to be the premiere guide for Civil War battlefield tours, and for excursions to many other historic places. Years later, Jim McPherson and I were having lunch and he told me that he and his wife had taken a tour of World War II Italy that Ed had led. He came away with a great understanding of the campaign and thoroughly enjoyed the tour. This from a Pulitzer Prize-winning historian!

---

[457] Online: https://www.nps.gov/alfl/index.htm.
[458] Online: https://home.nps.gov/cebe/learn/historyculture/the-union-stand-at-cemetery-hill.htm.

After Ed and I finished shooting at Gettysburg, I didn't see him for six months but we were in contact. The next time I saw him was in January 1993 when I collected him from a talk, he was giving at Arkansas Post National Monument.[459] We had a nice long drive from rural Arkansas to Vicksburg, Mississippi, where we were going to film the next day. Both Ed and I like professional football and had a great conversation on the drive. Although Ed has lived in Arlington, Virginia, for most of his adult life (and still does), he has never been a fan of the Washington Redskins,[460] and especially their former owner, Jack Kent Cooke. I was living in San Diego at the time and we both were rooting for the Chargers,[461] who were then in the playoffs. Their coach at the time, Bobby Ross, was a former coach at West Point. We liked his style.

Early the next morning we set out to shoot. It was just Ed, myself and the fog. Ed marveled at the way I was able to handle camera, sound, directing, etc. by myself. I was just trying to get good footage as we ranged along the Mississippi River from Port Gibson to the site of USS *Cairo* and other points in Vicksburg National Military Park in fog and light rain. I think that trip really solidified our friendship. Ed had another commitment and left but I remained in the area and obtained a lot greater footage on his recommendations.

Later that year we concluded filming at Petersburg. The documentary premiered on The Learning Channel[462] in January 1995 and has had a long run in all the home video formats. By the time it was finished there was nothing Ed would not do for me, or me for him. It was a smooth transition to book authorship; Ed the experienced book author and me, the filmmaker, collaborating on an excellent short history and battlefield guide, *Smithsonian's Great Battles and Battlefields of the Civil War* for William Morrow & Company.[463] We were in touch constantly by phone and (in those days) US Mail. I even got to know his late wife Margie pretty well, an

---

[459] Online: https://www.nps.gov/arpo/index.htm.
[460] Online: https://www.redskins.com/.
[461] Online: https://www.chargers.com/.
[462] Online: https://www.tlc.com/.
[463] Online: https://en.wikipedia.org/wiki/William_Morrow_and_Company.

accomplished historian herself, over the phone when I would call and she would take messages while Ed was off on a tour or a research excursion.

I really consider Ed my mentor is history. He has never hesitated to jump in and assist, in detail, with any of my writing projects; books, magazine articles, and online writings. He taught me that when estimating a number, it's "more than" not "over" and "decimated" only applies if every tenth man goes down. His precision and detail in writing are a manifestation of the idea that writing style is secondary to telling the story, something I heartily agree with. His characterizations bring the people of history to life. This style is also evident in his oral presentations, where time is a greater enemy than the word counts and column widths of written pieces. In writing and public presentation, he has truly earned the moniker of being an American treasure.

I see Ed whenever our busy bicoastal schedules permit. From brunch at his favorite Pentagon City restaurant (the Ritz Carlton) to tours and conferences; to visits to his attractive but modest house and its voluminous library of books and historical papers, time spent with Ed has given me some of the most cherished and memorable experiences of my life.

SHARON AND EARL CLOUGH

Sharon and Earl Clough are long-time tour-goers and friends who helped Ed Bearss when he was invited to a throw out the first pitch for a specialty game at National's Park.

Ed Bearss' entire life has focused on history, but he has another passion as well. Ed loves baseball. He attended the first All Star Game with his father in 1933 – Babe Ruth hit a home run in that game! For his 95th birthday, Ed was given tickets to the 2019 All Star Game at Nationals Park in Washington, DC and was also given the honor of throwing out the first pitch for the inaugural Armed Services Classic softball game that preceded the All-Star Game by a few days.

My name is Earl Clough. My wife, Sharon, and I have had the privilege of traveling with Ed for close to thirty years and we enjoy having Ed over to watch sports on our big TV – World Series, Super Bowls, All Star Games, etc.

While Ed used to play fast-pitch softball, it had been a few years (a lifetime) since he'd last thrown a pitch. I brought my glove and a couple softballs over to his place on the day we'd arranged a Washington Post interview, and the young reporter brought his glove as well. After sitting on the porch and hearing stories about that first All-Star Game,[464] the reporter, Ed's daughter Ginny, Ed, and I went out to Ed's side yard and warmed him up. As catcher, I can testify that Ed definitely "put some mustard" on some of those pitches, and he crowed "I feel young" right after a particularly effective pitch. This was caught on film and later shown on local television.

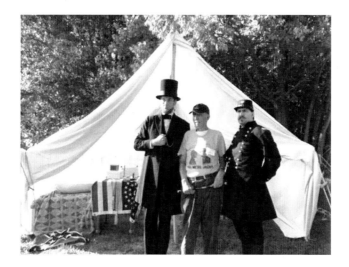

Ed Bearss and history. Photo provided from the Marty Gane collection and used with permission.

Speaking of television, our Mr. Ed became a media sensation for a week or more, with the *Washington Post* and ABC reporters coming to the house and interviews at Fox and WTOP (our local news radio station) among others as arranged by contacts at the American Battlefield Trust. Ed loved every minute of it – sharing his experience at that early [first (1933)] All-

---

[464] Online: https://en.wikipedia.org/wiki/1933_Major_League_Baseball_All-Star_Game.

Star Game and speculating that he might be the only person still living who attended that game.

Ed Bearss warming up for "First Pitch" at Nationals Stadium.

When we got to the Armed Services Classic,[465] MLB [Major League Baseball][466] rolled out the red carpet for Ed – parking spot right by the entrance to the stadium, fancy golf cart transport through the stadium, food and drink in the "green room," and upon request for "a place to warm up Mr. Bearss," we found ourselves warming up the Chief Historian Emeritus of the National Park Service within the Nationals' indoor batting cage. Wearing a brand-new Marine Corps t-shirt, Ed was ready. Even though he was handed a baseball, not a softball as he had practiced, Ed delivered a straight, one-bouncer to the catcher. It was all on the big screen, and AP photographer Nick Wass got a great shot of Ed as he released the ball. (That Associated Press photo now hangs on the wall in Ed's living room). We then watched the Airforce team beat Army's team 9-2.

---

[465] Online: https://www.mlb.com/news/all-star-armed-services-classic-announced-c279156092.
[466] Online: https://www.mlb.com/ and https://en.wikipedia.org/wiki/Major_League_Baseball.

Ed Bearss's first pitch. The ball is visible just leaving his hand. His daughter Ginny is with him. Note his name on the electronic sign behind the catcher's head. Public domain. Department of Defense video. URL: https://www.facebook.com/Deptof Defense/videos/10156615889615719/?t=3.

July 17th, we returned to Nationals Park to be escorted to the MLB suite for the All-Star Game. In a moving pre-game ceremony, twenty-nine Medal of Honor recipients were honored on the field. Much more than the food and drink spread in the suite, he appreciated the great seats and even more, the opportunity to meet some of the Medal of Honor recipients once the game started. At one point, Ed and I were seated outside the suite watching the game and a man came up from behind and tapped me on the shoulder with "Hi, I'm Cal Ripken." Cal was most charming, spoke at length with Ed, and introduced us to his fiancée (now wife). We also got to meet Johnny Bench. Ed told him about attending the first All-Star Game, and Johnny said, "I played in that game" to laughs. Ed, Ginny, her son Andy, and I all had a wonderful time as guests of MLB that night as the American League won 8-6 in the 10th inning. I don't think Ed ever stopped grinning during the almost two weeks of press and events. He was [and is] a rock star!

(1) Ed Bearss, Cal Ripkin and Earl Clough. (2) Ed Bearss and Johnny Bench. Permission for owned photographs from Sharon and Earl Clough collection.

Afterword

This third book in the trilogy that make up the Ed Bearss memoir is drawn from my personal experiences with the Pied Piper of American history. The experience of assembling these works has shown me the depth of character evident in this man from our "Greatest Generation." Through the years it took to assemble this work, I got to know Ed Bearss well, and in some details – at least for a time (until he could read them) – better than himself. Certainly, his recollections of past events, whether his alone at Suicide Creek; or at the 42nd General Hospital in Brisbane, Australia; in the National Park Service offices he occupied in Vicksburg and Washington, DC when not "walking the ground"; or the many places around the world on tour, is without a known equal. For me, I was able to do what his best tour goers seek to do, live vicariously through Ed Bearss to the moments, people and places we can only imagine. In this way, Ed Bearss leads us to these past times, historical figures and, of course, the ground they walked upon, and that is where the "Pied Piper" moniker fits best.

This expertise integrated in Ed Bearss's nature was derived over many years from those he respected, and his memoir describes them well. We can see what they brought to him that he valued enough to infuse himself with their best qualities. In so doing, he finely honed those skills over time, particularly is ability to carry the audience with him into the past. Because of this skill, as we see in his second memoir book, *Walking the Ground:*

Making American History, he was able to motivate our American Representatives and Senators to commemorate those whose voices are no more. His strong personal motivation certainly came from the success he was achieving in his career, but we know from his first memoir book, *Walking the Ground: From Big Sky to Semper Fi*, that it was sourced from a desire to give voice to those soldiers and Marines all around him at Suicide Creek on New Britain, who died silently, not making a sound, never able to speak to their love ones again or write their memoir, as he has done here.

Thousands of people respect and appreciate his life's work because of his third career, his history-tour leadership, only "hinted at" in the tours described in this third book. In some small way, I hope that this third book in his memoir trilogy brings Ed Bearss to the reader in a way that his childhood history and Park Service career narrative cannot do. I hope it brings a sense of the moment-to-moment Ed Bearss that those on tour with him are fortunate to experience. It is in these tour experiences that this Pied Piper of American history leads us toward the ever-improving summit of our culture, and showing the sacrifice that got us all to where we are today. Thank you, Edwin Cole Bearss, thank you, sir.

Robert Irving Desourdis
Olympia, Washington, February 2020

ABOUT THE EDITOR

Robert Irving (Bob) Desourdis
Book Developer, Editor, Co-Author,
Senior Editor and Homeland Security Series Editor

Bob Desourdis is a Master Solution Architect in IT and communications, working in Massachusetts and the National Capital Region for more than 40 years in post nuclear-attack and public safety communication systems. He evolved from a radio system engineer in 1980 developing software models for hypothetical post-nuclear-attack communications systems, then the more satisfying 'here-and-now' public safety communications, and finally as a Solution Architect in heterogeneous IT systems of all types. He has served communication senior scientist, division and operations manager, vice president of technology, and other titles over his career. He most enjoys working in small creative teams that envision, use 'trial and error', and innovate new ways of doing things based on well-proven techniques and capabilities. Most recently, he wrote a draft white paper on a project to evaluate and recommend steps to enhance public media support for public safety. He has written several technical books that span his career in communication-systems engineering.

He met Ed Bearss in 2011 on a tour, Western European Battlefields, by South Mountain Expeditions by Marty Gane. Bob heard about Ed Bearss desire to publish his 1992 NPS Interview and subsequently agreed to serve as the NOVA Homeland Security Series Editor, adding "Commemoration" of soldiers and First Responders to his series domain. This action set the stage for the creation of the Ed Bearss's memoir books from existing documentation, tens of hours of audio recordings, and hundreds of hours of tour video collected since 2011. He and Ed Bearss began work on the memoir books in late 2017.

Bob received his BS in Mathematics from the Worcester Polytechnic Institute (WPI) in Worcester, Massachusetts, in 1977 and an MS in Electrical Engineering in 1979. He received his MS degree in the Technology and Policy Program (TPP) from the Massachusetts Institute of Technology (MIT) in 1980.

Bob lives with his wife Betty near Olympia, Washington, recently moving from Fairfax, Virginia. He has three adult daughters Danielle Reese (nee Desourdis), Nicole Elizabeth and Amanda Michelle. His grandchildren Declan Robert and Reagan Louise are the work of Danielle and husband Jason Reese, a U. S. Army Doc (cardiologist), also living in Washington State. Jason contributed a chapter to Bob's first NOVA Science Publishers book entitled *Human Collaboration in Homeland Security*.

Bob is a fine-scale model builder. He has built aircraft dioramas for World War II pilots and aircrew, including a B-25B "Plane No. 5" for the family of a 1942 Doolittle Raider and C-47 "Texas Gal" for its crew chief, who towed an 82nd Airborne glider into France on D-Day. He built a Special Ops Blackhawk for his son-in-law Jason Reese, and a B-17G, B-24H and an Me-163 Komet for Barney Nolan. Barney's memoir of his Eighth Air Force experiences will be published in a forthcoming NOVA Science book. Bob also built Ed Bearss's Suicide Creek diorama used in Chapter 2 of the first book in Ed Bearss memoir, *Walking the Ground: From Big Sky to Semper*

(1) Cairo photo. Public domain. (2) 1/192nd-scale Cairo diorama by Desourdis. (3) Desourdis's Cairo and Suicide Creek dioramas. (4) Ed Bearss is pointing out his position on the ravine slope to Suicide Creek when he was hit.

Fi, and the USS *Cairo* diorama in his second memoir book, *Walking the Ground: Making American History*.

About the Editor

Ed Bearss and I with the *Cairo* diorama in his home after its presentation to him during his Birthday Bash in 2017.

INDEX OF TERMS

#

102nd Connecticut Regt, 201, 204
11th Virginia, 62
14th Virginia, 66
15th Massachusetts, 68
18th US, 112
19th Massachusetts, 68
1st Virginia, 62
24th Virginia, 62
26th North Carolina, 68, 69
26th Yankee Division, 201
27th US, 112
2nd US Cavalry, 100
328, Company G, 230
3rd Virginia, 62
42nd General Hospital, 277
42nd New York, 68
53rd North Carolina, 63
5th Virginia, 62
71st Pennsylvania, 66
72nd Ohio, 249
72nd Pennsylvania, 68
8th Missouri, 63

A

ABC, 272
Academic Travel Abroad, 13
Aisne-Marne, 211, 221, 222
Aisne-Marne American Cemetery, 221
Aisne-Marne Cemetery, 211
Algonkian, xxxviii
Allin alteration, 113, 114, 115
All-Star Game, 271, 272, 273, 274
Altaussee Salt Mines, 175
American Battle Monuments Commission, xvii
American Battlefield Trust, xvii, xviii, 246, 272
American Bicentennial program, ix
American Carnage
    Wounded Knee, 1890, 169
American Chateau-Thierry Monument, 211
American Marines in Belleau Wood, 191
American National Cemeteries, xix
American Southwest, xl
Anazasi ruins, xl
angle, xxix, 65, 154
Antietam, xii, xiv, xxii, xli, 17, 58, 221
Antietam Battlefield, xli

Arapaho, 103, 104, 113
archeology, 164, 166, 167, 169, 207, 208, 225, 235
Arlington, 8, 255, 270
Armistice, 208, 209, 210, 213
Army of Virginia, xiii
Army War Carnival, 238
Ash Hollow, 119
ATA, 13, 14
Attack on Pearl Harbor, xli

B

Baltimore and Ohio Depot, 79
Band-of-Brothers, 19
BAR, 4, 5
Battery No. 8, 35, 38
battle line, 64
Battle of
  Champion Hill, 51, 253, 254, 266
  Chickasaw Bayou, 25, 26, 27, 28, 30, 35, 39, 40, 49, 55
  Fredericksburg, 9, 33, 60
  Gettysburg, vii, xvii, xxviii, 11, 17, 19, 54, 57, 61, 63, 70, 71, 243, 246, 262, 263, 267, 269, 270
  Kernstown, 62
  Memphis, 21, 22, 23, 24, 33, 41
  Powder River, 120
  the Big Black, xlv, 50, 51, 55, 250, 252
  the Rosebud, xxvii, xxix, 118, 119, 123, 124, 125, 126, 128, 129, 130, 132, 135
  Verdun, xxix, 185, 188, 189
Battlefield touring, xix
Bear River Battlefield Massacre Site, 170
Bear River Battleground, 170
Bear River Massacre, 170, 171
Bearss Brigade, xi, xiv, xxxix, xlix, 267
beau ideal, 120

Belleau Wood, xxiv, xxix, xxxvi, 190, 191, 196, 197, 199, 200, 202, 205, 211, 215, 221
Benedict Arnold
  Path from Patriot to Traitor, 14
Best Western Historical Nonfiction, xxxviii
Better Times, 183
Bicentennial history program, x
Big Black River, xlv, 50, 250, 252
Big Black River Bridge, 50, 252
Big Horn River, 94, 111, 113
Big Horn Valley, 114
Big Piney, 96, 97
Big Piney Creek, 96
Big Sunflower River, 41, 44, 45, 46, 48, 49
Big Three, 210
Billings, Montana, 133
Bingham, 68, 69, 98, 100, 105
Bismarck, North Dakota, 117
Black Bayou, 41, 42, 43, 44
Black Crow, 111
Black Hawk, xv
Black Hills, xxxviii, 117
Black Hills State University, xxxviii
blitzkrieg, 218
Bloody Knife, 141
Blue Mountain College for Women, 250
Bolshevik Revolution, 211
Boston Custer, 151
Bows and arrows, 104
Box 78, 78
Boy Scout, xxxviii
Bozeman Trail, 91, 92, 93, 94, 96, 101, 103
Brandon, Mississippi, 249
Brandywine Road, 80
Brooklyn Dodgers, 7
Brownie points, 42, 121, 122
Browning Automatic Rifle, 4
Bruges, 175
Bruinsburg, 50
Brussels, 174, 176
Buffalo [Calf] Rode Woman, 126

Index of Terms

Buffalo Bill's museum, 15
buffalo hide, 123, 126
buffalo jump, 118, 121, 123, 127, 129

C

Cairo, 22, 24, 40, 43, 54, 243, 249, 250, 282, 283
California Volunteers, 170
Cambrai memorial site, 217
Canada, x
Cape Gloucester, xxxii, 173, 212, 264
Cape Gloucester, New Britain, 173
Carondelet, 24, 41, 42, 45
carrier pigeon, 202
causeway, 25, 27, 28, 30
Cedar Coulee, 154, 155
Cedar Creek, xv
Champion Heritage Foundation, 254
Champion Heritage Trust, 252
Champion Hill, xiii, xviii, xlv, xlix, 50, 51, 52, 55, 246, 251, 252, 253, 254, 255, 256
Champion Hill Battlefield, xviii, xlv, 252
Champion Hill Heritage Trust, 252
Champion House, 253
Changing History
    Virginia Women Through Four Centuries, 256
Chapultepec Castle, 60
Charlevaux Ravine, 202, 203
Charm, 250, 252
Chateau d'Hattonchatel, 204
Chateau Thierry, 196, 197
Chateau-Thierry American Monument, 211, 212
Chatel-Chehery, 205, 206
Cherokee, xv
Chevy Chase, 81
Cheyenne, 103, 104, 111, 112, 113, 116, 120, 121, 122, 127, 143, 157, 162, 163, 169

Cheyenne Memories, 162, 163, 169
Cheyenne Reservation, 163
Chickasaw Bayou, 25, 26, 27, 28, 30, 35, 39, 40, 49, 55
Chillicothe, 35, 36, 37
Chinn Ridge, xiii, 9
Church of Our Lady Bruges, 175
Cincinnati, 42
city of sin, 24
City of Verdun, 185
City of Vicksburg, 21, 25
City of Vicksburg, Mississippi, 21
City Point, 74
city-series gunboats, 22, 42
Civil War, ix, x, xii, xv, xviii, xxvii, xxviii, xxxv, xxxix, xli, xliv, xlv, xlviii, 8, 9, 10, 13, 15, 17, 21, 26, 53, 54, 64, 65, 70, 99, 106, 112, 134, 193, 202, 220, 221, 242, 243, 244, 245, 246, 248, 250, 252, 253, 262, 264, 265, 266, 267, 268, 269, 270
Civil War history, xxvii, 248
Civil War Preservation Trust, 245, 252
Civil War Round Table(s), xviii, 245, 246
Civil War roundtables, xv
Closed Hand, 162
clubs, 104, 143
Collected Stories of the Vicksburg Campaign, xlv, 249, 251, 253
Colorado, x, xi, xxxviii, 15
Commonwealth Cemetery, 218
Compiegne Armistice site, 209
Confederate, xi, xii, xv, xvi, xix, 21, 22, 23, 24, 25, 27, 28, 30, 32, 35, 36, 40, 41, 43, 45, 46, 47, 49, 54, 57, 58, 59, 62, 69, 73, 111, 244
Confederate Army of Northern Virginia, xii
confederate artillery, 28, 30
Confederate River Defense Fleet, 41
Confederate States of America, xv
Conference of Historical Journals, 256
Congressional committees, xviii
Continental [Divide, 127

Copse of Trees, 65, 66, 71
Council of War, 58
Counting Coups, 121
Coup stick, 121, 122
Crazy Horse, 99, 100, 101, 103, 106, 120, 124
Crow, 94, 111, 121, 124, 129, 134, 154, 157, 158, 166
Crow Agency, 94
CSS Charm, 250
CSS Paul Jones, 250
Curly, 157
Custom House, 24
Cut Belly, 162

D

Dakota Territory, 117
Dakotas, xi
Death Camps, 219
DeCourcy, 27, 28
Deep Ravine, 161, 163
Deer Creek, 41, 43, 44, 45, 46, 47, 48, 49
Delta Democrat Times, 4
Delta Queen, 3
Deluge in the Delta, 4
diaper, 178
Dictionary of Virginia Biography, 256, 257
District Government grounds, 81
Don Rickey, xxxviii
Douaumont, xxix, 186, 188, 189
Douaumont Ossuary, 188, 189
Drumgold-Snyder's and Hayne's Bluffs, 32
Dunkirk, 176

E

Eagle Bend, 42
Eagle Lake, 42
earthworks, 28, 30, 153, 166
Eastern Theater of the Civil War, xiv

Emmitsburg Road, 63, 65
Etowah, 29
Everton Congor, 84

F

FDR, xviii
Federals, xiv, 28, 39, 62
Fetterman Fight, xxix, 92, 96, 102, 105, 108, 109, 110, 111, 112
Fetterman Massacre, 96, 110, 118
First Manassas, 9, 23, 243
Flanders Field American Cemetery, 223
Flanders Fields Museum, 178, 179
Fleury, xxix, 186, 187
Fleury-devant-Douaumont, 186
Fort Douaumont, 185, 186
Fort Jackson, xv
Fort Ontario, xii
Fort Pemberton, 35, 38
Frederic Remington Museum, x, xii
Fredericksburg, 9, 33, 60
French Army, 202
Friends don't let friends split infinitives, 256
Ft. Abraham Lincoln, 117
Ft. C. F. Smith, 94, 111, 113, 114, 115
Ft. Laramie, 95, 104, 116, 119
Ft. McHenry, 111
Ft. Monroe, 61
Ft. Phil Kearney, 91, 92, 111
Ft. Phil Kearny Interpretive Center and Gift Shop, 92, 94

G

Galena Mafia, 112
Gane Atlas, xxv, 41, 116, 125, 128, 131
Garrett farm, 84
Garryowen, 137, 138, 139
German 7th Army, 199

Index of Terms 289

German Army, 186, 195, 219
Gettysburg, vii, xvii, xxviii, 11, 17, 19, 54, 57, 61, 63, 70, 71, 243, 246, 262, 263, 267, 269, 270
Gettysburg Address, 19
Girl Who Saved Her Brother, 124, 127
Goes Ahead, 157
Golden Colorado, 15
Goose Creek, 123, 132, 133
Grand Gulf, 31, 49, 50, 250
Grand Gulf Military Park, 250
Grant, vii, xviii, xxviii, 21, 25, 26, 29, 31, 32, 33, 38, 39, 40, 41, 42, 49, 53, 54, 55, 57, 76, 77, 78, 79, 112, 113, 117, 243
Great Hinds Street Missionary Baptist Church, 4
Great Plains, xxx, xxxviii, 91, 92
Great Sioux Nation, 117
Great Sioux Reservation, 117
Great War, vii, xxix, xliii, xlviii, 173, 177, 181
Greatest Generation, 277
Greece, featuring the WWII Battle of Crete, xli
Greek Classics, xli, 13
Greenville, Mississippi, 4
Guadalcanal, xvi, xlii
Guam, xvi, 3
gyrenes, 192

H

Hairy Moccasin, 157, 158
Hardin High School, 7
Harvard Alum, 13
Haskell College, 163
Hay party, 113
Hayfield Fight, 112
Height of Land, xvi
Henry 15-shot, 114
Herndon House, 78

Hero on The Western Front Discovering Alvin York's WWI Battlefield, xliii, 205
Higgins boat, 5
high-water mark, 68, 69
Hiking Hiram, 201, 204
Hiking Trail, 124, 126, 127, 128, 129
Hill 204, 211, 212
Hinds Junior College, 250
history interpreter, xxvi
HistoryAmerica, xxi, xli, xlii, xlviii, 1, 13, 14, 17
HistoryAmerica Tours, xxi, xli, xliii, xlviii, 1, 13, 14, 17
hostiles, 113, 117, 124, 129, 130, 132
Hotchkiss shell, 10
Hunkpapa, 103, 140
Hunley, 11

I

ID disc, 231, 232
Ieper, 177
Indian Maiden, 61
interpretation, xvi, xxii, xxiv, xxvi, xxix, 2, 51, 82, 150, 157, 162, 163, 191, 202, 226, 261
Intruder in the Dust, 71
iPhone, 228
Irish Brigade, 66
ironclads, 23, 35, 41, 43, 45
Iroquois, xxxviii
Island No. 10, xv
Italo-Ethiopian War, 173

J

Jack, xlviii, 16, 85, 197, 202, 270
John Stands in Timber, 162, 169
Joshua Chamberlain and the 20th Maine, 14
jumping the broomstick, 61

K

Kamikaze, 162
King Neptune, 3, 4
kiosks, xvi
Kirkwood House, 78
Klingle house, 64
knives, 104
Kollmar Creek, 125, 130
Kollmar ravine, 128

L

Lafayette Baker, 84
Lake Champlain, xvi
Lake Providence, 32, 40
Lakota, xi, xv, 103, 111, 112, 113, 121, 140, 166
Lame Deer, 127
lances, 104
Landscape Turned Red, xii
LaSalle Corbel, 61
Last Stand Hill, xxiii, 134, 151, 152, 157, 158, 159, 161, 163, 164, 168
left oblique, 63, 64
Library of Virginia, xxx, xlviii, 255, 256, 257, 258
lighter-than-air craft, 220
Little Big Horn, xxix, xlvii, 120, 133, 134, 135, 136, 138, 143, 147, 148, 149, 154, 155, 156
Little Bighorn, xi, xxxviii, 121, 133, 134, 137, 138, 142, 143, 149, 160, 162, 163, 166, 167, 169
Little Bighorn Battlefield National Monument, xxxviii
Little Piney, 96
Little Rebel, 23, 24
Little Rock, 40, 243
Little Round Top, xvi, 64
Little Turtle, xv
Little Whirlbird, 162
Lochnagar, 216, 217
Lochnagar Crater, 216
Lodge Trail Ridge, 96, 101, 102, 105
Logis Hôtel, 227
Lost Cause, 71
Louisville, 24, 42
Lovell, 23, 24

M

Madonna and Child, 175
Major League Baseball, 7, 273
Malta, xvi
Marias, 171
Marine Corps, 7, 31, 115, 196, 197, 198, 199, 200, 201, 259, 263, 264, 265, 273
Mary Baldwin College, 256
Mason, xlvi, 68, 69
Massacre at Boa Ogoi, 170
Matilda Champion, xlv, xlviii, 252, 253, 254
medical case, 164
medicine bundles, 131
Medicine Tail Coulee, 147, 148, 154, 155, 157, 158, 159
Memorial Museum Passchendaele 1917, 215, 216, 219
Menin Gate, 180, 181
Meuse Argonne, xxiii, xxix
Meuse-Argonne American Cemetery, 223
Military Forces Unification Equating the Marine Corps, 198
Mill Springs, Kentucky, xvi
Miniconjou, 103
Mississippi Department of Archives and History, xlv
Mississippi Division of Sons of Confederate Veterans, xlv
Mississippi flood of 1927, 4

Index of Terms

Mississippi River, 21, 25, 41, 49, 54, 250, 270
Missouri River, 117
MLB, 7, 273, 274
MLB All Star game, 7
Monarch, 22, 23, 24
Monmouth, New Jersey, xiv
Montana, x, xi, xxxv, xxxviii, 5, 7, 15, 18, 94, 113, 117, 118, 121, 122, 127, 134, 169, 243
Montfaucon American Monument, xxiii, 213, 214
Montsec American Monument, 212, 213
monuments, xvi, xxix, 64, 66, 69, 165, 175, 190, 211, 212, 246, 259
Moon Lake, 35, 36
mortars, 42, 46
MotionX GPS, 228
Mound City, 42
mowing machine, 114
Mud Island, 22
My Dear Wife
    The Civil War Letters of Sid and Matilda Champion, 251

N

Nathan Short marker, 135, 136
National, v, ix, xi, xxix, xxxi, xxxii, xxxv, xxxvii, xxxviii, xl, xlvii, 8, 13, 17, 18, 51, 69, 70, 73, 78, 95, 120, 134, 137, 166, 168, 170, 225, 241, 242, 245, 247, 262, 263, 269, 270, 271, 273, 277, 279
National Battlefield Parks, xxxii
National Geographic, xl, 13, 70
National Geographic Expeditions, xl
National Historic Landmark, 120, 170
National Historic Preservation Act, ix
National Park Service, v, ix, xxix, xxxi, xxxii, xxxv, xxxvii, xxxviii, xlvii, 17, 18, 166, 168, 170, 225, 241, 242, 245, 247, 262, 263, 269, 273, 277
National Theater, 78
national treasure, xii
National Trust for Historic Preservation, 13
Nationals Stadium, xxx, 273
Navy Yard Bridge, 81
Nebraska, xi, 111, 117
New Britain, 5, 6, 212, 278
New Mexico, xi, 15
New York Giants, 7
Newfoundland trenches, 215
Nez Perce, xv, 166, 169
Ninety Six, xv
Noisy Walking, 162
Nolan Group, xliii, 207, 208, 224, 225, 237, 238, 239
Normandy to the Rhine River, xli, 14
Northern Cheyenne, 162, 163
Northern Pacific railroad, 117
Nye-Cartright Ridge, 156

O

Office of the Chief of Military History, x
Ogdensburg, x, xii
Oglala, 103, 166
Oise-Aisne American Cemetery, 221
Okinawa, xv
Oklahoma, xi, xxxviii, 127, 243
optimism, 184, 185
Oswego, xii
Our American Cousin, 78, 79

P

Palace of Versailles, 210, 211
Pall Mall, 207
Papua New Guinea, 6
Paris, 191, 202, 210
Parrott, 37

PBS, x, 8
Pennsylvania Monument, 64
Pete Brown's HistoryAmerica Tours, xviii
Pete Shed, 18, 173
Pied Piper, vii, xxi, xxii, xxvii, xxviii, xxxv, xl, xli, xlviii, 1, 6, 17, 245, 247, 266, 277, 278
Pied Piper of History, xxi, xxvii, xxxv, 17
Pilot Knob, 96, 99
Pino Creek, 98
Pittsburg, 42
Plains Indian Wars, 119, 120
Plains Indians, 92, 96, 122, 162
Platte River, 117
Platte River Bridge, 117
Plenty Coups, 121, 122
Plum Point Bend, 23
Portugee Phillips, 93, 95
Prairie Dog Creek, 98, 101, 103, 107, 109, 123
Provost Marshall, 201
Prussian Army, 114
Pumphrey Livery Stable, 78, 80

Q

Quai d'Orsay, 210
Quebec, xvi
Queen of the West, 22, 23, 24

R

ramrod, 105, 106, 114
Rankin County, 250
Red Cloud, 99, 101, 103, 113, 115, 116, 127
Red Cloud Reservation, 127
Rees, 139
Remember crosses, 218
Reno, 94, 137, 138, 139, 140, 141, 142, 143, 145, 146, 147, 148, 149, 150, 151, 152, 153, 154, 155, 156, 157, 159, 164, 166, 167
Reno Creek, 140, 144, 149
Resolution of Commendation, xlv
Rest of the World, 13
Revolutionary War, xiv, xv
Rolling Fork, 41, 44, 45, 46, 47, 48, 49
romance novels, 29
Rosebud, xxvii, xxix, 118, 119, 123, 124, 125, 126, 128, 129, 130, 132, 135
Rosebud [Creek], 118, 135
Rosebud Battlefield, xxvii, 125, 128
Rosebud Fight, 123
Rubber Boat Incident, 4
Rubicon, 29

S

Sainte-Menehould, 227
Saltville, Virginia, xvi
Samoa, 3
San Diego, 3, 270
Sand Creek, 119, 169, 171
Sara Bearss Virginiana Conservation Fund, 257, 258
scalp, 101, 106
scalping, 104
scalping knives, 104
Sea Cloud, xl, 13
Second Day at Gettysburg, xvi
Second Manassas, xii
Segway, 174
Seminoles, xv
Seneca Falls, xi
Seventh Cavalry, 117, 118, 134, 135, 163
Sharkey County Courthouse, 47
Sharpshooter Ridge, 145, 146
Sherwood Foresters, 183
Shiloh, 18, 173
Sic Semper Tyrannis, 75
Sicily, xvi, xxxvi

Sioux, vii, xi, xxvii, xxix, xxxvii, xlvii, xlix, 91, 101, 103, 104, 110, 111, 116, 117, 119, 137, 140, 142, 143, 147, 166
Sioux Indian Wars, vii, xxvii, xxix, xxxvii, xlvii, xlix, 91
Sioux Reservation, 116, 117
Sioux War country, xi
Sitting Bull, 103, 147
skirmishers, 28, 30, 140
Slim Buttes, 120
Slot, xvi
Smithsonian, xii, xiv, xv, xviii, xl, 9, 13, 17, 203, 243, 267, 268, 270
Smithsonian Institution, 17
Smithsonian Resident Associates, 9
Somme American Cemetery, 222
South Carolina, xv, 35, 60
South Dakota, x, xxxviii, 117, 120
South Mountain, xxii, xxviii, xxix, xl, xli, xlii, xlvi, xlvii, xlviii, 14, 15, 16, 17, 21, 23, 54, 89, 91, 173, 174, 205, 227, 242, 280
South Mountain Expeditions, xxii, xxviii, xl, xlii, xlvii, xlviii, 14, 15, 16, 17, 21, 23, 54, 89, 91, 173, 174, 205, 227, 242, 280
South Pacific, x, xli, 5
Spanbroekmolen, 216, 217
Spanbroekmolen crater, 216
Spanish Civil War, 173
Spencer carbine, 86, 108
Spencers, 105, 114
Springfield rifle model 1863, 105
St. Lawrence River, xii
St. Mihiel Salient, 212
St. Patty's Day, 120
Star of the West, 35, 38
Star Saloon, 79
State of Tennessee, 226
State of Wyoming, 110
Stevenson, 44
Stonewall, xiii, 59

Suicide Boys, 162, 163
Suicide Creek, xxi, xxiv, 5, 6, 19, 173, 190, 202, 209, 212, 213, 239, 259, 277, 278, 282
Sullivant Hill, 96

T

Taft Monument, 79
Tallahatchie River, 35
Taltavull, 79
Tank, 217, 218
Tank, 218
Tecumseh, xv, 25
Texas, xi, xv, xxi, xli, xlviii, 1, 15, 268, 282
The Anazasi of the American South West, 14
The B. E. F. Times, 183
The Battle of 100 Slain, 119
The Battle of Britain, 14
The Battle of Little Bighorn, xli
The Bearss Brigade, xiv
The Cloth Hall, 178
The Kemmel Times, 183
The Morning and the Rest, 63
The Northern Cheyenne Breakout from Fort Robinson, 1878-1879, xxxviii, 169
The Sermon on the Mount, xvi
The Somme-Times, 183
The Wipers Times, 182, 183, 185
Thiepval Memorial, 189
Thoroughfare Gap, xiii
Thousand Islands region, xii
Tom, 122, 159, 160, 161, 208
Tomb of the Unknown Soldier, 122
Tommies, 177
Tongue River, 106, 113, 136
Tour Manager, 2
transcontinental railroad, 116
Trench newspaper, 182
trumpet, 102

U

U.S. Army, xv, xxxviii, 118, 169
U.S. Government, xxix, 26
U.S. Marine, x, xxix, 18
U.S. Marines, x
U.S. Medal of Honor, 205
Union, xi, xii, xiii, xvi, xxviii, 21, 22, 24, 25, 27, 28, 29, 30, 32, 35, 36, 41, 42, 43, 44, 45, 48, 51, 57, 58, 63, 64, 66, 67, 74, 77, 84, 111, 250, 254, 256
Union Army of Virginia, xii
Union artillery, xvi
Union Brown-water Navy, 22
Union cavalry, xvi
United States Army, xvii, 101, 122
United States Army Center for Military History, xvii
University of New Mexico, xlii
University of Oklahoma Press, xxxviii, 162, 169
University of South Dakota, xxxviii
University of Virginia, xli, 256
US Army Monuments Men, 175
US Army Signal Corps, 236
USS Cairo, 250, 270, 282
Utah, xi, 116

V

Valley of the Twin Forks, 207
Van Vliet's Hill, 118
Verdun, xxix, 185, 188, 189
Versailles, 210, 211
Vicksburg Campaign, vii, xviii, xxviii, 21, 26, 49, 53, 54, 55, 252
Vicksburg National Military Park, ix, xviii, xxxv, 8, 250, 270
village of Vigneulles, 204
Vimy Battle, 215
Vimy Ridge, 215

Virginia Brigade, 62
Virginia Foundation for the Humanities, 256
Virginia Historical Society, 256
Virginia Magazine of History and Biography, 256

W

Wagon Box Fight, 96, 99, 115
walking the ground, xxii, 2, 173, 226, 239, 258, 277
Walking the Ground
   From Big Sky to Semper Fi, xxi, xxiv, 18, 203, 278
   Making American History, xxi, xxvi, xxxi, xxxvii, 91, 170, 241, 278, 282
   Pied Piper of History, xxvii
Wall of Mirrors, 211
War of 1812, xii, xiv, 193
Washington Nationals, 7, 261
Washington Post, 89, 198, 263, 272
Washington Senators, 7
Water Carrier, 217
Weir Point, 146, 149, 150, 151, 155
West Point, xvi, 28, 33, 43, 47, 60, 62, 112, 148, 160, 268, 270
Western Front, xxx, xliii, 174, 185, 208, 217, 219, 223
Western History Association, xxxviii
White House, 74, 77
White Man Runs Him, 157
White Swan, 157
William D. McCain Publication Award, xlv
Winnibego, 111
World War I, x, xvi, xix, xxiv, xxix, xlii, 162, 173, 174, 176, 177, 185, 203, 208, 215, 218, 219, 220, 223, 224, 269, 281
World War II, x, xvi, xix, 162, 173, 208, 218, 219, 220, 269, 281
World Wildlife Fund, xl, 13

Index of Terms

Worldwide Web URLs, xxxi
Wounded Knee, xxxviii, 119, 120, 171
Wyoming, x, xi, 15, 91, 108, 113, 116, 117

Y

Yazoo City, 28, 41, 46
Yazoo City Road, 28
Yazoo Pass Expedition, 32, 35

Yazoo River, 21, 32, 39, 40, 41, 46, 49, 50, 250
Yellowstone [River], 117, 135
Yorktown, Virginia, xiv
Ypres, xxix, 177, 178, 179, 181, 182, 185, 219

Z

Zeppelins, 220

INDEX OF NAMES

A

Aisne-Marne, 211, 221, 222, 285
Argonne, Meuse, xxiii, xxix, 291
Armistead, Gen. Lewis Addison, 62, 67, 68, 69, 71
Axerodt, George, 78

B

Banks, General Nathaniel Prentice, 40
Banks, Nathanial, 112
Barnes, Dr. Joseph K., 88
Bearss, Margie Riddle, xxx, xliv, 248, 251, 252, 253
Bearss, Sara B., xxx, xlviii, 255, 257, 258, 293
Beckwith, James, 111
Benedict Arnold, xvi, 14, 286
Benjamin Berry's, 192
Benteen, Frederick William, 136, 149, 150, 151, 153, 154, 155, 164, 166, 167
Bingham, Capt. Henry Harrison, 68, 69, 98, 100, 105, 286
Bingham, Lt. Horatio, 98

Birdwell, Dr. Michael, 226
Blair, Francis P., 27, 28
Booth, John Wilkes, vii, xxix, 73, 79, 80, 83, 84, 85, 88, 89
Booth, Julius Brutus, 79
Bragg, General, 23, 24
Bridger, Jim, 99, 101, 111, 112
Brooke, Judge Francis T., 257
Brown, Capt. Frederick H., xviii, xli, xlii, xlviii, 2, 3, 4, 6, 13, 14, 22, 99, 101, 104, 105, 182, 292, 295
Brown, Pete, xviii, xli, xlii, xlviii, 2, 3, 4, 6, 13, 14, 292
Buchanan, Capt. Robert C., 23, 113
Buckner Jr, Lt. Gen. S. B., xv
Buckner, Lt. Gen. Simon Bolivar, xv
Burns, Ken, x, xiv, xxv, 8, 9, 17, 244, 262
Burns, Police Commissioner, 80, 81
Burroughs, Joseph, 81
Butler, General Benjamin Franklin, 40
Butowksy, Harry, xxvi

C

Calhoun, James, 156, 160

Carrington, Gen. Henry B., 93, 94, 96, 98, 99, 100, 101, 103, 109, 110, 111, 112
Carrington, Margaret Sullivant, 96
Champion, Sid Johnson (Sid V), xlv, 253, 254, 255
Charm, Paul Jones and Dot, 250
Clough, Earl, 271, 275
Clough, Earl and Sharon, xlix
Congor, Everton, 84, 288
Crook, Brig. Gen. l George, 120, 121, 123, 124, 125, 126, 129, 130, 131, 132, 133, 136
Crook, General George, xii, 123
Curry, David, 226, 230
Custer, Lt. Col. George Armstrong, 118, 134, 160

D

Danforth, Capt., 238
De Wolf, Dr. James Madison, 148
DeCourcy, John F., 27, 28, 288
DeKalb, Baron, 35, 36, 37
Deppen, Jim, 230, 231
DeRudio, Maj. Charles Camillo, 148
Doherty, Edward Paul, 87
Drake, Rebecca Blackwell, xliv, xlviii, 249, 251, 266

E

Early, Jubal Anderson, 63
Edwin Cole Bearss, ix, x, xiv, xxi, xxxviii, xli, xlviii, 1, 6, 245, 247, 268, 278
Ellet, Charles Rivers, 24

F

Faulkner, William, 71

Featherston, Brig. Gen. Winfield Scott, 47, 48
Ferraro, Marty, 15
Fetterman, Capt. William Judd, xxix, 92, 96, 97, 98, 99, 100, 101, 102, 103, 104, 105, 108, 109, 110, 111, 112, 114, 118, 119, 289
Fisher, Isaac, 101, 105, 107, 108, 109
Foch's, Marshal Ferdinand, 208
Ford, Henry Clay, 78
Fry, Brig. Gen. Brikett Davenport, 67

G

Gane, Martha, xxv, xxviii, xl, 2, 8, 9, 10, 11, 12, 15, 16, 23, 54, 95, 173, 174, 191, 205, 272, 280
Garnett, Richard Brooke, 62, 67, 71
Garrett, Jack, 85
Gibbon, Maj. Gen. John, 132, 135, 159
Gibbons, Floyd, 193, 195
Godfrey, Edward Settle, 153
Grant, General Ulysses S., vii, xviii, xxviii, 21, 25, 26, 29, 31, 32, 33, 38, 39, 40, 41, 42, 49, 53, 54, 55, 57, 76, 77, 78, 79, 112, 113, 117, 243, 289
Grant, Julia Boggs, 77
Grattan, Lt. John Lawrence, 119
Greene, Jerome A., vii, ix, x, xii, xxix, xxxvii, xlvii, 91, 169
Grummond, Lt. George Washington, 98, 99, 100, 101, 103, 104, 105, 109, 110

H

Hancock, Amoria, 63
Harris, Clara, 80
Hartzog, George B., 241
Herold, Davey, 79, 85
Herold, David, 74, 79, 82, 86
Hitler, Adolf, 198, 209

Hodgson, Benjamin Hubert, 147, 148

J

Jackson, Confederate General Thomas Jonathon, xiii, xv, 43, 50, 59, 60, 62, 289
Jones, Paul, 250, 252, 288

K

Kellogg, Mark, 121
Kelly, Michael, xxx, xlii, xlviii, 173, 174, 208, 226
Kemper, James Lawson, 62
Keogh, Capt. Myles, xi

L

la Bocage, Lucy, 192
Leister, Widow, 57
Lejeune, John Archer, 197
Liberty, Margot, 162, 169
Lighthizer, James, 246
Lincoln, Mary Todd, 77
Lincoln, President Abraham, xiii, xxiii, xxviii, xxix, 19, 31, 61, 62, 73, 74, 75, 76, 79, 80, 85, 88, 89, 112, 117
Littlepage, Maj. Gen. Carter, 44
Longstreet, Gen. James, xiii, 60, 62, 68, 71
Loring, Maj. Gen. William Wing, 38

M

Mackintosh, Donald, 148
Mangum, Neil, 168
Mattes, Merrill J., ix, xxxviii
McClellan, George B., 60
McClernand, Maj. Gen. John Alexander, 33, 40
McGilvery, Maj. Freeman, 64

Meade, Gen. George Gordon, xlv, 57, 58
Mills, Anson, 130
Montgomery, Capt. James E., 22
Murphy, John McLeod, 45

N

Neptune, King, 3, 4, 290
Noyes, Capt. Henry Erastus, 127, 130, 131, 132

O

O'Kane, Col. Dennis, 66

P

Padlow, Nurse Molly, 18
Patton, George S., xxvii
Pemberton, Lt. Gen. John Clifford, 26, 35, 37, 38, 39, 40, 43, 44, 46, 51, 289
Perce, Nez, xv, 166, 169, 292
Porter, Adm. David D., 39
Powell, Capt. James W., 74, 78, 79, 81, 99, 115
Powell, Lewis, 74, 78, 79, 81, 100, 115
Price, General, 23, 41

Q

Quinby, General Isaac Ferdinand, 38, 39

R

Ramseur, Major Gen. Stephen, xv
Rathbone, Maj. Henry Reed, 75, 80
Revere, Paul, 66
Reynolds, Brevet Maj. Gen. Joseph Jones, 120
Rickey, Don, xxxviii, 288

Ridge, Nye-Cartright, 156, 292
Rittenhouse, Capt. Benjamin Franklin, 64
Rogers, Jerry, 241
Rollins, John, 112, 113
Ross, Brig. Gen. Leonard Fulton, 38, 39, 270
Rupert, Harry, 224, 227, 232, 233, 236

S

Scott, Georges, 191
Seward, Secretary of State, xi
Shed, Pete, 18, 173, 292
Sherman, William Tecumseh, 25
Sibley, Colonel Berton W., 192, 193, 199
Smith, John E., 112
Smith, Lt. Cdr. Watson, 36
Spangler, Edmund, 79
Stalin, Joseph, 198
Stanley, Gen. David Sloane, 118
Stanton, Edwin McMaster, 87
Sternberg, Lt. Sigismund, 114
Stowe, Capt. Horatio, 98
Sumter, General, 23
Swanson, Wendy, xiv, xlix, 267

T

Terry, Gen. Alfred Howe, 55, 89, 132, 135, 136, 160, 254
Thompson, Erwin N., ix, xxxviii
Thomson, Bobby, 7
Truman, Capt. Harry S, 198, 245

U

Utley, Robert M., ix, xxxviii

V

Van Vliet, Capt. Frederick, 118, 132, 295
Vodra, William W., 246
Vollmer, Lt. Paul Jurgen, 236
von Boehn, Generaloberst Max, 199

W

Wallace, Capt. George Daniel, 143
Walsh, Senator Tom, 122
Warren, Gen. Gouverneur Kemble, 59, 66
Washburn, Elihu, 112, 113
Waugh, John C., xxi, xli, xlviii, 1, 6, 245, 247
Weir, Thomas Benton, 146
Wheatley, James, 101, 105
Whittlesey, Maj. Charles White, 202
Williams, Brig. Gen. Thomas, 29

Y

York, Sgt. Alvin Cullum, 205

Z

Zollicoffer, General, xvi